WHO'S WHO
in the
SECRET SERVICE

History's Most Renowned Agents

VINCE PALAMARA
Author of *Survivor's Guilt*

Who's Who in the Secret Service: History's Most Renowned Agents
Copyright © 2018 Vincent Michael Palamara

Published by:
Trine Day LLC
PO Box 577
Walterville, OR 97489
1-800-556-2012
www.TrineDay.com
publisher@TrineDay.net

Library of Congress Control Number: 2018948393

Palamara, Vincent Michael
–1st ed.
p. cm.

Epud (ISBN-13) 978-1-63424-182-3
Mobi (ISBN-13) 978-1-63424-183-0
Print (ISBN-13) 978-1-63424-181-6
1. United States. -- Secret Service -- Officials and employees. 2. Secret Service
-- United States. 3. Presidents -- Protection -- United States. 4. History/United
States/State & Local/General 5. United States. -- Secret Service. 6. Presidents
-- Protection. I. Palamara, Vincent Michael II. Title

First Edition
10 9 8 7 6 5 4 3 2 1

Printed in the USA
Distribution to the Trade by:
Independent Publishers Group (IPG)
814 North Franklin Street
Chicago, Illinois 60610
312.337.0747
www.ipgbook.com

TABLE OF CONTENTS:

INTRODUCTION

Some may ask "What makes these specific agents so special?" Indeed, why did I pick these agents, out of literally thousands from roughly 1865 to the present time, to profile? It is simply because, after many years of primary, intensive research, analyzing all the successful and unsuccessful attempts on presidents, looking at all the agents who made headlines and achieved fame or infamy, checking out the agents who wrote books and appeared on television, and weighing and considering various factors, I came to this subjective list. While some agents were obvious and seemingly unavoidable (Clint Hill, Jerry Parr, Tim McCarthy), others were, on the surface, much less obvious (Roger Warner, Harvey Henderson, Marty Venker). Again, I weighed and considered many factors.

As the reader will see, not everything is positive and laudatory with every entry. Indeed, some criticism arises here and there. After all, the assassination of President Kennedy on November 22, 1963 was and remains the Secret Service's greatest failure to date. That said, because the media spotlight was intense, many of these agents became familiar to a fair amount of the public, especially those who read books on Kennedy's life and death. In actual fact, agents involved in the assassination attempts on President Truman (11/1/50), the two attempts on President Ford (9/5/75 and 9/22/75), and the attempt on the life of President Reagan (3/30/81) also became familiar, to greater or lesser extents, to the public.

Sometimes, as with life itself, history is not fair (tell this to President Lincoln, who, before he left for Ford's Theater and his date with destiny on 4/14/1865, approved Treasury Secretary Hugh McCullough's plan to initiate an organization called the Secret Service). The agents/operatives who stood alongside President William McKinley on that dark day on 9/6/1901 when the president was assassinated are, by and large, lost to history (George Foster, Al Galagher and S.R. Ireland were their names. President McKinley did not care for the use of bodyguards and Secret Service agents but relented to the wishes of the Chief of the Secret Service, John E. Wilkie. Although the Secret Service had no official empowerment to protect the President, Wilkie exceeded his authority and assigned operative George Foster as McKinley's personal bodyguard, with Galagher and Ireland assisting on that fateful day). Likewise, the agents involved in the protection of President-elect Franklin Roosevelt on 2/15/1933 (Robert Clark, who was slightly wounded, among them), despite succeeding in their mission, are essentially forgotten now.

As with any subjective list such as this, there are arguably other agents who could have been included (and perhaps a couple who could have been excluded, as well). In addition, I recognize that there are many brave men and women who don't make the headlines yet perform their duties heroically and with just as much (or even more) skill and acumen as many of those listed below. Again, history shines a spotlight on a few and it is up to us to judge how they performed under the hot lights of media scrutiny and the court of public opinion.

Keeping all of these factors in sharp focus, in the final analysis, I chose these agents to spotlight because they are arguably the most interesting or famous or infamous (or a combination of all three).

1

Stu Stout

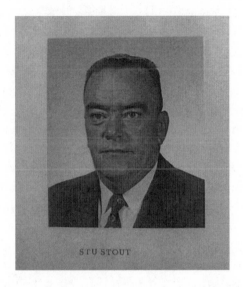

STU STOUT

Agent Stewart G. "Stu" Stout, who served from FDR to LBJ, looked so much like FBI Director J. Edgar Hoover that he would regularly be asked if he was the infamous head of the Bureau. "No, I work for another agency" he would respond. Stout, nicknamed "Slim" because he wasn't, previously served with the Pennsylvania State Troopers with fellow agents Floyd Boring and John Marshall.[1] Stout was one of the heroes who protected President Truman from would-be assassins on November 1, 1950. Former agent Frank Stoner had this to say about Stout regarding his part in protecting President Truman at Blair House on 11/1/50: "SA Stewart "Stu" Stout was inside the Blair House when the shooting started. He grabbed a Thompson submachine gun and ran upstairs to where the President was taking a nap. The President was looking out of the window and SA Stout told him to get under his bed, and then he took up a post at the top of the stairs. SA Stout was a much-decorated Army veteran who served in WW II, as were some of the other agents in the USSS at that time."[2] Former agent Darwin Horn wrote the author, "The Burke [pictured in his book] is Donald Burke who was Mrs. Eisenhower's

1. *American Gunfigh*t by Stephen Hunter and John Bainbridge, Jr. (2005), pages 147 and 161; ARRB interview with Floyd Boring 1996; *Reading (PA) Eagle*, 10/7/48.
2. Letter to author 2/15/04.

second agent. Stu Stout was in charge."[3] Horn later wrote, "Stu Stout was Mrs. Eisenhower's No. 1 agent. A no nonsense person who worked with [agent] Don Burke for many years with Mrs. Eisenhower."[4] Former agent Sam Kinney told the author: "He [Stout] was Mamie Eisenhower's first man." From Rex W. Scouten, former Secret Service agent who served with Stout and later was the White House Usher: "Dear Vince, Stewart Stout, following his retirement from the Secret Service was hired (by me) as an assistant Usher at the White House. He had a heart disorder – suffered a heart attack at the White House and died within a few hours."[5]

Former agent Winston Lawson wrote the author, "Stu Stout died in December 1974, a few years after retiring from USSS. He worked for a while after that in what is called the "usher office," which is adjacent to the large front foyer. He was a good friend and probably the nicest "gentleman" I ever knew. He went into real estate and then died suddenly in December 1974. He had been a state trooper in PA, joined the USSS during WWII, was drafted and came back to USSS. I was on his shift for a few years from probably 1961-1965. He was a wonderful man."[6]

Ironically, Stout rode in the hearse containing JFK's body from Parkland Hospital to Love Field. Stout had also been with Vice President Nixon in Caracas, Venezuela, in 5/13/1958 when the Vice President was attacked by an angry mob. The agents were decorated for valor for successfully protecting Nixon from assassination.[7] Stout was waiting for JFK at the Trade Mart when the assassination took place (Stout was one of three Shift Leaders at this time: designated ATSAIC).

Stu Stout jogged beside the JFK limousine the day before the assassination in San Antonio, TX:

---

3. E-mail to author dated 2/22/04.
4. E-mail to author dated 2/27/04.
5. Letter to author dated 5/28/98.
6. Letter to author dated 1/20/04.
7. *The Advance Man* by Jerry Bruno and Jeff Greenfield (1971), pages 79-81. H. Stuart Knight, Andrew P. O'Malley, Jack Sherwood, Wade Rodham, Ernest Aragon, Charles Taylor, Harry B. Hastings, Leroy M. "Roy" Letteer, John E. Schley, Robert Taylor, Dale Grubb, Emory Roberts, and the aforementioned Stu Stout received the Exceptional Civilian Service Award for their service in protecting Vice President Nixon in Caracas on May 13, 1958: *The Secret Service Story* by Michael Dorman (1967), p. 150; see also *The Advance Man*, p. 80; *Looking Back and Seeing The Future* by the AFAUSSS (1991), p. 68; *Washington Post*, 10/11/73.

As readers will know from my first and third books, agents did not ride on or near the rear of the limousine in Dallas on the day President Kennedy was killed, based on a totally fabricated "order" JFK never gave. In this regard, Stu Stout Junior wrote to myself on 11/1/10: "Vince. Thought I would mention that one of the influential people that attended the advance planning meetings for the Dallas trip was the Mayor of Dallas in 63 and I think it was Earle Cabell [Brother of Charles Cabell, the #2 man in the CIA fired by Kennedy for the Bay of Pigs disaster]. I distinctly remember during a conversation at the dinner table weeks following that surreal day, my father telling my mother that 'the Mayor thought agents riding on the back of the car (which was common protocol) would send a message and did not want his city to appear dangerous to the world through the media. He asked for subtle security exposure if and where possible.' On that day only two individuals would have been able to direct such an order and that would have been the President himself or Floyd Boring SAIC. In my opinion, and you know about opinions, if you find out who else was in that chain of command 'during that moment' you will be able to rationally determine why the agents jumped down for a portion of that politically motivated route through the city. Take care Vince and please don't give up."

Stout was later a charter member of the AFAUSSS, the Association of Former Agents of the United States Secret Service, in 1969.

Stout died without speaking to anyone: not the FBI, the Warren Commission, or the HSCA, which acknowledged his death in a memorandum released by the ARRB.[8]

I have enjoyed much social media contact with Stout's son, Stu Stout III, as well as other surviving family members, many of whom are appreciative of the fact that I keep Stu Senior's name alive via numerous photos I have found, collected, and shared with them. As Stu Stout III wrote to myself on 5/1/2010: "I can't thank you enough for sharing these wonderful pictures of my father. The work you obviously put into the creation of Presidential History photos is remarkable. Taking the time to search for pictures that included my father and sending them to me is one of the kindest actions a stranger has ever done for myself and my family. I am inspired and truly thankful. Regards, Stew."

Stew Junior returned the favor with this remarkable photo of himself as a boy with his father, yet another image bearing a remarkable resemblance between his dad and Hoover:

8. See chapter 11 of my first book *Survivor's Guilt* (2013).

2

MICHAEL TORINA

Michael W. Torina

Chief Inspector Michael Torina was about as important and influ-ential an agent or official that the Secret Service could ever boast about, for it was he that *actually wrote the Secret Service manual itself.*[1] Torina contributed significantly to a book about the Secret Service in 1962 which stated: "If the President is to appear in a parade, agents and policemen are assigned posts atop buildings and on the street along the parade route."[2] I corresponded with Torina on 12/5/97 and 2/23/04, respectively, and the former agent/official confirmed the veracity of what was written in that book, although he took pains to not say too much more: "I am not in a position to comment on our concerns in dealing with Presidential security matters." That said, he did contribute significantly to the aforementioned book about the Secret Service written in 1962, in which it is plainly stated, "Agents of the White House Detail ride in the same car with the President. Others will walk or trot alongside, while still others ride in automobiles in front of and behind the Presidential car … if exceptionally large crowds are expected … the Secret Service may call upon the Armed Forces to station troops along the line of march."[3] Torina

1. *The United States Secret Service* by Walter S. Bowen & Harry E. Neal (New York: Chilton, 1960), page 209.
2. *What Does A Secret Service Agent Do?* By Wayne Hyde (New York: Dodd, Mead, and Co., 1962), p. 28 (and acknowledgments).
3. *What Does A Secret Service Agent Do?* by Wayne Hyde (1962), page 28 (and acknowledgments) On the same page is a picture of agents walking beside JFK's car in 1961.

also told author William Manchester in 1961 that wherever a Presidential motorcade must slow down for a turn, the entire intersection must be checked in advance.[4] Needless to say, none of these security measures were used for the fateful Dallas trip of 11/22/63.

Born in Birmingham, Alabama, he graduated from Woodlawn High School and Alverson Business College. He was employed as a court reporter with assignments in Federal, State and City Courts as well as regulatory agencies. In 1937, he was appointed Clerk-Stenographer in the Birmingham office of the Secret Service. Assignments in Columbia, SC, New York City, Chicago, and Washington, DC followed. He was promoted to Special Agent, Special Agent in Charge, Inspector and Chief Inspector. During the Roosevelt and Truman administrations, he was a member of the White House Secret Service detail. He retired after 30 years of service and was then appointed Director of Security with United States Banknote Corporation and held that position for six years. He was a charter member of the Association of Former Secret Service Agents (AFAUSSS) and was the organization's first elected president.[5]

Torina's importance to history and the Secret Service is of legendary proportions. It was an honor to have corresponded with the gentleman. Torina passed away at the ripe old age of 96 on 8/21/2008.

---

4. *The Death of a President* by William Manchester, page 32.
5.   http://www.legacy.com/obituaries/washingtonpost/obituary.aspx?n=michael-w-torina&pid=116192074

3

James K. Fox

James Fox

You are probably familiar with PRS (Protective Research Section) agent James K. "Jack" Fox – at least some major item he is directly related to – and not even realize it. For it was the late researcher Mark Crouch who obtained several Kennedy autopsy photos from Fox (on, of all days, the day Reagan was shot on 3/30/81) and later made available to both director Oliver Stone for use in the movie *JFK* and to director Wolfgang Peterson for *In The Line of Fire*, among other projects, not to mention countless books that contain these disturbing images.

During interviews conducted on 1/28/92 and 9/23/92 respectively, I obtained startling new information from the late agent's sole confidante (Fox died in 1987). I learned from Crouch that Agent Fox stated that the story-reported widely by the news media[1] – of the Secret Service agent

---

1. All three major television networks, ABC, NBC, & CBS, reported that, "A Secret Service agent and a Dallas policeman were shot and killed" on 11/22/63. Eddie Barker, of CBS affiliate KRLD-TV, noted, "The word is that the President was killed, one of his agents is dead, and Governor Connally was wounded." ABC News in Washington reported, "A Secret Service agent apparently was shot by one of the assassin's bullets." ABC's Bill Lord stated, " [I] did confirm the death of the Secret Service agent … one of the Secret Service agents was killed … Secret Service agents usually walk right beside the car," And that, "One of the Secret Service agents traveling with the President was killed today." The Associated Press (AP) was quoted on WFAA (ABC):"A Secret Service agent and a Dallas policeman were shot and killed some distance from where the President was shot." At 12:45 p.m. CST, KRLD-TV

who died on 11/22/63 was true! According to Crouch, Fox was working in the Executive Office Building, where the PRS was headquartered, on 11/22/63, when he was asked by SAIC of PRS Robert Bouck to ready a detail of four to six agents to assist in retrieving the body and casket of the unnamed Secret Service agent. Fox told Crouch, "We lost a man that day – our man," and qualified his remarks by stating that he was not referring to JFK. Author Harrison Livingstone reported in his 2000 online book, *Stunning New Evidence*, that Jim Pearsu of the Secret Service believed there was indeed a dead agent.

Fox had also photographed the Presidential limousine in the White House garage at 4:00 P.M. on 11/23/63 with fellow PRS employee Howard K. Norton.[2] Author David Lifton wrote, "In 1981, I received a letter from Maryland radio journalist Mark Crouch saying he knew someone who had a set of the autopsy photographs, the same photographs that were at the National Archives. He subsequently introduced me to James K. "Jack" Fox, formerly a photographer with the Intelligence Division of the Secret Service. Documents from the House Assassinations Committee establish that Fox was one of a few officials who had access to the processing. On three occasions, he supervised their processing. According to Fox, shortly after the assassination, he was told by Secret Service Agent

---

reported that a Secret Service agent had been killed along with the President. At 1:23 p.m., CST, CBS's Walter Cronkite reported, "A Secret Service man was also killed in the fusillade of shots." Seth Kantor, a reporter for Scripps-Howard, would write in his notebook, which was published by the Warren Commission "They even have to die in secret." [20 H 410] At 2:14 p.m., the AP again made note: "A Secret Service Agent and a Dallas policeman were shot and killed today." At 2:40 p.m., The Dallas Police radio, channel two, also carried the story: "One of the Secret Service men on the field—Elm and Houston, said that it came over his Teletype that one of the Secret Service men had been killed: 17 H 749 (CE 705). The *Dallas Times Herald*, dateline November 22, 1963, added, "From the Secret Service office in Dallas – a spokesman could neither confirm nor deny the report: 'All I've heard is the same reports you've heard.'" However, at 3:40 p.m. Assistant Secretary of the Treasury Robert A. Wallace reported, "No Secret Service man was injured in the attack on President Kennedy," a denial of sorts, but it does not indicate if one was killed, or if there was violence at another location. Still, these stories could have supplied the Secret Service with the much-needed jurisdiction to take over and steal the body of JFK from the Dallas authorities, which in fact is what they did. Remember, while the murder of the President was not a federal crime in 1963, the murder of a Secret Service agent was [18 U.S. C. 1114]. Interestingly, journalist Seth Kantor reported, "A Western Union man who had been with us since we came down from Andrews Air Force Base came into the [Parkland Hospital] office. A nurse asked him about a report that a Secret Service agent had been killed out on the street. He said that it was true. This was one of the immediate rumors, which sprung up. It took several days for this particular rumor not to be believed in Dallas itself (Fellow in Jaggars-Chiles-Stovall who got it from a friend who got it from a postman supposed to have been at the death scene that the shot and bleeding SS man was in on the plot to kill the President.)"[20 H 410]. Jaggars-Chiles-Stoval employed Lee Harvey Oswald from 10/12/62 until 4/6/63. This company did photographic work for the U-2 spy program, and Oswald's starting date of employment coincided with the Cuban Missile Crisis [*Encyclopedia of The JFK Assassination* by Michael Benson (2002), pp. 27 and 123]. See chapter 9 of my first book *Survivor's Guilt* for even more on this issue.
2. CD 80, p. 3; RIF# 180-10001-10041 (see also *Murder In Dealey Plaza* by James Fetzer (2000), pp. 428-430).

Roy Kellerman, 'Here, make a set of these for yourself. They'll be history someday.' Fox showed me the pictures he had, and later I was able to obtain a set."[3]

Secret Service Assistant Director (and former Inspector) Thomas J. Kelley wrote to Harold Weisberg, "On or about November 27, 1963, Bouck gave the [autopsy] photographic film to Secret Service employee, James K. Fox, who took the film to the U.S. Navy Photographic Laboratory. The black and white film was processed, black and white negatives were developed, and colored positives were made from the colored film. The processing and development was done by Lieut. V. Madonia, U.S. Navy, at the laboratory. Fox remained with the film at the laboratory and all the photographic film was returned to Mr. Bouck the same day. The processed film was placed in a combination lock-safe file; the combination was known only to two persons. A few days later, black and white prints were made by Mr. Fox in the Secret Service photographic laboratory. On or about December 9, 1963, Mr. Fox took the colored positives back to the U.S. Navy Photographic Laboratory and observed while enlarged color prints were made. All the color positives and prints were returned by Fox at 6 p.m., the same evening and returned to the locked safe."[4] Regarding the autopsy photographs, "Bouck said that James Fox was his photographer at the White House and believes that he processed the black and white prints ('little snapshots'). Bouck also said, 'I believe they had nothing to do with the big prints or the color ones.' Bouck said that James Fox processed one or two or several rolls of color film at another facility."[5]

Fox was interviewed 8/7/78 by the HSCA's Andy Purdy. Purdy's notes on the call: "Who developed film? He did black and white at Secret Service lab. Color was done at Naval Processing Center – recalls Lt. Madonnia [sic] (He wrote [a] memo on it.) White House photographer [Robert L. Knudsen] was in drying room. He (Fox) checked and there was film on each side of color film holders. (Some black [and] white missing). Negatives put in files 4-5 days. Bouck then ordered him to have prints made. He and Knudsen did it. Two women in drying room passed out when [film] came through [most likely Saundra Kay Spencer and Carol Ann Bonito].[6] He did not help Knudsen put prints in holders. Recalls one

3. 7 HSCA 23-24; *Best Evidence* by David Lifton (1981), p. 703.
4. 5/19/70 letter from Secret Service Assistant Director Thomas J. Kelley to Harold Weisberg: see *Post Mortem* by Harold Weisberg (1975), page 274; RIF#180-10109-10368: 2/67 Secret Service statement signed by Kellerman, Bouck, Edith Duncan (secretary), Fox, and Kelley (see also *Post Mortem*, p. 558).
5. 8/6/77 HSCA interview of SAIC of PRS Robert I. Bouck (RIF# 180-10097-10141).
6. For more on Knudsen, Spencer, Bonito, and others, please see the 1998 edition of *High Treason* by

or two sets of prints being turned over to Bouck. (It was four years after assassination that he was asked for statement.) Admiral George Burkley told Fox to have prints made up. He went to Bouck for okay. He said fine but would need special arrangement for color. Knudsen was not there when black and white done. No metal probes present; doctors were taking measurements, ruler and hands visible in autopsy photos."[7]

Author Harrison Livingstone wrote, "Mark Crouch tells us that on the night of December 6 or 7, just two weeks after President Kennedy was murdered, Robert Bouck went through his safe in the presence of James K. Fox, another Secret Service agent, and burned much of the photographic and X-ray evidence in the assassination of President Kennedy. If true, this was a great crime, but Bouck denies that it ever happened."[8]

James Fox reappeared in the media during the 51rst anniversary of the JFK assassination with a news story entitled "Betrayed! Secret Service Photographer Secretly Tried To Sell JFK Autopsy Pics."[9] The article states: "The agent, Jim Fox, was desperate for money when he enlisted self-proclaimed JFK expert, Mark Crouch, to broker the black-and-white photos on his behalf, an audiotape has revealed. "They are quite gross and definitely of Kennedy. There's a bullet in his head," according to the audio recording of a reporter who was approached about buying the photos. The recording indicated that the pictures raised questions in the newsman's mind – deepening the mysteries surrounding the murder. The wound in the back of JFK's head was the size of an egg, according to accounts. But after seeing the pictures, the reporter noted, "It's more like the size of four eggs. Plus, there is an incision over the eye that raises questions."

Needless to say, James Fox will always be remembered for his connection to the JFK assassination and what he reported and what he later shared with the public.

Harrison Livingstone, pp. 416-418, 418-420, 421-425, 428-432, 493-497, 498-500, and 501-536. See also *The Men Who Killed Kennedy*, 2003: episode entitled "The Smoking Guns."
7. RIF# 180-10077-10107.
8. *High Treason 2* by Harrison Livingstone (1992), p. 322. Bouck's denial is based on Livingstone's investigator's (Richard Waybright) report dated 11/16/91 [p. 628].
9. http://radaronline.com/exclusives/2014/11/secret-service-agent-sells-jfk-autopsy-pictures/

JERRY PARR

J erry Parr was one of the true heroes of the Secret Service, protecting
President Reagan by pushing him into the limousine on 3/30/81
as assassin John Hinckley took aim at the President (agents Ray
Shaddick and Tim McCarthy also deserve much credit for their valor
and performance on this date, as well). Simply put, if Parr did not make
the decision to take a wounded President Reagan to George Washington University Medical Center, Reagan would have perished. *Washington
Post* reporter – and all around good guy – Del Wilber wrote the definitive
book on the Reagan assassination attempt, *Rawhide Down* (I have spoken
to and corresponded with Del many times). Parr himself, who I had the
pleasure of speaking to in 1995, wrote a great book himself called *In The
Secret Service* (written with the help of his wonderful wife Carolyn, whom
I had the pleasure of having some social media contact with). Sadly, Jerry
passed away on 10/9/2015.

Parr's interest in joining the Secret Service originated as a boy after
watching *Code of the Secret Service* (1939) starring Ronald Reagan as agent

"Brass" Bancroft.[1] After joining the service, from 1962 to 1968, Parr conducted 15 foreign and 65 domestic protective surveys for various Presidents and Vice Presidents, and worked with security, intelligence and law enforcement professionals in all 50 states and in 37 countries.[2] From 1969 to 1978, he worked for the Foreign Dignitary Division as a mid-level supervisor on Humphrey, Agnew and Ford details. As Deputy Special Agent in Charge, Foreign Dignitary Division, he directed security for 56 foreign heads of state.[3] From 1978-1979, he was Special Agent in Charge of the Vice Presidential Protective Division, where he directed security for Vice President Mondale. In 1979, Parr moved to the Presidential Protective Division, where he was Special Agent in Charge and Head of the White House Detail.[4] There, he directed security for Presidents Carter and Reagan.

Parr, a major consultant on the *In The Line of Fire* movie, told Larry King on 7/14/98, "The critical factor [in Dallas] ... was the fact that he [JFK] ordered the two agents off the car ... which made him very vulnerable to Lee Oswald's attack." With regard to exactly who makes the decision regarding the agents' proximity to the President, Agent Jerry Parr also told Larry King: "I would say it was the agent in charge who makes that decision." Indeed. For anyone who has read my first book *Survivor's Guilt* or my third book *The Not-So-Secret Service*, I contend that it was the agents themselves who made the decision to remove themselves from the rear of the limousine and, contrary to Parr's second-hand assertion, JFK had nothing to do with this.

In any event, the bravery and heroism of Agent Parr on 3/30/81 will never be forgotten.

---

1. *Inside The Secret Service*, Discovery Channel, 1995.
2. *Boston Globe,* October 9, 2015.
3. *LA Times,* 9 October 2015.
4. *In The Secret Service* by Jerry and Carolyn Parr (2013).

JAMES ROWLEY

A native of New York, Rowley received two law degrees from St. John's University in Jamaica, NY, and became an investigator with the NY State Banking Department.[1] Rowley went on to become an FBI agent, joining their ranks in 1936, after dictating an application for the agency to his sister and then having it sent to J. Edgar Hoover personally. First assigned to the Charlotte, North Carolina office, he was then transferred to Boston. Rowley went to New York, quit the FBI, and briefly practiced law. Rowley joined the Secret Service in October 1938, transferred to the White House in 1939 and remained there until 1973, having been both SAIC of the WHD (1946-1961) and Chief of the Secret Service (1961-1973), replacing the "retiring" U.E. Baughman.[2]

---

1. *Washington Post*, 11/2/92.
2 Rowley Truman Library oral history, 9/20/88.

Today, the James J. Rowley Training Facility in Beltsville, MD serves as the nerve center for Secret Service training. Rowley is arguably the most well-known Chief/Director of the agency to date, mainly due to his length of service, his tenure during the JFK assassination, and for leaving during the Watergate crisis. The *Washington Post* reported on 9/2/61: "Oh, My!" gasped Mrs. Rowley as the ad-libbing bystander sidled over to greet them with easy effusion. It was obvious that President Kennedy's presence at the ceremony was as unexpected as it had been unannounced … Kennedy quipped, 'He (Rowley) hasn't lost a President in all [his time with the Secret Service]. On a record like that, he deserves a promotion." Two years later, Rowley, would become the first and only Secret Service Chief to lose a President.

In a humorous aside, Rowley told the JFK Library this anecdote about JFK:

> It was our custom to present the president with a gold [Secret Service] badge, and so on the occasion that I went in to, as a result of an appointment that Ken O'Donnell set up for us, I and my staff had this appointment, went in to the president's office and the ceremony in which we presented the badge, and the president listened very politely and all and looked at the badge. And with a straight face said, "Well, I guess now this entitles me to work the midnight shift at Middleburg [the Kennedy residence in Virginia]."[3]

Based on a tip from Agent Gerald Behn, the author was able to contact Rowley on 9/27/92. However, although cordial, the former chief was too ill to be interviewed thoroughly about the events of 11/22/63 (see chapter 12 of my first book *Survivor's Guilt* for more on Rowley). Rowley died at 84 of congestive heart failure on 11/1/92.

---

3. James Rowley Oral History, JFK Library, 3/29/76.

6

GERALD BEHN

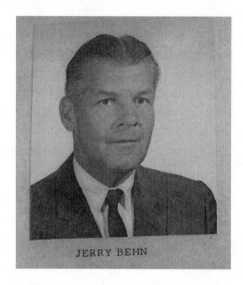

JERRY BEHN

E ven though I may be the harshest critic of the "Kennedy Detail," I have a lot of respect, admiration and fascination with Jerry Behn, who served from FDR (1939) to LBJ (1967) and was widely respected and admired by all of his colleagues. He was not in Dallas and I hold no suspicion toward him. He was, forgive my fan boy dialect, a cool looking dude who seemed to know what he was doing and had the respect and know-how to carry out his duties. If Behn would have been in Dallas, I believe the outcome for President Kennedy would have been much better. I spoke to Behn three times on 9/27/92 and the information I gleaned from the cordial former agent was of extreme importance to my work. The former agent told me that President Kennedy did not tell the agents to remove themselves from the rear of his limousine and that the motorcade route was changed for Dallas.[1] Behn passed away on 4/21/93.[2] I spoke to his daughter Sandra and wife Jean later on, as well.[3]

---

1. See my first book *Survivor's Guilt.*
2. *Washington Post*, 4/23/93.
3. Jean Behn told me on 11/18/95 that Jerry did not like William Manchester's book, *The Death of a President,* and confirmed that she also did not believe that JFK had ever conveyed to Jerry the idea of having the agents not ride on the rear of the limousine. In a follow-up letter dated 11/28/97, she stated, "The only thing I can tell you is that Jerry always said 'Don't believe anything you hear and only half of what you read.'"

Behn was born in Forest Park, Illinois, and raised in Flint, Michigan. He had an illustrious career in the Secret Service beginning in 1939, fresh from his graduation with fellow classman Robert Bouck from Michigan State University, where he played freshman football and was a member of the boxing team. He was a member of Mortar and Ball, Officers' Club and the Lambda Chi Alpha Fraternity. Behn began his tenure with the agency in the Detroit field office, followed by a stint in the Washington field office, then a stretch protecting FDR, Jr. down in Charlottesville, VA. Behn joined the White House Detail just before FDR's third inaugural. He would go on to protect Presidents Truman and Eisenhower before ultimately becoming the Special Agent in Charge of the White House Detail in September 1961, the same time the former SAIC, James Rowley, became the Chief of the Secret Service, replacing U.E. Baughman.[4]

Behn lost his position as SAIC to Rufus Youngblood in January 1965, although one could argue that, like Attorney General Robert Kennedy, Behn was a lame duck after the assassination. Youngblood was now in favor. Behn went, along with former SAIC of the V.P. Detail H. Stuart Knight, to the Special Investigations Division as SAIC, a position he held until January 1967, when he retired from the agency to join the Post Office, working under former JFK aide Bill Hartigan, the same man who would conduct Behn's and Boring's JFK Library Oral History. Behn worked for the Post Office for four years after leaving the Secret Service and was a charter member and president of the Association of Former Agents of the U.S. Secret Service, founded by Floyd Boring.[5]

Behn appeared on the game shows *What's My Line* on 12/27/59[6] and *To Tell The Truth* on 2/26/62.[7]

Gerald Behn and Bob Bouck as they appeared as 1939 graduates of MSU:

---

4. Behn's JFK Library oral history, 2/24/76.
5. *Washington Post*, 4/23/93.
6. https://www.youtube.com/watch?v=sso3PL-sLbk
7. https://www.youtube.com/watch?v=QVwf9t32dTQ

FLOYD BORING

FLOYD BORING

Floyd M. Boring was born in Salamanca, New York, on 6/25/15, and raised in DuBois, Pennsylvania.[1] He went to DuBois High School and, afterward, joined the Pennsylvania State Police, serving from 1936 until 1942. During part of this time, he served with fellow future agent Stewart Stout.[2] Boring then joined the security division of the National Tube Company in McKeesport, PA, in 1942, remaining for a little over a year.[3] Boring joined the Secret Service on 11/9/43, first assigned to FDR Jr. and the kids. He then went on to become part of the Protective Research Section (PRS) in the White House before joining the White House Detail (WHD) on 3/1/44. Whether it was fate or pure coincidence, Boring was close by when four successive presidents died or had brushes with death. He was "outside the window when [FDR] had his stroke" down in Warm Springs on 4/12/45. Boring was temporarily in charge of the WHD (along with Stu Stout) the day two Puerto Rican nationalists attempted to assassinate Truman at Blair House on 11/1/50.[4] He was close

---

1. The author was born 6/25/66 in Pittsburgh, PA.
2. Boring's JFK Library oral history, 2/25/76 [released 1998].
3. Boring's JFK Library oral history, 2/25/76 [released 1998].
4. Floyd Boring was interviewed by Chief U.E. Baughman for his book *Secret Service Chief* (1962), pp. 68-69, and by David McCullough for *Truman* (1992), pp. 364, 385, 434-435, 802, 808-810, and 908

at hand when President Eisenhower had his stroke and, as we know, he was in charge of planning the Texas trip when JFK was assassinated.[5] Boring's code name was Deacon (later used by President Jimmy Carter).[6] He served in the Secret Service until March 1967, when he retired as an Inspector during the Johnson administration. As an ex-agent Boring went on to do security work for the United Nations, Milton Kayle, G. Ross Perot, and, finally, Motown Records).[7] Boring has a rich background; he was President Truman's temporary chauffeur and, as mentioned above, in charge of the Presidential detail on 11/1/50. While Truman was sleeping in Blair House during the renovation of the White House, two Puerto Rican Nationalists launched their assassination attempt with guns ablaze. That night, Boring and his comrades fired some of the few shots ever fired "in anger" by Secret Service agents in their long history of protecting the nation's presidents.[8] One of the would-be assassins, Oscar Collazo, was wounded by Boring,[9] who told the author, "Collazo said the guy in the grey suit had hit him. Well, I was the only guy wearing a grey suit."

Boring was in charge of Secret Service planning of the entire Texas visit for President Kennedy from Washington D.C.[10] On three different occasions between 1993 and 1997, Boring told me: "[JFK] was a very easy-going guy ... he didn't interfere with our actions at all. He was a very nice man; he never interfered with us at all. President Kennedy was very cooperative with the Secret Service." Boring also told the JFK Library on 2/25/76: "Of all the administrations I worked with [FDR-LBJ], the president and the people surrounding the president were very gracious and

regarding President Truman. See also *Looking Back and Seeing the Future* (1991), p. 51 (Boring was interviewed 4/16/91).

5. Boring's Truman Library oral history, 9/21/88 Regarding the death of FDR, Boring added: "I'll tell you why I remember [the death of FDR]; there was a move on foot for [Chief] Frank J. Wilson to remove all the agents from the White House Detail. I had been on the White House Detail, and that was kind of worrisome to me. But I found out that I wasn't one of the people they were shooting for, so I stayed there."[Page 5] Regarding Eisenhower, Boring commented: "I never really particularly cared for the guy until he got out. When he got out, then I got fairly fond of him." [p. 62] In regard to 11/22/63, Boring said: "... I was off duty and washing windows at the house." [p. 64].

6. *The Death of a President*, Manchester, pp. xxi and 61; *Air Force One: The Planes and the Presidents-Flight II* video/ DVD (1991).

7. Boring's 9/18/96 ARRB interview; *20 Years in the Secret Service* by Rufus Youngblood (1973), p. 178. Author's three interviews with Jerry Behn 9/27/92; Boring's Truman Library oral history.

8. Author's interviews with Floyd Boring, 9/22/93 and 3/4/94 See also the 1995 Discovery Channel documentary *Inside The Secret Service* and the 1997 PBS documentary *Truman*, based on David McCullough's book of the same name (Rex Scouten also appeared on the latter program). On both programs, Boring's remarks were confined to Truman and Eisenhower.

9. See also Boring & Rowley Oral Histories, Truman Library. Later pardoned by President Jimmy Carter, Collazo passed away in 1994.

10. *The Day Kennedy Was Shot* by Jim Bishop (1968; 1992 edition), p. 558; 4 H 342; author's interviews with Floyd Boring, 9/22/93 & 3/4/94; author's interviews with Sam Kinney 3/5/94 & 4/15/94. Floyd Boring oral history, Truman Library; Floyd Boring oral history, JFK Library.

were very cooperative. As a matter of fact, you can't do this type of security work without cooperation of the people surrounding the president."

Floyd Boring passed away on 2/1/2008 at the age of 92.

EMORY ROBERTS

EMORY ROBERTS

A native of Cockeysville, Maryland, Roberts had previously served with the Maryland State Police, the Baltimore County Police, and as an investigator for the Office of Price Administration. Roberts was appointed to the Secret Service in January 1944, in Baltimore, and also served in the Washington field office before joining the White House Detail during the Truman era. Roberts was awarded the Exceptional Civilian Service Award for outstanding service while protecting Vice President Nixon in June, 1958, in Caracas, Venezuela.[1]

Mr. Roberts served as the commander of the agents in the follow-up car for both the Florida and Texas trips in his position as one of three shift leaders of the White House Detail (the other two were Stewart G. Stout, Jr. and Arthur L. Godfrey, both also on the Texas trip with Roberts). As readers of my first and third books well know, I hold Roberts in contempt for his actions and inactions on 11/22/63, as he recalled two agents (Donald Lawton and Henry Rybka) at Love Field, ordered the agents not to move when the shooting began, and even recalled an agent (Jack Ready) who began to move to the president's aid during the assas-

1. *Washington Post,* 10/11/73; *The Death of a President* by William Manchester, p.165; David Clark, Archivist, Harry S. Truman Library & Museum: Reathel M. Odum Papers, Box 10. Odum was Secretary to Mrs. Truman: 1945-1953; A picture of Roberts protecting Nixon in Caracas can be found in *Know Your Government: The U.S. Secret Service,* by Gregory Matusky and John P. Hayes, p. 36.

sination. Roberts shift was also the one containing the most agents who drank the early morning of the murder.

If that weren't enough, Roberts was also made appointment secretary for LBJ soon after the assassination while still a member of the Secret Service, an unprecedented and disturbing move, to say the least. Roberts died 10/8/73.[2] It is safe to put Roberts in the "infamous" category.

---

2. *Washington Post*, 10/11/73.

CLINT HILL

CLINT HILL

Former agent Chuck Zboril told me on 11/15/95: "We were close-mouthed for so long ... the only one who really did any of the talking was Clint Hill ... Clint Hill is the one who did a lot of the interviewing." Indeed, Hill testified to the Warren Commission in 1964; was interviewed on 11/18/64 and 5/20/65 by author William Manchester for his massive 1967 best-seller *The Death of a President*; famously spoke at length to Mike Wallace for *60 Minutes* in December 1975 and again in November 1993; spoke to The History Channel's *The Secret Service* (1995; also a home video); spoke to the Discovery Channel's *Inside The Secret Service* (1995; also a home video); spoke to the National Geographic's *Inside the U.S. Secret Service* (2004; also a DVD still available); contributed and wrote the Foreword to the 2010 best-selling book *The Kennedy Detail* (as well as doing the book tour, all the television and media spots, and the Emmy-nominated documentary – later a DVD – of the same name); as well as authoring (with his girlfriend Lisa McCubbin[1]) the best-selling books

---

1. Lisa McCubbin's current Amazon bio: "Lisa McCubbin is an award-winning journalist who has been a television news anchor and reporter, hosted her own radio show, and spent more than five years in the Middle East as a freelance writer." Lisa McCubbin's 2010-era bio (when she only had one book, not four, under her belt and before her romance with Clint Hill): "In the aftermath of the attacks on 9/11, McCubbin provided compelling reports to KGET-TV (NBC) as a foreign correspondent in Saudi Arabia. *Later, as the Saudi government came under increasing Western media scrutiny,*

Mrs. Kennedy and Me (2012), Five Days in November (2013), and *Five Presidents (2016).* The last three books also include the inevitable media barrage, television appearances, and international book tours. Some would say Hill has cried all the way to the bank and has profited more than anyone else ever has over the death of President Kennedy. Hill drank the night before the assassination and failed to protect JFK; that is the bitter truth.[2]

That said, many view Hill as a hero who attempted to save the life of the First Lady, Jacqueline Kennedy, and one could argue that at least he attempted to do something in defense of the president, unlike his stoic and unmoving colleagues.

During former Kennedy era agent Clint Hill's 11/19/10 Sixth Floor Museum oral history, the former agent revealed the full, unvarnished truth about JFK: he did not order the agents to do anything; they did what they wished to do, security-wise: "He can tell you what he wants done and he can tell you certain things but that doesn't mean you have to do it. What we used to do was always agree with the President and then we'd do what we felt was best anyway."

I myself have mixed emotions about Hill. I want to think of him as some kind of hero, as he seemed genuinely tormented (well, at least back in 1975 – he smiles so much now) during his *60 Minutes* interview in 1975. Yet, I have a hard time squaring that image with the latter-day portrait of a man who regularly signs assassination photos that end up for big bucks on Ebay, as well as the massive amounts of money (some would say blood money) Hill has garnered from all his best-selling books. There are other reasons, as well, but they are too voluminous to mention here.[3]

One can argue forcefully that Clint Hill is the most famous agent of the Secret Service. He certainly is the most over-exposed.

---

the Saudi Minister of Foreign Investment hired Lisa McCubbin as a media consultant to train leading business people and members of the Saudi government to deal with the Western press. She currently splits her time between the Middle East and Colorado with her husband and two teenaged sons." [Emphasis added] What is up with the Saudi Government 'thing'? Attacks on 9/11, McCubbin provided compelling reports to KGET-TV (NBC) as a foreign correspondent in Saudi Arabia. Later, as the Saudi government came under increasing Western media scrutiny, the Saudi Minister of Foreign Investment hired Lisa McCubbin as a media consultant to train leading business people and members of the Saudi government to deal with the Western press. She currently splits her time between the Middle East and Colorado with her husband and two teenaged sons." WHAT is up with that Saudi government 'thing'???"

2. See my first book *Survivor's Guilt* and my third book *The Not-So-Secret Service* for much more.

3. In addition to my books *Survivor's Guilt, JFK: From Parkland to Bethesda,* and *The Not-So-Secret Service,* readers are encouraged to view my major CTKA online reviews of all of Hill's and McCubbin's books and projects: http://www.ctka.net/reviews/kennedydetailreview.html and http://ctka.net/reviews/slick_propaganda.html and http://www.ctka.net/reviews/MrsKennedy_Hill_Review_Palamara.html and http://www.ctka.net/2016/book-review-five-presidents/five-presidents-by-clint-hill-with-lisa-mccubbin-a-review.html

BILL GREER

Whether by design or "accident of history," agent William R. "Bill" Greer will always go down in history as the man most responsible for the success of the JFK assassination, a view that holds true whether one believes the assassination of President Kennedy was the act of a lone man (Oswald) or a deadly conspiracy of some sort. Simply put: if Greer would have hit the accelerator instead of the brakes during the shooting, President Kennedy would have survived Dallas; sad but true. Sixty witnesses, ten police officers, seven Secret Service agents, thirty-eight spectators, two Presidential aides, one Senator, Governor John Connally, and Jackie Kennedy, plus the Zapruder film, document Secret Service agent William R. Greer's deceleration of the presidential limousine, as well as his two separate looks back at JFK.[1] Greer denied all of this to the Warren Commission. By decelerating from an already slow 11.2 mph, as even Gerald Posner admitted, Greer contributed greatly to the success of the assassination. When we consider that Greer disobeyed a direct order from his superior, Roy Kellerman, to get out of line before the fatal shot struck the President's head, it is hard to give Agent Greer the benefit of the doubt. As ASAIC Roy H. Kellerman said, "Greer then looked in the back of the car. Maybe he didn't believe me."[2] Clearly, Greer was at fault, and felt remorse. In short, Greer had survivor's guilt.

Presidential Aide Ken O'Donnell rode in the follow-up car: "... If the Secret Service men in the front had reacted quicker to the first two shots

1. See chapter 8 (on Greer) in my first book *Survivor's Guilt.*
2. *The Death of a President* by William Manchester, p.160.

at the President's car, if the driver had stepped on the gas before instead of after the fatal third shot was fired, would President Kennedy be alive today?" The aide also reported, "Greer had been remorseful all day, feeling that he could have saved President Kennedy's life by swerving the car or speeding suddenly after the first shots."[3] Presidential aide Dave Powers, in the follow-up car, wrote: " ... At that time we were traveling very slowly ... At about the time of the third shot, the President's car accelerated sharply."[4] On 11/22/88, Powers was interviewed by CBS reporter Charles Kuralt. Powers remarked on the remorse Greer felt about not speeding up in time to save JFK's life and agreed with Kuralt that, if Greer had sped up before the fatal head shot, JFK might still be alive today. This is a very dramatic and compelling short interview.[5] The ARRB's Tom Samoluk told me that, during the course of an interview he conducted in 1996 in which the Board was in the process of obtaining Powers's film, Powers said that he agreed with my take on the Secret Service.

Mary Gallagher reported in her book, "She [Jackie] mentioned one Secret Service man who had not acted during the crucial moment, and said bitterly to me, 'He might just as well have been Miss Shaw!'"[6] Jackie also told Gallagher, "You should get yourself a good driver so that nothing ever happens to you."[7] Secret Service agent Marty Venker confirmed that the agent Jackie was referring to was Agent Greer. "If the agent had hit the gas before the third shot, she griped, Jack might still be alive."[8] Later, author's C. David Heymann and Edward Klein further corroborated that the agent Mrs. Kennedy was referring to was indeed Greer.[9] Manchester wrote, "[Mrs. Kennedy] had heard Kellerman on the radio and had wondered why it had taken the car so long to leave."[10]

While Greer certainly did not shoot JFK (that asinine theory will not go away), his actions and inactions made President Kennedy an easy target. Greer passed away on 2/23/85. I spoke to his son Richard on 9/17/91, 10/7/91 and 9/23/92.[11] When first asked, "What did your father think of JFK," Richard did not respond. When asked a second time, he answered,

3. As quoted in *Crossfire* by Jim Marrs (1989), p. 248, based on a passage from *Johnny, We Hardly Knew Ye* by Ken O'Donnell and Dave Powers, p. 31. See also 7 H 450; *Johnny, We Hardly Knew Ye*, page 44.
4. 7 H 473-475.
5. https://www.youtube.com/watch?v=oyW1dad-oBo
6. *My Life With Jacqueline Kennedy*, p. 342.
7. *My Life With Jacqueline Kennedy*, p. 351.
8. *Confessions of an Ex-Secret Service Agent* by Johann Rush, page 25.
9. *A Woman Called Jackie* (New York: Lyle Stuart, 1989), p. 401; *Just Jackie: Her Private Years*, pages 58 and 374.
10. *The Death of a President* by William Manchester, p.163.
11. See chapter 8 (on Greer) in my first book *Survivor's Guilt*.

"Well, we're Methodists ... and JFK was Catholic." Bill Greer was born and raised in County Tyrone, Ireland, immigrating to America in February 1930, when he was about 18 years old.

Conspiracy realists and lone-nut true believers rarely agree on anything. However, one item they are in mutual agreement: because of Greer, JFK died that awful day in Dallas. Because of this, Greer is both famous and infamous, all at the same time ... and always will be.

PAUL PATERNI

Deputy Chief Paul J. Paterni, Chief Rowley's direct assistant was a major behind-the-scenes player in the aftermath of the assassination (similar to Floyd Boring). Paterni was a member of the OSS, the predecessor of the CIA, during WWII and served in Milan, Italy with fellow OSS men James Jesus Angleton, and Ray Rocca, later liaison to the Warren Commission.[1] Even more alarming is the fact that Chief Inspector Michael Torina wrote to me stating the following: "Specifically, Paul Paterni (my very good friend) served [in the Secret Service] from late 1930's through mid-1960's"[2], meaning, Paterni was a member of the OSS at the same time he was a member of the Secret Service.

Paterni's plate was full in the immediate aftermath of the assassination:

> 1: While at his desk in the White House on 11/22/63, Paterni was asked by Chief James Rowley to arrange with the Immigration Service to close the border.[3]

> 2: He assigned Inspector Thomas Kelley to go to Dallas to speak to Lee Oswald. Kelley would not only end up talking to Oswald mo-

1. Julius Mader, *Who's Who in the CIA* (Berlin: Julius Mader, 1968); *Cloak and Gown*, p. 363; Burton Hersh, *The Old Boys: The American Elite and the Origins of the CIA* (New York: Scribner's, 1992), p. 182.
2. Letter to author 12/5/97.
3. 5 H 451; See also 3 HSCA 359, 390.

ments before Ruby silenced him forever, but would also end up, like Rocca, liaison to the Warren Commission (Kelley would also later testify to the HSCA – this time as recently-retired Assistant Director).[4]

3: Paterni was involved with Boring in the critical limousine inspection at the White House garage the night of the assassination when skull fragments, bullet fragments, and vehicle damage were "noted" hours before the FBI would get their hands on the car. As we know, some skull fragments disappeared, many questions remain regarding the bullet fragments, and the limousine, which was reported to have had a hole in the windshield, was sent away to be rebuilt.[5] Apparently, Paterni and Boring beat Chief Rowley and Kellerman to the punch in regard to overseeing this inspection.[6]

4: Paterni was involved in the investigation of Lee Harvey Oswald's income tax check on 11/22/63.[7]

5: Paterni was given all the information SAIC Forrest Sorrels of the Dallas office had on 11/22/63 regarding Lee Harvey Oswald and his interrogation.[8]

6: Paterni was also involved in the PRS (Protective Research Section) investigation of threats against JFK, which reported no activity in Dallas before the murder.[9]

7: Paterni checked on the CIA connections of assassination suspects Thomas Mosely and Homer Echevarria for the Chicago field office. He had also served in the Chicago office as SAIC in the 1950's.[10] In a possible connection, assassination suspect and Oswald associate W. Guy Bannister had been the SAIC of the Chicago FBI office during the 1950's.[11] The Mosely-Echevarria matter was then unexpectedly dropped by Paterni's headquarters: The field office agents, Joseph Noonan and Ed Tucker, both former White House Detail agents, were to send all memos, files, and notebooks to Washington and not discuss the case with anyone.[12]

---

4. 3HSCA357, 454 (referring Kelley's 6/1/64 Affidavit to the Warren Commission).
5. CD80, pp.2-3 (see also HSCA RIF# 180-10102-10212: 3-page chronology of the presidential limousine); 1/6/64 letter from Chief James J. Rowley to the Warren Commission's J. Lee Rankin re: the presidential limousine; 5H67; 7H354, 403; 13H65; see also *The Day Kennedy Was Shot* by Jim Bishop, pp.511-512, 546, 637; *Best Evidence* by David Lifton, p. 359.
6. Manchester, p. 390. 8/24-8/25/77 HSCA interview of Roy Kellerman.
7. Jerry Rose, "The Feds Spring Into Action," *The Fourth Decade*, May 1996; as Rose states, "Why [was] Deputy Chief Paterni [willing to] indulge [Sorrels] in this curiosity?"
8. 7 H 354.
9. 3HSCA340.
10. R.I.F. #180-10074-10079: 8/8/78 HSCA interview of Lem Johns. Johns had worked under Paterni from 1957-1959.
11. See, for example, *Oswald and the CIA* by John Newman (1995) pp. 289-290.
12. R.I.F.#180-10104-10331; R.I.F. #180-10087-10137; 3 HSCA 371, 372-379, 383-389.

Interestingly, Jackson N. Krill, former OSS, Naval Intelligence, and top-ranking JFK/LBJ era Secret Service official (and who was also a Chief Inspector like Michael Torina), was the man who debriefed the agents after the assassination, basically advising them not to talk.[13]

Incongruously, Paterni appeared on the game show *What's My Line* on 1/28/62.[14]

Chief Inspectors Michael Torina and Jackson Krill with Assistant Chief Russell "Buck" Daniels, who was replaced by Paul Paterni in 1961:

---

13. For example, see 2/28/78 HSCA interview of Agent Robert Jamison. Krill had been in the Kansas City, MO office and was close to President Truman's brother: Rowley Oral History, Truman Library, p. 31.
14. https://www.youtube.com/watch?v=5GydR4aQMXc

GERALD BLAINE

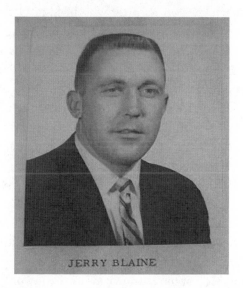

JERRY BLAINE

Gerald Blaine was an agent who served from 1959-1964 and later wrote the 2010 book (with Lisa McCubbin) *The Kennedy Detail*. As readers of my critical review of Lisa McCubbin's first of four "co-authored" books well know,[1] I am thoroughly convinced that it was my 22-page letter to Clint Hill in 2005 that awoke a sleeping giant. Hill, then 73 and with zero want or desire to write a book (a sort of badge of honor that he carried for decades), was angered by my letter, a "cliff notes" version of the basics from my then self- published first book critical of the JFK-era Secret Service entitled *Survivor's Guilt*. It is important to empha- size the fact that Hill had an unlisted address and phone number at the time; it was only through the good fortune of an unsolicited bit of help via a colleague of Hill's, former agent Lynn Meredith, that I was able to obtain this then highly-sought bit of information. As I discovered during my June 2005 conversation with Gerald Blaine, Clint shared the contents of my private letter to his fellow former agent, a man who, I soon found out, was his best friend for many years and who was, by any measurable standard, an obscure agent of the Secret Service who was on the Texas trip (but not in Dallas), having served a meager five years with the agency.

---

1. http://www.ctka.net/reviews/kennedydetailreview.html

It was during this same summer of 2005 that two things happened: Gerald Blaine began writing his book[2] and Clint Hill, writer of the Foreword to the book (and participant in the book tour and numerous television programs), destroyed his personal notes he had in his possession for decades.[3] It was also during this very same time that Lisa McCubbin, an obscure former television reporter who lived in Qatar in the Middle East for six years as a freelance journalist, began helping Blaine with the writing of his book. McCubbin was born after the assassination and was friends with the Blaine family; in fact, she had dated Blaine's son.[4] In an unexpected turn of events, McCubbin (born in 1964) would start a romantic relationship with Hill (born in 1932), although Hill is still married.[5] As I have written at length about in both my first book *Survivor's Guilt*, my third book *The Not-So-Secret Service*, and in several CTKA reviews (not to mention countless blogs and posts online), her work *cannot* be trusted with anything controversial. Sure, you can take it to the bank when she writes about harmless historical items such as Hill's many interactions with Jackie Kennedy and other *Redbook/Reader's Digest* type moments, but her work should be viewed with a jaundiced eye when the Kennedy assassination is mentioned.

Hill, Blaine and McCubbin are much aware of my work; no delusions of grandeur here. Apart from my aforementioned 22-page letter that opened Pandora's box, Hill and Blaine have discussed my work on C-SPAN with CEO Brian Lamb (in Hill's case, twice)[6]; Blaine sarcastically names me as a Secret Service "expert" on pages 359-360 of his book (and quite a few other pages are a direct response to my work); I am credited at the end of a 2013 television program in which Hill briefly addresses my "allegations" (McCubbin also participated as well)[7]; Blaine had his attorney send me a threatening letter[8]; McCubbin, who contacted me about my blog, gave my first book a one star on "GoodReads.com" and has even admitted on C-SPAN of finding information that contradicted Blaine (almost certainly my work)[9]; Blaine added my book as an item "to read" on

---

2. http://www.ctka.net/reviews/kennedydetailreview.html
3. https://www.youtube.com/watch?v=3gRhG3ya7JE
4.   https://www.youtube.com/watch?v=IYpY8zl_wwA   and   https://www.youtube.com/watch?v=EmCEx-f0dfl
5. http://www.irishexaminer.com/lifestyle/features/why-i-blame-myself-for-jfks-death-248893.html
6. https://www.youtube.com/watch?v=IbD1shPmla8 and https://www.youtube.com/watch?v=bqE0rPJyGl
7. *JFK: The Final Hours* 2013, National Geographic (also a DVD); see: https://www.youtube.com/watch?v=zNXJKs9xAMI
8. http://www.ctka.net/reviews/kennedydetailreview.html
9. https://www.youtube.com/watch?v=lgB2mnmiU-s

"GoodReads"; Blaine and Hill friend (and former agent) Chuck Zboril, much aware of my blog, gave my first book a one-star review on Amazon; former agent Ron Pontius mentions one of my articles without naming me on the television documentary; and I have been treated to petty harassment by several other personal friends of Blaine, both at home and at my former place of employment.

As I pointed out in my first book *Survivor's Guilt* and in my third book *The Not-So-Secret Service*, Blaine cannot be trusted for the following reasons[10]:

Blaine falsely claims he and his fellow agents "break their silence" in his book, as if the numerous other books and television documentaries that came out years before his book did not exist.

Blaine falsely claims that President Kennedy ordered the agents off the limousine, a matter I have thoroughly debunked…in fact, so did Blaine: he told me on 2/7/04 that President Kennedy was "very cooperative. He didn't interfere with our actions. President Kennedy was very likeable – he never had a harsh word for anyone. He never interfered with our actions." If that weren't enough, Blaine told me on 6/10/05 the alleged JFK remark about "Ivy League charlatans" made to Floyd Boring (which Boring told me was not true) came "from the guys … I can't remember who [said it] … I can't remember." Thus, Blaine confirms that he did not hear the remark from JFK.[11]

There are no footnotes, endnotes, sources, or a bibliography to be found in his book, many of the agents are deceased and cannot corroborate or defend themselves, and we are supposed to take Blaine, writing in the third person, at his word on matters involving what the deceased agents allegedly did and said.

Blaine admitted that he purposely avoided fellow agents Larry Newman, Tony Sherman, and Tim McIntyre (who rode in the follow-up car on 11/18/63 and 11/22/63) because they "broke the code" by talking about JFK's private life, a flagrant example of avoiding unpleasant truths that go against his way of thinking (yet agent Joe Paolella, who also said the very same things, was not avoided). Likewise, fellow agent Abraham Bolden was avoided. Is this good history? I avoided no agent whatsoever in my quest to find each and every one of the Kennedy Detail.

---

10. See also: http://www.ctka.net/reviews/kennedydetailreview.html
11. Interestingly, the Secret Service made an effort "…to ascertain whether any [movie news] film could be found showing special agents on the ground alongside the Presidential automobile at any point along the parade route." Commission Document No. 87, page 434. Shortly after the assassination on 11/22/63, before a television audience of many millions of people, ABC's Ron Gardner reported, "Secret Service agents normally walk directly beside the car. We can't see any in these pictures."

Blaine falsely states that "the Secret Service was not authorized to override a presidential decision." This is false – the exact opposite is true.

Blaine waxes on about an alleged meeting that was held on 11/25/63 to discuss the alleged order JFK never gave in the first place. There is no documentation whatsoever that this meeting took place, all the participants (save Blaine) are now conveniently deceased, many of them debunked the substance of this so-called meeting, and one agent told me there was no meeting and that the notion that there was a meeting is "horseshit."

Blaine predictably blames JFK for the removal of the bubbletop, yet fellow agent Sam Kinney was adamant to me – on three different occasions – that he was solely responsible for its removal and that no one else had anything to do with it. The top was also used a lot more (in good weather) than Blaine claims.

Blaine covers up the infamous drinking incident involving *nine* agents of the Secret Service, including Clint Hill, Paul Landis, Glen Bennett, and Jack Ready!

Blaine doesn't even touch the issue of the Secret Service and their involvement in removing motorcycle coverage for JFK on 11/22/63.

Blaine *also* does not deal with the issue of the press and photographer's displacement from the motorcade.

Incredibly, as documented in agent Andy Berger's report,[12] Blaine writes on page 233, with regard to Parkland Hospital: "A representative of the CIA appeared a while later." The importance of this is left unstated;

Blaine never mentions JFK's Military Aide, General Godfrey McHugh, a devout Kennedy loyalist who was relegated to the distant VIP car in the Dallas motorcade[13] and who stated that he was asked by the Secret Service "for the first time" to "ride in a car in the back [of the motorcade], instead, as normally I would do, between the driver and the Secret Service agent in charge of the trip."[14]

On pages 221-222, Blaine, referring to the president's physician, Admiral George Burkley, writes: Normally the admiral rode in a staff car in the motorcade, or in the rear seat of the follow-up car, but he and the president's secretary, Evelyn Lincoln, had misjudged the timing of the motorcade's departure from Love Field and wound up scurrying to the VIP bus. He was furious for not having been in his normal seat but had *nobody to*

---

12. 18 H 795 ; See also see Bill Sloan, *Breaking the Silence,* pp. 181–5; *The Man Who Knew Too Much,* pp. 570–1; Michael Benson, *Who's Who in the JFK Assassination* (1993), pp. 40–41.
13. Along with General Ted Clifton, the other military aide who often rode in the front seat of the limousine between the driver and the agent in charge.
14. CFTR radio (Canada) interview 1976 Interview with McHugh conducted late 1975 via phone.

blame but himself." Yet, both Dr. Burkley and JFK's secretary Evelyn Lincoln were adamant that it was the Secret Service who were at fault for the displacement of both Burkley and Lincoln.[15]

In yet another matter Blaine chose to ignore, Dallas Sheriff Bill Decker, who rode in the lead car with Lawson and Sorrels, told his men to in no way participate in the security of the motorcade.[16] Blaine also is seemingly unaware of the following, as noted by reporter Seth Kantor: "Will Fritz's men called off nite [sic] before by SS. Had planned to ride closed car w/ machine guns in car behind Pres."[17]

On page 224, Blaine writes: "It was very rare for both the president and vice president to be together at the same time in the same place." This is an understatement – being in the same *motorcade* was unique![18] As HSCA attorney Belford Lawson succinctly put it: "Why for the first time in American history were the President and Vice-President together in the same motorcade?"[19]

Blaine ALSO ignores the fact that the roofs along the route were not manned or checked on 11/22/63, as they normally were. SAIC of the Nashville office Paul Doster told the *Nashville Banner* back on May 18, 1963 that "a complete check of the entire motorcade route" was done for JFK's trip to Nashville. In addition, Doster stated: "Other [police] officers were assigned atop the municipal terminal and other buildings along the route. These men took their posts at 8 a.m. and remained at their rooftop stations until the president and his party passed." The roofs of buildings were also guarded in Tampa on November 18, 1963,[20] four short days before Dallas, in addition to San Antonio on November 21, 1963.[21]

On page 201, regarding agent Bill Greer, the driver of JFK's car in Dallas, Blaine writes: "And, God forbid, if he [Greer] ever did have to make

---

15. Bishop, pp. 109–110, 134; Manchester, pp. 131–2. See also *The Flying White House*, p. 209 (O'Donnell seems to get the blame for Burkley's lack of proximity); Burkley's October 17, 1967 JFK Library oral history; RIF#154–10002–10422; July 5, 1978 HSCA interview of Evelyn Lincoln.

16. Roger Craig, *Two Men in Dallas* video; *No More Silence* by Larry Sneed (1998), p. 224; 21 H 547, 572: DPD Stevenson Exhibit; 22 H 626; *No More Silence*, p. 337.

17. 20 H 391; see also 4 H 171-172 (Curry); 11 HSCA 530.

18. Author's interview with Bolden, September 16, 1993; Lawson: 4 H 336. SA Kinney told the HSCA on February 26, 1978 that it was "unusual for LBJ to be along."

19. RIF#180–10093–10320: May 31, 1977 Memorandum from HSCA's Belford Lawson to fellow HSCA members Gary Cornwell and Ken Klein (revised August 15, 1977).

20. RIF#154–10002–10423: Secret Service Final Survey Report, Tampa, FL—underpasses controlled by police and military units; Sheriff's office secured the roofs of major buildings in the downtown and suburban areas; agents on limo; Salinger with Kilduff; close press and photographers (including Stoughton in follow-up car); McHugh in between Secret Service agents in front seat of limo.

21. RIF#154–10002–10424: Final Survey report, San Antonio—Forty members of the military police from Fort Sam Houston, Texas: traffic control, motorcade route security, and intersection control; police helicopter utilized along route; many flanking motorcycles.

a sudden getaway, he knew the 7,500-pound car with its 300-horsepower engine just didn't gather speed as quickly as he would like." Yet, agent Roy Kellerman testified under oath to the Warren Commission: "I have driven that car many times, and I never cease to be amazed even to this day with the weight of the automobile plus the power that is under the hood; we just literally jumped out of the God-damn road."

On pages 230-231, Blaine seeks to pass the blame on to others once again, this time in the form of JFK's Chief of Staff, Ken O'Donnell: "Ken O'Donnell agreed ... that Johnson should return to Washington as soon as possible and that yes, he should leave Dallas on Air Force One." However, O'Donnell denied this, telling author William Manchester: "The President and I had no conversation regarding Air Force One. If we had known he was going on Air Force One, we would have taken Air Force Two. One plane was like the other."[22] In fact, when Arlen Specter of the Warren Commission asked O'Donnell, "Was there any discussion about his [LBJ] taking the presidential plane, AF–1, as opposed to AF–2?" O'Donnell responded: "There was not."[23] In this regard, O'Donnell later wrote in his book *Johnny, We Hardly Knew Ye* that a Warren Commission attorney – the aforementioned Arlen Specter – asked him to "change his testimony so that it would agree with the President's": an offer O'Donnell refused.[24]

Blaine (on pages 350 and 352) seeks to cast away ANY notion that the Secret Service agents believed there was a conspiracy, yet there is the record that says differently – former agents Jerry O'Rourke, Sam Kinney, John Marshall, Abraham Bolden, and Maurice Martineau believed there was a conspiracy, as well.[25]

On page 216, Blaine describes the shooting sequence in this manner: "... the first shot strikes the president, the second shot strikes Governor Connally, and the third shot strikes JFK in the head ... " There is no acknowledgement of the Warren Commission's fictional single bullet theory or the known missed shot that struck bystander James Tague! This is a pattern Hill and Blaine repeat on national television[26] and in Hill's 2016 book *Five Presidents*. On page 217, Blaine writes that agent Clint Hill saw "a bloody, gaping, fist-sized hole clearly visible in the back of his head," clear evidence that JFK was struck by a shot from the *front*, as also

---

22. Jim Marrs, *Crossfire*, pp. 296–7. See also Bishop, p. 259, and Manchester, pp. 234–5.
23. 7 H 451. See also *Johnny, We Hardly Knew Ye*, pp. 35, 38.
24. Marrs, p. 297. In fact, as noted by researcher David Starks in his 1994 video *The Investigations*, while Specter's name appears in the hardcover version of O'Donnell's book, it was deleted from the mass-market paperback (p. 41)!
25. *Survivor's Guilt*, chapter 7.
26. Fox News 11/12/10: see http://www.youtube.com/watch?v=frWYGPZe9YQ

confirmed by Hill's report[27] and Warren Commission testimony,[28] not to mention the reports (plural) from fellow agent Paul Landis (whose contents were *confirmed by Landis to the HSCA*),[29], no matter what Landis or Blaine say now (see pages 225 & 352-353), as well as the statements made by agent Sam Kinney to me (and, ironically, in *Blaine's own book*, pages 216 & 218, regarding blood hitting his windshield!) *and* agent Win Lawson, who also "saw a huge hole in the back of the president's head."[30] Blaine also uses this same language later in the book (page 258): Now the men who just four and a half hours earlier had seen the back of President Kennedy's head blown off hauled the casket holding his dead body..." Finally, regarding Hill, Blaine describes his friends' recollections of the autopsy (page 266): "Six inches down from the neckline, just to the right of the spinal column, there was a small wound, a hole in the skin. ... All Clint could see was that the right rear portion of President Kennedy's head was completely gone.;

On pages 264-265, Blaine related how he almost shot President Johnson on 11/23/63 with his Thompson submachine gun, a tale of dubious merit that garnered much press before the release of the book. One witty writer wrote me: "Hill's book is called *Five Presidents*. Perhaps Blaine's book should have been called *Three Presidents: One We Let Die and Another I Almost Killed.*"[31]

Blaine seems to be unaware of the following, as reported by the Assassination Records Review Board in 1998: "Congress passed the JFK Act of 1992. One month later, the Secret Service began its compliance efforts. However, in January 1995, the Secret Service destroyed presidential protection survey reports for some of President Kennedy's trips in the fall of 1963. The Review Board learned of the destruction approximately one week after the Secret Service destroyed them, when the Board was drafting its request for additional information. The Board believed that the Secret Service files on the President's travel in the weeks preceding his murder would be relevant."[32]

---

27. Hill's November 30, 1963 report: 18 H 740–5. (See also the 2004 National Geographic documentary, *Inside the U.S. Secret Service*.)
28. 2 H 141, 143.
29. Landis's report dated November 27, 1963: 18 H 758–9; Landis's detailed report dated November 30, 1963: 18 H 751–7; HSCA Report, pp. 89, 606 (referencing Landis's interview, February 17, 1979 outside contact report, JFK Document 014571).
30. See article in *The Virginian-Pilot*, June 17, 2010, by Bill Bartel: http://hamptonroads.com/2010/06/do-you-remember-where-you-were-he-does-jfk#rfq
31. E-mail from John Brewster 5/3/16.
32. ARRB Final Report (1998), p. 149.

Blaine states that President Eisenhower almost always rode in a closed car, yet the exact opposite is true. In point of fact, Ike often rode in an open limo – just do a Google image search. Ironically, Blaine's friend, Clint Hill, corroborated my research on this point.[33]

Blaine, during an earlier interview with myself, thought SAIC Gerald Behn was on the Tampa trip, yet it was Floyd Boring! This seemingly innocent error is highly disturbing because Blaine speaks so authoritatively about what transpired on the Tampa trip, even using unsourced direct quotes from memory. How can Blaine write so authoritatively that he heard Boring over the radio relaying JFK's alleged instruction to remove Zboril and Lawton from the rear of the limousine in his book when, several years before, he told me it was *another* completely different agent on the trip? Likewise, his good friend, former agent and *Kennedy Detail* contributor Chuck Zboril, also on the Tampa trip (riding on the rear of JFK's limo, no less), erroneously thought Roy Kellerman was in charge of the Tampa trip and riding in the front seat of the presidential limo! Again, this is disturbing for the very same reasons, as Zboril vigorously defends Blaine's views in media appearances.[34] How can Zboril support Blaine's later-day Boring story when he thought it was yet *another* agent on the trip?[35] How can both Blaine and Zboril, with a straight face, endorse the

---

33. *Five Presidents* by Clint Hill – a review by Vince Palamara: http://www.ctka.net/2016/book-review-five-presidents/five-presidents-by-clint-hill-with-lisa-mccubbin-a-review.html

34. "Zboril was sure that Kellerman, who wasn't even on the Florida trip, was present in Tampa: "I thought it was Roy Kellerman, not Boring, in the car on the Tampa trip...that's my recollection." *Survivor's Guilt*, page 294 [author's interview with Chuck Zboril 11/15/95]. Interestingly, a 6/1/77 photo of Zboril with President Jimmy Carter and Vice President Walter Mondale comes with the caption stating that "Zboril was a young agent scheduled to be on the back of President John F. Kennedy's limousine on the day he was assassinated in Dallas, Texas" [Alamy.com; Ken Hawkins Pictures].

35. Postscript: it is a total non-issue about Boring telling the agents to not ride on the rear of the limousine right before the Texas trip. I BELIEVE this indeed happened (page 43 of my first book) and I also have no doubt that, if I was given the chance to speak to many of Blaine's colleagues circa late 1963-1965 (or perhaps even later), those gentlemen would have "rained on my parade" in droves and told me the fib that JFK ordered the agents off his limo (bottom of page 52 of my first book). The point is the credibility of this action by Boring, NOT that Boring performed this action of telling the agents not to ride there (albeit disobeyed by Agent Clint Hill- 4 times- on Main Street in Dallas!). By credibility, I mean that I do NOT believe JFK had anything to do with this- this was a decision made by Floyd Boring for reasons that appear sinister yet, at the same time, seem hard to fathom (according to what Tampa motorcycle officer Russell Groover told me, the point is a moot one: agents did not ride on the rear of the limo during the FINAL LEG of the long journey because the limo was going at a fast rate of speed in a residential area. In any event, both Groover and Congressman Sam Gibbons both told me that they heard no order from JFK. Even believing Boring's 1996 "story" to the ARRB, what JFK allegedly conveyed to him was hardly an order of any kind... and it was one that Hill ignored in any case). It was only with the advent of time, the release of films, photos, records, the ARRB, the internet, etc., as well as contacting White House aides/ non-Secret Service agents like Dave Powers with no horse in the race (no reason to lie and cover-up) that the truth came out. Take your pick: were the agents lying in 1963-1965 or were they lying to myself? Does lying=credibility? Does lying destroy one's belief in someone's integrity? You be the judge. My verdict is my book. [Please see chapter one of my first book for much more].To blame JFK for

story they attribute to Boring in Blaine's book when both thought it was another person substituting on the trip? I think this is perhaps the biggest clue – the smoking gun – as to the lack of credibility in Blaine's book.

Blaine, in an online video, said that fellow agent Art Godfrey "gave his blessings" to his book, yet by his own admission, Mr. Blaine did not even begin his book until over three years *after* Mr. Godfrey passed away![36]

Blaine states in an online video that he "has never spoken to an author of a book,"[37] yet he spoke to both William Manchester and myself. Manchester's book references a 5/12/65 interview. What's more, Mr. Blaine is thanked by Mr. Manchester in his other JFK book *One Brief Shining Moment*. Thus, Mr. Blaine is 2 for 2: he is in both Manchester JFK books. In addition, Mr. Blaine spoke to myself in both 2004 and 2005, as well as corresponding via e-mail during this time, as well. And, incidentally, Blaine *told* me he spoke to Manchester. In an online video, Blaine falsely states that he specifically never spoke to Mr. Manchester[38]

I could go on, but you get the point.

---

his own death is a vulgar, shameful, and cowardly thing to do … repeat that once again, former agents: vulgar, shameful, and cowardly. Thank God I spoke to Gerald Behn on 9/27/92 (6+ months before his death) and, on several occasions between 1993 and 1997, Floyd Boring, among many others (Win Lawson and Art Godfrey, to name a few more). Otherwise, there would be no reason for Blaine's 2010 book and the public would just believe the lies from late 1963-1965 instead.

36. https://www.youtube.com/watch?v=U_YqC5NJASA
37. https://www.youtube.com/watch?v=IbD1shPmla8
38. https://www.youtube.com/watch?v=LxZVgPlt05o

13

RUFUS YOUNGBLOOD

Youngblood revealed to me that he was in the very same WWII Air Force unit, the 91st Bomber Group, as Howard Donahue, the man responsible for the book *Mortal Error*, which alleged that a Secret Service agent accidentally killed JFK; small world, indeed.[1] In fact, Donahue sent the author a blow-up of a color photo of himself talking to Rufus Youngblood at an Air Force WWII conference in Memphis, Tennessee back in 1996. In the enclosed letter, he wrote the following to Youngblood: " … I am puzzled about the number of spectators who claimed to have smelled gunpowder." Youngblood answered, "So did I after the last shot." Youngblood now joins the list of those witnesses who smelled street-level gunpowder in Dealey Plaza. Interestingly, while others slept or were out drinking in Fort Worth, Youngblood left in the early morning hours of 11/22/63, supposedly to visit a childhood acquaintance,[2] a detail not mentioned in his LBJ Library oral history, his book, or anywhere else since he noted it in his report.

1. *Survivor's Guilt*, chapter 10.
2. 18 H 681-682.

On 10/22/92, Youngblood confirmed to the author, "There was not a standing order" from JFK to restrict agents from the back of the limousine – the agents had "assigned posts and positions" on the back of the President's car. On 2/8/94, Youngblood added, "President Kennedy wasn't a hard ass ... he never said anything like that [re: removing agents from limo and the like]. As a historian, he [Manchester] flunked the course – don't read Manchester." Youngblood knows of what he speaks: he was interviewed by Manchester on 11/17/64.

Youngblood protected Presidents Truman thru Nixon, although he best known for his time protecting LBJ, both as Vice President and as President. He is the author of the 1973 book *20 Years in the Secret Service: My Life with Five Presidents*. Youngblood was the right man for Vice President Johnson, at the right place and at the right time to see both his career and infamy skyrocket. Although official history tells us that Youngblood received a medal for his fast actions on 11/22/63,[3] covering LBJ, who wasn't even a target, after the first shot sounded, Senator Ralph Yarborough, who sat in the same car as the agent and LBJ, said that this never happened. Dave Powers agreed with him.[4] Youngblood never left the front seat, and the agent and the Vice President were listening to a walkie-talkie with the volume set too low for the Senator to hear what they were picking up!

It is clear that, early on, LBJ was fond of only one Secret Service agent: Youngblood. Johnson said, "Youngblood was tougher and better and more intelligent than them all. Not all the Secret Service are sharp. It's always worried me that they weren't. They are the most dedicated and among the most courageous men we've got. But they don't always match that in brains. But the problem is, you pay a man four or five hundred dollars a month and you get just what you pay for."[5] In fact, LBJ called Youngblood "the dearest of all."[6]

---

3. Youngblood received the Exceptional Service Award on 12/4/63, the day after Clint Hill received the same award [*20 Years in the Secret Service*, p. 144-146].
4. Manchester, p. 166. *The Killing of a President* by Robert Groden (1993), p. 37. *Crossfire*, pp. 249-250.
5. *Reaching For Glory: Lyndon Johnson's Secret White House Tapes* by Michael Beschloss (2002), 1964-1965, page 703.
6. *20 Years in the Secret Service*, page 230.

14

WINSTON LAWSON

WIN LAWSON

Winston Lawson served from the Eisenhower era until the early Reagan days, October 1959 to June 1981[1]; quite a span of time. He is best remembered for being the lead advance agent for the fateful Dallas trip on 11/22/63 when President Kennedy was assassinated (agent David Grant assisted Lawson with the advance). Though Agent Sam Kinney told me that Lawson has "regrets" over 11/22/63, as the agent was "the first Secret Service advance man ever to lose a President," sentiments related by Lawson himself in the 1995 documentary *Inside The Secret Service*, as with Agent Greer, there are two sides to the story. Lawson admitted before the Warren Commission that he had been an Army counterintelligence agent before joining the Secret Service.[2] Amazingly, Lawson related in the aforementioned 1995 documentary *Inside The Secret Service* that fellow agents had come to him, not to Grant, nor to anyone else, after the assassination and said, "If it had to happen, I'm glad it happened to you." As author Melanson stated, "The

1. Letter to author dated 2/17/04
2. Manchester, page 312; 4 H 318; see also RIF# 180-10093-10320: 5/31/77 Memorandum from HS-CA's Belford Lawson to fellow HSCA members' Gary Cornwell & Ken Klein (revised 8/15/77).

words seem curious, if not cruel."[3] Lawson quickly added, amidst his tears, "They really didn't mean that in a bad way."

Lawson was involved in all the details of the security arrangements for Dallas, as well as a couple other important matters[4]:

Lawson checked the Protective Research Section (PRS) files for threat subjects and found none.

Lawson told both the Warren Commission and the House Assassinations Committee that he could not recall giving instructions to watch building windows, "although it was his usual practice to do so." Dallas Police Captain Lawrence confirms that no instructions were given.

The press and photographer's flatbed truck was cancelled at the last minute and the reporters and photographers were moved further back and, quite literally, out of the picture.

Military aide Godfrey McHugh was asked for the first time not to ride in the front seat of JFK's limousine (between the driver and SAIC in the passenger seat).

Dr. Burkley and Evelyn Lincoln were shoved further back in the motorcade, over the doctor's protests. Other than the trip to Rome, this was the only time Burkley did not ride close to the president.

The ambulance that should have been on standby in case of injury to JFK was gone from the scene a few minutes before the shooting, carrying an alleged seizure victim to the hospital.

The motorcycle police officers that had "originally been instructed to ride right beside Kennedy" received a change in plans "about five or ten minutes before the motorcade left Love Field." Lawson is, once again, the principal suspect. Even so, the motorcycle officers were flanking Kennedy's car until just before the turn onto Elm Street, then inexplicably dropped back just before the shooting commenced.

Agent Lawson was present during part of Lee Harvey Oswald's interrogation by the Dallas Police Department.

Lawson accompanied FBI Agent Vincent Drain with all the packaged evidence in both the JFK and J.D. Tippit killings aboard USAF plane #276 at 3:10 a.m., C.S.T., 11/23/63, arriving at Andrews Air Force Base at 6:30 a.m. E.S.T. [5] Sheriff Bill Courson later said, "In my opinion, and in the opinion of several others around here, the Secret Service made a bunch of fools of themselves in the whole assassination,

---

3. *The Secret Service: the Hidden History of an Enigmatic Agency* by Philip Melanson (2002), p. 87.
4. See chapter 12 from *Survivor's Guilt.*
5. Lawson's report dated 12/1/63 [CD 3 Exhibits].

especially when they confiscated evidence and tainted it by breaking the chain of evidence."[6]

Both JFK and LBJ were permitted to be in the same city, in the same motorcade, and in slow-moving open vehicles in close proximity to each other. This violation of Secret Service regulations was unheard of until that day.

Lawson told the HSCA he "acknowledged that Lt. Col. George Whitmeyer, who was part of the Dallas District U.S. Army Command, who Lawson said 'taught Army Intelligence' and who rode in the pilot car, 'wasn't scheduled' to be in the motorcade, as Lawson's scheduled motorcade list, bears out.[7] Mr. Lawson denied that the presence of Col. Whitmeyer had anything to do with Lawson's prior service in the CIC, Army Counter Intelligence Corps." Lawson is now a member of the Association of Former Intelligence Officers, or AFIO. This organization was founded by CIA propaganda specialist David Atlee Phillips.[8]

Agent Lawson, Agent Louis Sims (Chicago office, later of Watergate tape "fame"), and a CIA operative who knew Oswald and was also allegedly privy to the assassination plot, Richard Case Nagell, all served at Fort Holabird, MD in the 1950's.

To his eternal credit, Lawson wrote to me on 1/12/04: "I do not know of any standing orders for the agents to stay off the back of the car. After all, foot holds and handholds were built into that particular vehicle. I am sure it would have been on a 'case by case' basis depending on event, intelligence, threats, etc. Jerry Behn as Special Agent in Charge of the White House Detail ... would have been privy to that type of info more than I. However, it never came to my attention as such. I am certain agents were on the back on certain occasions." The agent should be certain of that last understatement. He rode on the back of the limousine on the 7/2/63 Italy trip. Coming from one of the chief architects of security planning in Dallas, this is very important. Lawson himself told author Phil Melanson on 2/20/02: "There's always gonna be a political side versus a Secret Service side. Sometimes you win and sometimes you lose."[9] They lost big in Dallas.

---

6. *No More Silence* by Larry Sneed (1998), p. 505.
7. 17 H 615.
8. *Encyclopedia of the JFK Assassination* by Michael Benson (2002), p. 216.
9. Melanson (2002), p. 88.

15

ABRAHAM BOLDEN

Agent Abraham Bolden served from the Ike era to the LBJ era and is the author of a great book from 2008 called *The Echo From Dealey Plaza*. Bolden, the first African-American agent who served on the White House Detail, also served with distinction in the Chicago field office. Bolden is a hero to many, especially because he was unjustly framed for a crime he did not commit in order to shut him up not long after the JFK assassination. Bolden was a rich source of information for me, as I have spoken to and corresponded with Abe numerous times between 1993 and 2017 (I have also enjoyed much social media contact with Abe and his family).

In addition to Abe's excellent book, I devoted a whole chapter to his story in my first book *Survivor's Guilt*. A sample of what Abe had to convey to me: "I knew from experience that the lax attitude concerning protective assignments, the deep disrespect for Kennedy prevalent within the

Service, and the propensity to consume hard liquor prior to assignment were the actual murderers of our president. Oswald did not kill Kennedy ... the attitudinal violence of the Secret Service did! No one could have killed our President without the shots of omission fired by the Secret Service. Observe the feet of [four] Secret Service agents glued to the running boards of the follow-up car as bullets [sic?] pierce the brain of our President!!!"

"If any person had the ability, love, and compassion to better the condition of all peoples of America, it was John F. Kennedy. Oft times during my assignment at the White House, he would approach me and ask, 'How are they treating you?' or 'How do you like the detail?' He introduced me to every member of his cabinet saying, 'This is Mr. Bolden. I brought him here to make history and to open a door for his people.'[1] Abe had this to say about myself on 4/10/12: "Vince Palamara is the foremost authority on the secret service in the 60s. He is a personal friend of mine and a very good researcher."

In reference to Kennedy's alleged "requests," Mr. Bolden told the author on numerous occasions in 1993-1996 that he "didn't hear anything about that ... I never believed that Kennedy said that [ordering removal of agents]. Bolden later wrote a scathing review of former agent Gerald Blaine's book *The Kennedy Detail*, in which he writes: "I was dismayed at the continued attempts by former agents to deny culpability in the assassination of President John F. Kennedy ... I was hoping that the former Kennedy body guards would show a modicum of contriteness in the book instead of trying to blame Kennedy's assassination on the President himself."

Mr. Bolden, who was imprisoned on trumped-up charges of trying to sell a government report on a counterfeiting case, is adamant that he was innocent and framed by the Secret Service. Anyone who reads Abe's book and studies the case agrees with him. Abe has quite a legion of fans and supporters. In a letter to Josiah Thompson dated 12/26/67, Attorney John Hosmer outlined his case: "Some peculiar and remarkable things happened before and during the trial ... three Secret Service informers were the witnesses against Bolden. One of whom, Joseph Spagnoli, later in his own trial, admitted perjury at the behest of the Government, and Bolden's alleged co-conspirator, a man he had arrested twice (Frank W. Jones), was never brought to trial ... the 'shaft' was put to Bolden by the Secret Service and by my Government." A fellow agent from the Chicago

---

1. Letter to author dated 10/30/93.

office, Conrad Cross, told the HSCA "he believes Bolden was set up" but did not know by whom.[2] Bolden further wrote: "I surmised that the actual reason for my arrest was due to the fact that Kennedy was assassinated and that I could not be depended upon to keep quiet about my complaints [of laxity, etc.] regarding the Secret Service.... In August 1964, an all-white jury returned a verdict of guilty on all counts against me and on September 4, 1964 [shortly before the issuance of the Warren Report], I was sentenced to serve 6 years in federal custody.

"In January 1965, Joseph Spagnoli, the counterfeiter contacted by Frank Jones on May 11,1964, was on trial in the court of J. Sam Perry [,] the same judge who had heard both of my trials. This was the same judge who had interrupted the deliberation of the jury in my 1rst trial in order to coax that jury into returning a verdict of guilty.

"During the examination of Joseph Spagnoli by his attorney Frank Oliver, Spagnoli admitted in open court that he had committed perjury in "the Bolden trial." Spagnoli produced a yellow sheet of paper that he admitted stealing from the office of the U.S. Attorney during a pretrial conference. Judge Perry asked Spagnoli if he understood that he was admitting to perjury to which Spagnoli replied, 'Yes, sir.' He openly confessed that the government attorney Richard Sykes solicited the perjured testimony. The change of dates appearing on the stolen paper and the change of times of Jones' contact with Spagnoli were all in the handwriting of Assistant U.S. Attorney Richard T. Sykes.

"Efforts to get a hearing on the perjury matter before Judge Perry by my attorney Raymond Smith proved unsuccessful and the case went to the 7th Circuit Court of Appeals in 1965. During the argument before the U.S. Court of Appeals the issue of Spagnoli's perjury was brought up. Judge Luther Swygert summoned Attorney Richard Sykes into the courtroom and point blank asked Sykes if he had solicited perjury in the Bolden trial. Sykes' reply was, 'Your honor, I refuse to answer that question on the grounds that it may tend to incriminate me.'"[3]

The head of the Chicago office (and Abe's boss), Maurice Martineau, did not wish to talk about Abe when I spoke to him[4]: "As far as Bolden is concerned, I'd rather not discuss it. He was a blight on the agency." Interestingly, Mr. Martineau revealed that he "was subpoenaed to testify before" the HSCA, which he declared "a lot more valid than the Warren Commission." (Abe also spoke to the HSCA). He believed "there was

2. HSCA interview of Conrad Cross [HSCA RIF# 180-10104-10324].
3. Letter to author dated 10/30/93.
4. Author's interviews with Martineau, 9/21/93 & 6/7/96.

more than one assassin" on 11/22/63, stemming from the HSCA's report, his own role in the investigation, his extensive experience with firearms, and his own gut feelings on 11/22/63, "As soon as I learned some of the details … " When the author conveyed to him Agent Kinney's own beliefs of conspiracy, including Agent Kinney's qualification that his own "outfit was clean," Mr. Martineau stated: "Well … ah … (long pause) … I've got some theories, too, but, ah … without any actual data to back them up, I think I'll keep them to myself." Interestingly, like Kinney and Martineau, Bolden also believes there was a conspiracy.

16

ARTHUR GODFREY

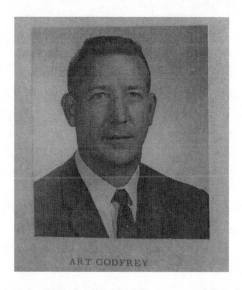

ART GODFREY

Arthur Lincoln "Rawhide" Godfrey, one of the three Shift Leaders of the Kennedy detail, was a genuine war hero of the highest order. He served in the Army in Europe during WWII, and his decorations included two Silver Stars, a Bronze Star, and a Purple Heart. He received a Silver Star for rescuing a soldier and carrying him back to friendly lines in Italy while under enemy fire; a real "Saving Private Ryan" hero. Godfrey protected Presidents Truman through Nixon on the White House Detail and is one of my favorite agents of all time (how could you *not* like this man?). I spoke to Art twice and corresponded with him once; great guy.

Fellow agent Darwin David Horn, Sr., described Godfrey as "a very good friend who enjoyed protection so much he stayed there for his entire career."[1] This was later confirmed to me via an e-mail from former agent Walt Coughlin. For his part, former agent Gerald Blaine said of Godfrey, "He won two Silver Stars in Yugoslavia during WWII."[2] Former agent Sam Sulliman said that Godfrey "had quite a war record."[3] Indeed.

---

1. E-mail to author dated 1/30/04.
2. Author's interview with Blaine, 2/7/04.
3. Author's interview with Sulliman, 2/11/04.

Regarding Agent Art Godfrey, author Anthony Summers, who also interviewed the agent, wrote, "Godfrey ... had been unusually close to both Nixon and [Bebe] Rebozo. After retiring in 1974, he had visited the disgraced president at San Clemente and watched the Grand Prix with him at Long Beach. Rebozo even asked Godfrey to work for him. As late as 1994 Godfrey was a member of the February Group, an association of diehard Nixon loyalists."[4]

The former agent told me on 5/30/96, regarding the notion that JFK ordered the agents not to observe standard procedures, which included removing themselves from the rear of the limousine: "That's a bunch of baloney; that's not true. He never ordered us to do anything. He was a very nice man ... cooperative." Godfrey repeated this to me on 6/7/96. Asked if Aide Ken O'Donnell issued any similar orders, Godfrey said emphatically, "He did not order anyone around." As just one example, Godfrey was on the Italy trip mentioned in Floyd Boring's report and agents frequently rode on the rear of the limousine, one of whom was none other than Winston G. Lawson.[5] In a letter dated 11/24/97, Godfrey stated the following: "All I can speak for is myself. When I was working with President Kennedy he never asked me to have my shift leave the limo when we were working it," thus confirming what he had told the author over the phone on two prior occasions.

---

4. *The Arrogance of Power: The Secret World of Richard Nixon* by Anthony Summers (2001), p. 247 (See also photo section re: picture of Godfrey).
5. Italy film clip, courtesy Jim Cedrone of the JFK Library; newly discovered still photos from Naples in *John Fitzgerald Kennedy: A Life In Pictures* by Yann-Brice Dherbier & Pierre-Henri Verlhac (New York: Phaidon Press, 2003), pp. 183 & 231. Corbis stock photos discovered by the author in 2005 (and also forwarded to former agents' Blaine, Coughlin, & O'Rourke). Godfrey wrote to the author: "I did the advance in Rome and the Vatican and Bob Lilley did the advance in Naples. I think NATO was there then."

17

ROY KELLERMAN

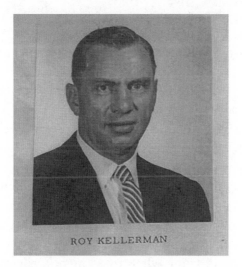

ROY KELLERMAN

Incredibly, ASAIC Roy Kellerman told the following to FBI agents' James Sibert & Francis O'Neill on the night of the murder of JFK: "The advanced security arrangements made for this specific trip were the most stringent and thorough ever employed by the Secret Service for the visit of a President to an American city."[1] Perhaps *this* is why JFK reassured a worried San Antonio Congressman Henry Gonzalez on 11/21/63 by saying: "The Secret Service told me that they had taken care of everything – there's nothing to worry about."[2] If that weren't enough, President Kennedy told an equally concerned advance man, Marty Underwood, on 11/21/63: in Houston, "Marty, you worry about me too much."[3]

Kellerman, who served from FDR to LBJ, is a real paradox. On the one hand, he was ineffective during the assassination and failed to protect the president, yet he also gave testimony that goes against official history. As most students of the assassination know, Roy stated to the Warren Commission on 3/9/64: "There have got to be more than three shots, gentleman"[4] and that a "flurry of shells" came into the car in rapid succession.[5]

---

1. FBI RIF#124-10012-10239; Kellerman would go on to deny ever saying such a thing: 18 H 707-708.
2. *High Treason*, page 127; *Two Men In Dallas* video by Mark Lane, 1976.
3. *Evening Magazine* video 11/22/88; interview with Marty Underwood 10/9/92.
4. 2 H 78.
5. 2 H 74, 76, 77.

Kellerman also testified, "There was in the early – this was on the day [11/22/63] in Parkland Memorial Hospital, and this information comes from Dr. George Burkley … I asked him the condition of Governor Connally, and have they removed the bullet from him … Dr. Burkley said that to his knowledge he still has the bullet in him. … This was after we got into the hospital after the shooting, sir, between then and 2 o'clock."[6] Dr. Robert R. Shaw, Connally's surgeon, spoke at a press conference: "The bullet is in the leg … it hasn't been removed … it will be removed before he goes to the recovery room."[7]

According to his widow June, Roy "accepted that there was a conspiracy." This was based on June overhearing Roy's telephone conversation with someone from the HSCA in approximately 1977 or 1978. "I'll accept that" was Roy's telephone reply to the Committee.[8] Like Bill Greer, Roy is often added to the list of those witnesses who reported that the right rear of JFK's head was blasted, indicating a shot from the front, and for good reason: the drawings of JFK's wounds he gave to HSCA investigators on 8/24/77 show that exactly.[9] Finally, one of Kellerman's two daughters told Harold Weisberg in the 1970's: "I hope the day will come when these men [Kellerman and Greer] will be able to say what they've told their families."[10] In a letter to the author dated 12/2/97, Mrs. Kellerman wrote, "Roy did not say that JFK was difficult to protect," which confirms my two prior telephone interviews with her conducted on 3/2/92 and 9/27/92, respectively. Kellerman did not mention JFK's alleged desires even once during his very lengthy, two-session interview with the Warren Commission,[11] not to mention his reports and his later HSCA and private researcher contacts.

LBJ had this to say about Kellerman: "This fellow Kellerman … he was about as loyal a man as you could find. But he was about as dumb as an ox."[12]

---

6. 2 H 91.

7. Dr. Robert R. Shaw Press Conference (Connally's surgeon), 7:00 CST 11/22/63 on WFAA/ ABC (see also *Treachery in Dallas* by Walt Brown, p. 158: video snippet provided to author). Here is the video in question: https://www.youtube.com/watch?v=aQ8NJwq58Fg

8. Author's interview with June Kellerman 3/2/92; *Vanity Fair*, Dec. 1994, p. 88 – information provided to authors.

9. HSCA interview of Kellerman, 8/24-8/25/77 Kellerman: 2 H 80-81, 93. Greer: 2 H 124, 127, 128.

10. This was revealed in a letter to the author from noted author/researcher Harold Weisberg from 3/92.

11. 2 H 61-112.

12. *Reaching For Glory: Lyndon Johnson's Secret White House Tapes, 1964-1965* by Michael R. Beschloss (New York: Simon & Schuster, 2002), p. 703.

The News and Courier – Jan 30, 1969

not go voluntarily.

But Roy Kellerman, now an FBI agent after serving in the Secret Service, was ordered to testify at the trial of Shaw, 55, who Garrison has charged with plotting with Lee Harvey Oswald and pilot David W. Ferrie to murder Kennedy.

Kellerman was sitting beside Bill Greer, driver of the presidential limousine, in Dallas on Nov. 22, 1963, when Kennedy was shot. Two other FBI agents previously were ordered to appear at the Shaw trial.

In this news article, it is claimed that Kellerman became an FBI agent after retiring from the Secret Service and was scheduled to appear in the Jim Garrison case.

18

DON LAWTON

I am responsible for making Don Lawton "famous." In 1991, I discovered (well, actually, I popularized) a segment from WFAA/ABC video depicting the Love Field Dallas airport arrival of President and Mrs. Kennedy. This particular clip I later showed during major conference presentations in 1995, 1996 and 1997, as well as on The History Channel. In the video, one can see agent Donald J. Lawton[1] jogging at the rear of the limousine on JFK's side only to be recalled by none other than Emory P. Roberts, who rises in his seat in the follow-up car and, using his voice and several hand-gestures, orders Lawton to cease and desist.[2] As the ARRB's Doug Horne wrote in a memo dated 4/16/96, based on viewing the aforementioned video shown during the author's presentation at

---

1. 25 H 787
2. Author's discovery, shown at the following major national research conferences: COPA '95, COPA '96, Lancer '97, as well as on *The Men Who Killed Kennedy: The Smoking Guns,* 2003. As the ARRB's Doug Horne wrote in a 4/16/96 memo: "The author viewed this videotape at a symposium in 1995 [by Vince Palamara, presenter]."

a 1995 research conference: "The bafflement of the agent who is twice waved off of the limousine is clearly evident. This unambiguous and clearly observed behavior would seem to be corroboration that the change in security procedure which was passed to SA Clint Hill earlier in the week by ASAIC Floyd Boring of the Secret Service White House Detail was very recent, ran contrary to standing procedure, and that not everyone on the White House Detail involved in Presidential protection had been informed of this change." In regard to the Love Field video, former agent Larry Newman told me he "never saw that before." This clip has become a You Tube sensation and was later shown on the 2009 Discovery Channel documentary *Secrets of the Secret Service*. Most everyone who sees the clip is impressed- Emory Roberts rises in his seat, uses hand gestures, and obviously says something to Lawton before Lawton speaks. Only then does Lawton stop, turn, and raise his arms three times high in the air in response to what Roberts said and did. Agent Landis even makes room for Lawton on the running board and none of the people in the car can be seen reacting positively to what Lawton is expressing.

Agent Don Lawton told me on 11/15/95: "JFK was very personable … very warm. Everyone felt bad. It was our job to protect the President. You still have regrets, remorse. Who knows, *if they had left guys on the back of the car* … you can hindsight yourself to death [Emphasis added]." A friend of Lawton's said he felt guilty and kept saying 'I should have been there [on the back of the car].' "[3]

Lawton passed away 4/5/13.

VINCE MROZ

Agent Vince Mroz, along with Floyd Boring and Stu Stout, was one of the heroes of 11/1/50, the day two Puerto Rican Nationalists attempted to assassinate President Truman when he was staying at Blair House during the renovation of the White House. Vince protected Truman (starting in 1949, the year after he entered the Secret Service), Eisenhower, part-time with JFK (9 months), LBJ, and Nixon, retiring as Deputy Assistant Director of the Uniformed Division in 1974. During an interview conducted on 2/7/04, Mroz said that President Kennedy was "friendly, congenial – he was really easy to get along with … just like Truman." When asked point blank, if JFK had ever ordered the agents off the car, Mroz said forcefully, "No, no – that's not true." When asked a second time, the former agent responded with equal conviction: "He did not order anybody off the car."

In December 1951, President Truman, described as being "deeply moved," decorated Mroz and Floyd Boring with silver lapel buttons for their roles in saving him. He said they were "two straight-shooting secret service agents."

Agent Mroz became the head of the Charleston, West Virginia and Kansas City, Missouri field offices, also having served in both the Chicago, Illinois and Springfield, Illinois field offices. Mroz later became an Inspector in headquarters.[1]

Mroz passed away 7/22/08.

---

1. *American Gunfight* by Stephen Hunter and John Bainbridge, Jr (2005), page 325.

DAN EMMETT

Dan Emmett served from 1983 to 2004 in the Secret Service and is the author of what I consider to be the very best Secret Service memoir to date, *Within Arm's Length* (I am mentioned on the cover of the original edition of Dan's fine book). Dan was praised by fellow agent Dan Bongino for his teaching skills when Emmett was an instructor[1], saying Dan was "as tough a human being as I had ever encountered," as Dan has a fine reputation for teaching many agents who went on to careers in the Secret Service. A former Marine and CIA agent, Dan's career in the Secret Service spanned 21 years protecting three presidents (four, if you count being a young post stander with President Reagan). I have spoken to and corresponded with Dan many times; great guy.

Dan has done a very good job expressing his point of view during numerous media appearances between 2012 and the present time. Dan is often called upon to offer his candid opinions with regard to various Secret Service scandals and intrigue that has unfortunately come the agency's

---

1. Dan Bongino's *Life Inside The Bubble* (2013), page 20.

way as of late. The former agent does not pull any punches and is quite eloquent. He has appeared on CNN, Fox News, and other media outlets, and a fair amount of his appearances are archived online.[2]

Dan is on record as stating the following:

> The office of the presidency for the last couple of years has not been as secure as it has been in years past. This goes back to a complete failure in leadership from the director's seat all the way down to middle management. It's not out of question that a Secret Service agent, or even two or three, might get drunk and act stupid on a trip, but it was beyond imagination during my career that a supervisor would get drunk and act stupid on a trip. I've been very critical of the Secret Service with impropriety after impropriety over the last couple of years, and I have no dog in the fight. I'm just calling them as I see them. When the leadership is not good, the troops do not perform up to standard. There cannot be a worse tragedy for the nation than losing a president. We must make sure that never happens again. After 9/11, we got agent candidates at the academy that were so substandard they never would have been hired before. I watched the quality of a class of 24 agents in training that would produce before 9/11 about 18 super-solid future agents and about six that were average, to a class of 24 agents in training after 9/11 that would produce about eight agents that were average and 16 who were sub-standard.

Regarding the first female Secret Service Director, Julia Pierson, Emmett said: "Barack Obama was going to have a female Secret Service director and that was the end of the story. Julia Pierson was a fine agent. We came on the job together, and I consider her to be a friend. But she was not director material. When she got the position, I feared it would not end well, because she lacked a strong sense of being a leader. The Secret Service is filled with great managers and she was probably a great manager. But just because you keep being promoted does not make you a good leader. You can't sit in your office on the eighth floor, do nothing but hold meetings, and expect that everything is going to go well."[3]

---

2. See, for example: https://www.youtube.com/watch?v=xEqQ4XGOjBs and https://www.youtube.com/watch?v=aajwZIWCP7A and https://www.youtube.com/watch?v=Gf7SQSzzqbw
3. WND 12/7/14 Secret Service experts worry about Obama's safety.

DAN BONGINO

Dan Bongino is a somewhat controversial former agent who regularly makes the media rounds – on television and in various internet news articles – regarding anything related to the Secret Service and President Obama, often espousing right wing views. Bongino is the author of three books, *Life Inside the Bubble* (2013), *The Fight* (2016), and *Protecting The President: An Inside Account of the Troubled Secret Service in an Era of Evolving Threats* (2017). Bongino was a New York Police Department officer from 1995 to 1999. He joined the Secret Service in 1999, serving on PPD for Presidents George W. Bush and Barack Obama before leaving the Secret Service in 2011 to run for the Senate.

Bongino is also hosts radio shows and has been outspoken at times in criticism toward President Obama, sometimes to the regret of former colleagues in the Secret Service.[1] Bongino is once again running for Congress, this time in Florida.[2]

---

1.   http://abcnews.go.com/Politics/secret-service-agent-turns-obama-runs-congress/story?id=20807235

2. http://www.wcbm.com/2016/06/10/dan-bongino-running-for-congress-in-florida/

JOE CLANCY

J oe Clancy is a former SAIC of the Secret Service for President Obama and the Director from 10/1/14 to 3/4/17, retiring early in the Trump administration. "Joe Clancy is deeply respected within the federal law enforcement community. He has served with distinction inside the Secret Service, and he has done well respected work outside the Secret Service too," said Mark Filip, a former federal judge and deputy attorney general in the George W. Bush administration. "Ultimately, Joe Clancy struck the right balance of familiarity with the Secret Service and its missions, respect from within the workforce, and a demonstrated determination to make hard choices and foster needed change. I am confident Joe will continue this management approach."[1]

Dan Emmett, a member of the agency's elite counter assault team – often referred to as CAT – had put himself and his squad into an observation position when Clancy's voice came over the radio. "Hawkeye from command post," Clancy said. "Be advised that numerous North Korean soldiers have been observed moving into their sector of the bridge armed with AK-47 rifles."

The situation presented deadly security implications that could erupt into a diplomatic firestorm and, if handled crudely, maybe even war. But Clancy remained cool and collected as President Bill Clinton arrived, visited the crossing and left none the wiser. "He's unflappable," Emmett says of Clancy, recounting the standoff. "I've never heard him swear. He's not emotional, other than the fact that he was a little bit louder than normal that day when he told me the guys were coming up with AKs."

---

1. CNN, 2/18/15.

"At the same time, as a leader, his people on CAT liked him a lot because he led in a quiet manner, by example. He never asked his team to do anything he could not do or would not do himself. He's a very serious man. But he's also a very good man, a very kind man. He's not full of himself, he has no ego. He's just a solid guy who does his work."[2]

Within the Secret Service, he is still well known and highly regarded. Fellow agents call Joe Clancy "Father Joe" because he looks the part of a priest but also because of how he goes about his business. Clancy has a good relationship with both Obamas.

A news article from Clancy's hometown reported the following:

> Joseph Clancy once patrolled the backfield as a football player for Archbishop Carroll High School, helping the Patriots win the 1971 city championship. The Haverford [PA] native was charged Wednesday with a far greater responsibility — repairing the agency that protects the president of the United States and other political dignitaries... Clancy, 59, traces his roots to Delaware County, where he attended St. Denis in Haverford before graduating from Archbishop Carroll in 1973. He attended West Point before transferring to Villanova University, where he graduated in 1978 with a political science degree. He taught at Father Judge High School in Philadelphia before joining the Secret Service.
>
> Clancy ascended the agency's ranks to head the Presidential Protection Division. He previously served as the director of national special security events and led a squad of agents at the Secret Service's field office in New York. "He's always taken his job seriously and he prefers to remain anonymous," said Clancy's brother, Kevin. "He's not going to be happy about me talking — but I'm not going to lie. He'll be happy not to be in the press after this."
>
> Clancy retired from the Secret Service in 2011. He spent the previous three years working for Comcast, becoming the cable giant's executive director of security in May. Now, he's headed back to Washington.
>
> "We were happy to have him back in the Philadelphia area and we were just getting used to having him around," said Kevin Clancy, who spoke with his brother when Joe called Wednesday to check on their father.
>
> Clancy is tasked with restoring the reputation of a 6,700-member agency that is best known for protecting the president. Confidence in the agency's ability to fulfill that mission eroded in recent

---

2. http://www.usnews.com/news/articles/2014/10/08/who-is-joe-clancy-the-new-secret-service-acting-director

weeks as revelations of security breaches surfaced. In addition to an intruder successfully entering the White House, Obama allegedly shared an elevator in Atlanta with an armed guard who was not authorized to be around him.

"Almost anyone who has read the news is shocked by these lapses," said David Barrett, a Villanova political science professor who specializes in the presidency and the history of the CIA. "The No. 1 priority is getting the agency back into an operational mode, but he also has to think about the public."

Improving the performance of the Secret Service will boost public confidence in the agency, Barrett said. That Clancy has an intricate knowledge of the agency's protocols, standards and personnel will help him ensure the agency functions properly, he added.

"He sounds like he has the temperament, the experience, the ability," Barrett said. "He sounds, to me, well-situated to bring this agency back into a better operational mode."

Joe McNichol, who coached Clancy at Archbishop Carroll, noted Clancy captained the team in 1972, his senior year. He said Clancy probably was "the best conditioned athlete we had at the time." His character also was notable, he said.

"He's a great person, he really is," McNichol said. "The Clancys — they were raised well. ... I've got nothing but kind words for him, believe me. He's exceptional. He's just a wonderful person."

Various national and local leaders took to Twitter to offer their support of Barrett, including Haverford police and Archbishop Carroll President the Rev. Edward Casey.

"I knew Joe Clancy when he led the presidential detail," Tweeted David Axelrod, a former adviser to Obama. "You could not find a better person to repair the Secret Service."

Comcast also issued a statement praising Clancy as distinguished for his "integrity and strong management skills."

"During more than three years at Comcast, he was an integral part of our security team and we are sad to see him leave," the statement read. "We are highly confident he will be an outstanding interim leader for the Secret Service and we wish him the very best."[3]

The Secret Service scandals that are (hopefully) all in the past now:

November 22, 1963: NINE agents, including Clint Hill and three others on the Secret Service follow-up vehicle, went drinking and

---

3. http://www.delcotimes.com/general-news/20141002/haverford-native-joseph-clancy-tapped-to-head-secret-service

carousing in the early morning hours, having a detrimental effect on President Kennedy's protection. The President was assassinated a short time later in what was and is *the* biggest scandal in the Service's history. Hill was not reprimanded but promoted (twice-SAIC of WHD and Assistant Director), awarded a medal, retired early with full government pension, and has gone on to fame and fortune as the author of four books with his young girlfriend co-author. The protection of Kennedy was horrid- JFK was literally left a sitting duck during that dark day 50 years ago.

November 2009: A Washington couple, Tareq and Michaele Salahi, crash Obama's first state dinner. The Secret Service later acknowledges that officers never checked whether they were on the guest list. A photo emerges showing that they shook hands with the president. Mark Sullivan, the director at the time, says that he is "deeply concerned and embarrassed" by the breach. The Salahis parlay their fame into an undistinguished career in reality TV.

November 2011: A man with a semiautomatic rifle parks in front of the White House and fires at the building, with Sasha Obama inside and Malia Obama on her way home. A Secret Service supervisor, mistaking the shots for car backfire, orders officers to stand down. The service does not figure out that shots hit the building for four days, and only then because a housekeeper noticed broken glass. The president and first lady are infuriated.

April 2012: Eight Secret Service agents doing advance work for a presidential trip to a summit in Colombia lose their jobs after allegations that some took prostitutes from a strip club back to their hotel rooms. A Justice Department investigation finds that two Drug Enforcement Administration agents arranged one encounter between a prostitute and a Secret Service officer. Obama later says: "When we travel, we have to observe the highest standards."

May 2013: A Secret Service supervisor leaves a bullet in a woman's room at the Hay-Adams hotel, which overlooks the White House, and allegedly tries to force his way into the room to retrieve it. An investigation finds that the supervisor and a colleague sent sexually suggestive emails to a woman subordinate. The supervisor loses his job, and the colleague is reassigned. A Secret Service spokesman says: "Periodically we have isolated incidents of misconduct, just like every organization does."

March 2014: Three Secret Service agents responsible for protecting Obama in Amsterdam are placed on leave after a night of drinking, in violation of Secret Service rules. One of the agents is passed out drunk in a hallway. The newspaper reports that the three are part of what is known as the counter assault team, a last line of defense responsible for fighting off assailants if the president or his motorcade comes under attack.

Sept. 16, 2014: In perhaps the most chilling of the Secret Service lapses, a security contractor with a gun and an assault record gets on an elevator with the president during a trip to Atlanta. The contractor used his cellphone to take video of Obama and did not stop when Secret Service agents told him to. The Secret Service only learns that the man has a gun when he is fired on the spot and turns it over. Obama was not told.

Sept. 19, 2014: An Iraq war veteran with a knife jumps the White House fence, dashes through the North Portico doors and makes it deep inside the building, into the East Room, before he is tackled, and only then by an off-duty Secret Service agent. The Secret Service first says only that the man was apprehended after getting in the door. A congressman says that a security alarm was disabled because staff nearby found it too noisy.

23

ROBERT DEPROSPERO

R obert DeProspero is arguably one of the most respected protection agents the United States Secret Service has ever been honored
to employ.[1] Agent Joe Petro said Bob was "as good a protection
agent as the Secret Service has ever had."[2] Jerry Parr said: "I was blessed
with great deputies ... Bob DeProspero on PPD."[3]

Bob graduated from West Virginia University (WVU) with a Bachelor's
Degree (BS) in physical education in 1959 and a master's degree (MA)
in education in 1960[4] and later joined the United States Secret Service
(USSS), serving from 1965-1986.[5] He was the Special Agent In Charge
(SAIC) of the Presidential Protective Division (PPD) during a large part
of the President Reagan era (January 1982 to April 1985), succeeding
Jerry S. Parr.[6] Parr chose an excellent replacement: DeProspero was the
perfect agent to head Reagan's detail in the wake of the assassination attempt. Fellow former agents Walt Coughlin, Jerry Kivett, Howell Purvis,
Robert Snow, Darwin Horn, Mike Maddaloni, and a host of others waxed
on about DeProspero's virtues to me in unique interviews that I conducted between 1991 and 2007. Walt wrote the following: "Have known Bobby for many years. Very disciplined – no nonsense guy-wrestled [at] West
Va. U. Very good protection guy – Bobby is respected." Former agent

1. See, for example, the book *Standing Next To History* (2005) by former Secret Service agent Joseph
Petro, pages 140-142, 202-204, & 206-207.
2. *Standing Next To History* (2005), page 141.
3. *In The Secret Service* (2013), page 189.
4. Please see: http://alumni.wvu.edu/awards/academy/1995/robert_deprospero/
5. 6/14/05 e-mail from George D. Rogers, Assistant Director, Office of Government and Public Affairs, to Vince Palamara.
6. Please see: *New York Times*, 1/4/82 and *Washington Post*, May 15, 1998, page A01.

Mike Maddaloni wrote, "Bobby D was…very quiet, short in stature, but a weightlifter who was very powerful." Former agent Bob Snow wrote the author: "I know Bobby De. He was one of the best." Former agent Jerry Kivett wrote the author: "I served on occasions with Bob … and have high regard for [him]." Former agent Howell "Hal" Purvis likewise wrote, "He was a dedicated agent and well respected by his peers … I thought he was the best." Former agent Bob Ritter wrote: "DeProspero had a reputation of being an effective and fair supervisor, who elicited the best from those under him. With a poker face and reserved demeanor, DeProspero kept his subordinates guessing. He said little, but when he did – you listened. Never knowing for sure where they stood with DeProspero, most agents gave more than they might have otherwise. DeProspero's managerial style presented no problem for [me]; [I] always gave [my] best."[7]

DeProspero devised several very important and innovative security measures during his time in the Secret Service (while SAIC of PPD) that are used to this very day: the "hospital agent" (stationing an agent at the nearest primary trauma hospital on a presidential movement),[8] to which he received from the agency, among his many other awards, the prestigious Special Recognition for the Establishment of the Presidential Trauma Protocol,[9] as well as the creation of magnetometer (metal detector) checkpoints to screen every individual who could get a view of the president, earning yet another agency award, Special Recognition for Improved Security Measures.[10]

As a result of his outstanding achievements as SAIC of PPD, DeProspero was appointed assistant to the director in the Office of Training,[11] directing both a 20 million dollar expansion of the physical training facility and the administration of literally hundreds of courses.[12]

The tremendous influence of DeProspero's time and talents in the Secret Service can still be felt today: not only have many of the assistant

---

7. *Breaking Tecumseh's Curse* (2013), page 432.
8. *Standing Next To History* (2005), page 141. See also *Syracuse Herald Journal*, 4/10/85: "AN AWESOME JOB- Agent was willing to die to keep Reagan alive WASHINGTON (AP) As the man who walked one step behind President Reagan for 4 years, Robert L. DEPROSPERO began every day knowing he could be called upon to place his body between the president and a bullet. There never was any doubt that he'd do it. "I always felt I was the guy," he said." Also, please see: Philadelphia Inquirer, 6/27/98; *NY Times*, 5/19/82; *Frederick Post*, 4/3/84.
9. http://alumni.wvu.edu/awards/academy/1995/robert_deprospero/
10. *Standing Next To History*, page 141; see also: http://alumni.wvu.edu/awards/academy/1995/robert_deprospero/
11. *Standing Next To History*, page 202; excerpt from DeProspero retirement party as shown in the AFAUSSS newsletter (Bob is listed as ATD: Assistant To the Director)- see: http://robertdeprospero.blogspot.com/
12. http://alumni.wvu.edu/awards/academy/1995/robert_deprospero/

directors, deputy directors, and even some directors of the Secret Service (Lewis C. Merletti, Brian L. Stafford, Barbara S. Riggs, Stephen M. Sergek, George Opfer, and David G. Carpenter, to name a few) come out of DeProspero's PPD,[13] Robin L. Deprospero (Philpot), whom I have spoken to and corresponded with, is currently the chief of the Personnel Security Branch, Special Investigations and Security Division, of the Secret Service, extending the proud legacy of the Deprospero family from the 1960's through and including the millennium and beyond.[14]

On 4/10/11, I received the shock of my life and a most pleasant surprise – Bob DeProspero himself wrote to me out of the blue: "Vince, I have been watching your work for many months. Am impressed with your research, accuracy and willingness to "tell it like it is." In retrospect, should have talked to you instead of Del [Wilber]. Bob DeProspero."[15]

Unbeknownst to Bob at the time, it was I who started his Wikipedia page (since amended by others)![16]

Bob and I continue to correspond since and I have become Associate Producer of a major forthcoming documentary on his life and career called *The Man Behind The Suit*. In addition, his daughter Robin, currently in the Secret Service, contacted me via e-mail and phone in order to give me the honor of adding my praise of her father ("as the foremost civilian literary expert on the U.S. Secret Service") to the written nomination of a very prestigious award Bob received!

---

13. *Standing Next To History*, page 203; personal research of the author.
14. http://wvutoday.wvu.edu/pdf/Sep171998.pdf See also: http://a257.g.akamaitech.net/7/257/2422/01jan20061800/edocket.access.gpo.gov/2006/pdf/E6-13942.pdf
15. DeProspero is mentioned in both Del Wilber's book *Rawhide Down* and former agent Bob Ritter's book *Breaking Tecumseh's Curse*.
16. https://en.wikipedia.org/wiki/Robert_DeProspero

24

EDMUND STARLING

Colonel Edmund W. Starling is something of a legend within the Secret Service. Serving Presidents Wilson thru FDR, Starling was the SAIC of the WHD for a point in time during the FDR era and was the author of the book *Starling of the White House*, which came out two years after he died on 8/3/44. Colonel Starling, a native of Kentucky, began his career as a Deputy Sheriff in Hopkinsville and later became a special agent for the railroads, gaining fame when he trapped a desperate criminal known as "The California Kid." Following this feat, his expert horsemanship and unerring trigger finger became legendary. Special assignments given to him by President Theodore Roosevelt led to his appointment to the White House Secret Service staff in 1914. He became chief in 1935. Often referred to as "the one man the President has to obey," he had supervised almost all presidential trips since Wilson's administration. Colonel Starling was married in 1933 to Mrs. Ida Lee Bourne White, a hostess in a Washington radio station. He had traveled more than 1,000,000 miles in this country and abroad with the five Presidents under whose administrations he served before his retirement in September 1943. Colonel Starling was credited with saving the life of Georges Clemenceau, French Premier, at the time of the Versailles peace conference, in which he accompanied President Woodrow Wilson. He was riding within the car immediately behind Clemenceau's car when he saw an onlooker aim a gun at the Premier. Quickly drawing his own gun, he shot the weapon out of the man's wrist.[1]

There's a natural tendency to think of the Secret Service as above reproach, especially concerning the notion of any possible bad blood between their own ranks. However, as far back as 6/1/67, during ex-agent George Drescher's Herbert Hoover Library oral history, Drescher, the SAIC of the WHD right before Rowley, made the comment: "[Col. Edmund] Starling [SAIC of WHD during the 1930's] wrote a book. He was a phony. He was the biggest phony in the world, the way he used to parade."

---

1. *Cincinnati Enquirer,* 8/4/44.

25

GLEN BENNETT

From the HSCA's 1/30/78 interview summary we learn the following details about Bennett's background in the Secret Service: "Glen Bennett stated that he joined the Secret Service on 10/5/59. He trained at the Treasury School and Secret Service school. The training period was seven weeks. About two of the weeks were devoted to Presidential Protection; other training included counterfeiting and forgery. The protection segment would have been interspersed with the other training. Training included the "History of Assassinations"; manuals as reading materials. They got more or less "on the job training," working in and around the White House. Bennett's first assignment was Cleveland, Ohio, where his SAIC was Michael Burger. His second assignment was Washington, D.C. in the Protective Research Section. Robert Bouck was the Chief of PRS. Bennett stated that there were five agents in PRS at that time. He stated that they would receive intelligence and had liaison with FBI, CIA, ATF, the military, U.S. Customs and local police departments. They would have an index file on 3 x 5 cards broken down into geographical areas. East-1, Mid-West-2, S.W.-3, and West 4. The advance men would be the moving force on all trips. They would handle original pre-trip survey and reports, both pre-trip and post-trip.... He said that the FBI worked with PRS on the investigation into the assassination."[1]

From Bennett's alleged contemporaneous handwritten notes from 11/22/63: "... I heard a noise that immediately reminded me of a firecracker. Immediately, upon hearing the supposed firecracker, looked at

---

1. RIF # 180-10082-10452.

the Boss's [JFK's] car. At this exact time I saw a shot that hit the Boss about four inches down from the right shoulder; a second shoot [sic] followed immediately and hit the right rear high of the Boss's head."[2] From Bennett's typed report dated 11/23/63: "… I heard what sounded like a firecracker. I immediately looked from the right/crowd/physical area and looked towards the President who was seated in the right rear seat of his limousine open convertible. At the moment I looked at the back of the President I heard another firecracker noise and saw the shot hit the President about four inches down from the right shoulder. A second shot followed immediately and hit the right rear high of the President's head … We peered towards the rear and particularly the right side of the area."[3] From Bennett's HSCA interview: "He remembers hearing what he hoped was a firecracker. He then heard another noise and saw what appeared to be a nick in the back of President Kennedy's coat below the shoulder. He thought the President had been hit in the back. Glen Bennett stated that he believes the first and second shots were close together and then a longer pause before the third shot … Bennett stated that he does not recall any agents reacting before the third shot … Bennett stated that he believes he saw the nick in the President's coat after the second shot."[4]

So, what's the problem? Although the autopsy photo, the death certificate signed by Dr. Burkley, FBI Exhibit 60 (JFK's shirt), FBI Exhibit 59 (JFK's jacket), the autopsy face sheet (which was "verified" by Dr. Burkley), the Sibert & O'Neill Report, Secret Service Agent Clint Hill's report, the testimony of Secret Service agent Hill, the testimony of Secret Service agent Bill Greer, the testimony of Secret Service agent Roy Kellerman, the 1/27/64 Warren Commission executive session transcript and Nurse Diana Bowron's recent statements corroborate Bennett's alleged eyewitness observation within an inch or two, Phil Willis' photo #5, the Hugh Betzner photo, the Zapruder film, and the James Altgens photo depict Bennett looking away from Kennedy![5] During the HSCA era, Bennett worked in the Intelligence Division.[6]

---

2. 24 H 541-542.

3. 18 H 760.

4. 1/30/78 HSCA interview with Bennett [RIF#180-10082-10452].

5. *Best Evidence* by David Lifton, autopsy photo 5. Photo 18 17 H 25-26. Photo 17. 17 H 45. *Cover-Up* by Stewart Galanor, page 128. *Postmortem* by Harold Weisberg, p. 310 & 532-536. 18 H 744-745. 2 H 143. 2 H 127 and RIF#180-1009910491: 2/28/78 HSCA interview. 2 H 93. *The Killing of a President* by Robert Groden, p. 118. *Killing The Truth* by Harrison Livingstone, p. 183. 21 H 770. *Mortal Error* by Bonar Menninger, photo 14 blow-up. *Image of an Assassination* video/DVD 1998: sprocket hole area. 21 H 781-782.

6. 12/14/77 letter from Secret Service Legal Counsel Robert O. Goff to the HSCA's G. Robert Blakey, RIF #180-10112-10218.

Finally, some vital data via Ancestry.Com:

Glen Arthur Bennett:

Born 12 July 1928 McDonald PA Washington Co.;

Died 4 April 1994 632 Woodlawn Dr. Bradenton, FL Manatee Co. 34210-3038 Age 65 years;

Interred 13 April 1994: Arlington National Cemetery - Section 3-Kk, Row 23 Site 3;

Parents: Peter A. Bennett & Madge Kennedy;

SSGT US Army: 23 Sept 1946 to 22 March 1948;

Glen's wife Glenna Mae (Klein) Bennett:

 Born 30 June 1931 Dover, OH Tuscar Co.;

Died 21 June 2000 Bradenton, FL age 68 years;

Interred 9-29-2000 at Arlington - same section as Glen;

Parents: Robert Klein & Janet M. Williams; Step-father: George Aebersold.

26

MIKE REILLY

M ike Reilly started his career with the Secret Service, after a few years as head of the legal division of the Farm Credit Association in Washington, D, C., in 1935. He stepped into the job as chief of the service with the outbreak of World War II, the day after the Japanese bombed Pearl Harbor. There were only three men who preceded Reilly in the job. Joseph W. Murphy, the first Secret Service chief protected Teddy Roosevelt, William Taft and Woodrow Wilson; Dick Jervis, who served during the terms of Warren Harding, Calvin Coolidge, Herbert Hoover and Franklin Roosevelt; and Edmund Starling, who worked as chief for part of the early term of Franklin Roosevelt. Reilly was responsible for arranging the meetings Roosevelt attended at Yalta, Casablanca and Tehran. It was at Tehran that he had his hardest job in protecting President Roosevelt. The Germans, hearing of the meeting, dropped 38 paratroopers into the foothills near Tehran. All 38 were trained assassins and all of them were after Roosevelt and Churchill. Six of the assassins were captured, but the balance of 32 continued to plague the Secret Service men the entire stay. Reilly lined the streets with military from the American Consulate to the meeting place, and then literally sneaked the Chief Executive down alleys and to the meeting while the troops acted as a diversion to the German agents. The rest of the Germans were captured a week after the President and Churchill left Tehran.[1]

---

1. *Desert Sun* (Palm Springs, CA), 12/29/58.

Reilly was also the author of the 1947 book *Reilly of the White House*. Reilly's book contains many gems, including this was: "Incidentally, every schoolboy knows that the White House Secret Service boss can order the President of the United States not to go here or there if he chooses … presidents usually accept the laws of the land and follow Secret Service advice with little or no question."[2] Another one: There were two inviolate rules. The man running or riding at the President's shoulder never left that position unless relieved. The other, if a situation got out of hand, empty all cars and get as much Secret Service flesh between the crowd and the Boss as possible.[3] Reilly also wrote: "He [an agent] was derelict in his duty if he permitted the Chief Executive of the United States to get in any place or position where his life was endangered."[4]

Reilly passed away in June 1973. Interestingly, his 1947 book was reissued in different formats in 2014 (paperback), 2015 (hardcover) and 2017 (kindle).

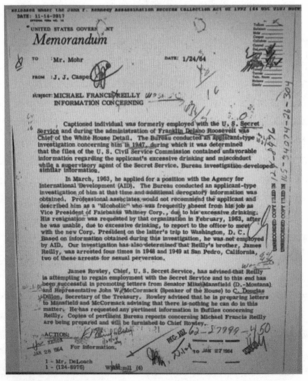

(Via the FBI/ NEW JFK DOCUMENT RELEASES) So FDR's Secret Service Detail Chief, Mike Reilly, was a drunk and his brother was a perv, huh?

---

2. *Reilly of the White House* by Mike Reilly (1947), pages 13-14.
3. *Reilly of the White House*, page 24.
4. *Reilly of the White House* (1947), page 96.

27

FORREST SORRELS

During interviews conducted on 1/28/92 and 9/27/92, the 90-year-old former agent refused to discuss the JFK assassination. Sorrels would only say, "The Warren Report stands." Sorrels passed away 11/6/93. However, Sorrels stated in his report dated 11/28/63: "I looked towards the top of the terrace to my right as the sound of the shots seemed to come from that direction."[1] Sorrels also told the Warren Commission, "I just said, 'What's that?' And turned around to look up on this terrace part there, because the sound sounded like it came from the back and up in that direction ... as I said, the noise from the shots sounded like they may have come back up on the terrace there."[2] Sorrels also recognized the first shot as gunfire, not a firecracker.[3] According to Orville Nix, a Dealey Plaza eyewitness who filmed the assassination and a good friend of Sorrels, the agent told him that the shots came from the grassy knoll.[4]

1. 21 H 548.
2. 7 H 345-346.
3. *The Death of a President* by William Manchester, p. 155.
4. *Rush to Judgment* film by Mark Lane; see also *Who's Who in the JFK Assassination* by Michael Benson (1993), p. 314.

Sorrels had led President Roosevelt over almost the same route as Kennedy took on 11/22/63, the crucial difference being the hazardous Elm Street turn. Sorrels testified to the Warren Commission: "Main Street is right through the heart of the city. It is the best choice for parades. It gives an opportunity for more people – tall buildings on the side of the street – and it is almost invariably – every parade that is had is on Main Street. The one in 1936, when President Roosevelt was there, was the same route in reverse, so to speak."[5]

From an FBI report dated 11/27/63: "At approximately 10:30 P.M. today a telephone call was received from a female individual who refused to furnish her identity. She advised she is a member of the local theatre guild and that on numerous occasions she has attended functions or speeches where Mr. Sorrels, Head of the Secret Service, Dallas, has spoken. She maintained that Mr. Sorrels should be removed from his position as he was incompetent and did not have the ability to protect the president. She stated he was definitely anti-government, against the Kennedy administration, and she felt his position was against the security of not only the President but the United States. During the time this individual furnished the information set out above an effort was made to determine her name and address however she declined." [Signed] Inspector Tom Kelley Secret Service 9:20 A.M. 12/2/63."[6]

---

5. 7 H 337.
6. FBI RIF#124-10164-10019.

28

STU KNIGHT

H. STUART KNIGHT

H. Stuart Knight, like fellow agent Art Godfrey, was quite a war hero. Knight served with distinction during WWII, earning numerous medals, including the Combat Infantry Badge, two Purple Hearts, a Bronze Star, a Silver Star and a Presidential Unit Citation. Knight served in the Secret Service from 1950 to 1982.[1] Knight became the 15th director of the Secret Service in 1973, appointed by President Richard M. Nixon, whose life he probably saved 15 years earlier when a mob attacked the car of the then-vice president in Caracas, Venezuela. Mr. Knight's promotion marked an effort to return luster to the name of the then-108-year-old agency after it was tarnished in the Watergate scandal. Knight was also the man in charge during two unsuccessful assassination attempts on President Gerald R. Ford in 1975 and an attempt that wounded President Ronald Reagan in 1981. Mr. Knight also vowed not to write a tell-all book. "A great deal of our effectiveness is based on the mutual respect and trust we have with the people we protect," he said. "I think I would erode that respect even if I wrote vignettes, telling tales out of school." [2]

---

1. According to his tombstone at Arlington National Cemetery. Most sources state 1950-1981.
2. *Washington Post*, 11/30/81 and 9/12/2009.

On November 3, 1963, the day before the formal wheels were set in motion by agent Floyd Boring for the Texas trip, Vice President Lyndon Johnson began his tour of the Benelux countries. This was to be Stu Knight's last trip as head of the Vice-Presidential Detail; Chief Rowley announced that Rufus Youngblood would replace him near the end of November 1963.[3] Youngblood's first trip with LBJ as the de-facto leader of the V.P. Detail was Texas.[4] Youngblood later stated, "Stu's transfer and my promotion were to become effective Monday, November 25 1963."[5] Why wasn't Knight on the Texas trip? Where was Knight, and where was Behn? They were ostensibly both back in Washington.

I contacted Knight on 10/22/92, and again on 2/8/94, but he refused to discuss the matter at any length, referring me instead on both occasions to Public Affairs agent Jack Warner. Good biographical information on Knight can be found in former agent Harry Neal's book *The Secret Service in Action*.[6]

Knight passed away on 9/7/2009.

---

3. *20 Years in the Secret Service* by Rufus Youngblood (1973), pp. 96-97; see also 4 H 342 and 17 H 618.

4. During an interview with the author conducted on 2/7/04, V.P. LBJ agent Jerry Kivett, who went to Dallas on 11/19/63 and stayed there to conduct the advance work for LBJ's trip to the Bottler's Association, said he "wasn't sure" that Knight was the SAIC of the V.P. LBJ Detail at that specific time, a further indication of how far out of the loop Knight apparently was ... and how close the timing of Youngblood's promotion was planned pre-11/22/63 and made a reality on 11/22/63.

5. Youngblood, p. 97.

6. Neal, pp. 137-140.

29

DAVID GRANT

DAVE GRANT

Agent David Grant was Clint Hill's brother-in-law. Grant was also the assistant advance agent for the ill-fated Texas trip for President Kennedy. As mentioned before, Hill, still legally married to his wife Gwen, has been in a relationship with his co-author, Lisa McCubbin, for a number of years now. Apparently, there was some bad blood – perhaps caused by the aforementioned relationship – between fellow agent David Grant, Clint Hill's brother-in-law, and Clint Hill (Perhaps the bad blood from Grant also included Gerald Blaine, as well. The connection between Grant and Hill was mentioned in a passing comment from Gerald Blaine to myself in June 2005 and also later mentioned in Blaine's 2010 book). Grant, who passed away 12/28/13, turned down the producers of *The Kennedy Detail* movie – including Clint Hill – because he felt the Hollywood lawyers "were trying to buy his memories," yet he gladly agreed to appear on a BBC television program about Kennedy's trip to England.[1/2] I was amazed that Hill failed to mention his relationship to Grant in his two books and in his many media appearances in print, on the radio, and on

1. http://www.bbc.co.uk/ariel/24944881
2. Excerpts appear here: https://www.youtube.com/watch?v=h1nIqthuIUY and https://www.youtube.com/watch?v=XsuuXMmTcPU

television. In fact, both agents – Hill and Grant – appear, albeit separately, on *The Kennedy Detail* 2010 television documentary and, again, nothing was mentioned concerning this startling connection. What really did it for me was the fact that Clint Hill is omitted from the obituary of David Grant, while Hill's wife Gwen is not; very telling, indeed.[3]

When I asked former agent Winston Lawson about Agent Grant's role in the planning of JFK's motorcade route, Lawson attempted to defend his comrade, stating that Grant "wasn't there at the beginning" of the motorcade planning.[4] This statement does nothing to elaborate on either of two subjects:

> 1. Grant's arrival in Texas on 11/18/63, after which the route was changed.[5]

> 2. Lawson's Final Survey Report of 11/19/63, which includes this statement: "This survey was conducted by SA Winston Lawson and SAIC Forrest Sorrels, and assisted by SA David Grant, from November 13 through November 22, 1963 … "[6]

In fact, in the 1995 documentary *Inside The Secret Service*, Win Lawson stated that he had arrived first in Dallas, as the second advance person, David Grant, unacknowledged, arrived just a few days before the event. It appears that Lawson has a habit of attempting to minimize the importance of his partner's role in the planning of the event(s). He then went on to say that he was the first and only advance agent to ever lose a president. What about his partner, David Grant? Like Boring's role, Agent Grant's presence was unknown to the public, and most of the research community, until the author discovered and pointed this out in 1991. In addition, Lawson wrote the author, "In fact, David Grant [,] who [arrived] quite late in the advance, came to help me. He had been on advance in Florida I believe. He was senior to me and would have been in charge in Dallas if he had gone there before me."[7] Perhaps Mr. Grant was more "in charge" than Lawson knew.

Former agent Gerald Blaine told me on 6/10/05: "I was supposed to go from Tampa to Dallas [on 11/18/63]," stating further that the agent who went in his place, David Grant, was dating Clint Hill's sister-in-law at the time (the two went on to be married, thus making Hill and Grant brothers-in-law). This was the first time this interesting connection was revealed.

3. http://www.fairfaxmemorialfuneralhome.com/obituary/David-B.-Grant/Springfield-VA/1326770
4. Author's interview with Winston Lawson, 9/27/92.
5. 18 H 789.
6. 17 H 601.
7. Letter to author dated 1/20/04.

In the aforementioned BBC documentary, David Grant discusses JFK and the day he was assassinated:

> "It should never have happened [...] anyone that was there has got a degree of guilt that they feel but I don't feel responsible for him being assassinated. I regret deeply him being assassinated and wish that it never happened. And I wish that I could have done something to prevent it, but I couldn't."

Better security arrangements during the advance would have helped. He discussed coming face to face with Lee Harvey Oswald: "Arrogant... sneer on his face. As far as whether he or said anything in my presence, he was asked why did you shoot the President? Point blank, and he just shook his head." Oswald always denied killing JFK and said he was just a patsy. When asked about that fateful day in Dallas and why he didn't have the bubble top down on the car (as they did in England when he did the advance there), he said they wanted it off for 'exposure': "The President's staff wanted it off for exposure... you can't argue with them unless you've got a good argument." This is directly contradicted by what former agent Sam Kinney adamantly told me on three different occasions- "I am the sole responsibility of that ... Yes, I was." Asked if Kennedy ordered it to be taken off, Sam said, "that is not true." In regard to SAIC of the Dallas office, Forrest V. Sorrels, who was alleged to have removed the top by Jim Lehrer,[8] Sam was equally adamant: "I knew him [Sorrels] very well – he had nothing to do with it." As far as any regrets over his decision, Sam said, "That's one of my thirty-year concerns – whether I made the right decision or not." Kinney went on to say that "only thing the bubbletop may have prevented. It may have distorted Oswald's sight or possibly a ricochet ... it might deflect a bullet."

---

8. *A Bus of My Own* by Jim Lehrer, p. 83.

PAUL LANDIS

PAUL LANDIS

Agent Paul Landis, like Clint Hill, was a member of the First Lady Detail. Paul Landis rode on the running board of the follow-up car during the fateful Dallas motorcade of 11/22/63. He is on record as stating one shot appeared to come from the front in two reports in the Warren Commission volumes that were later endorsed by Landis to the HSCA: "My reaction at this time was that the shot came from somewhere towards the front."[1] His second report: "I still was not certain from which direction the second shot came, but my reaction at this time was that the shot came from somewhere towards the front, right-hand side of the road."[2] Landis to the HSCA: "Landis confirmed to the committee the accuracy of his statement to the Warren Commission."[3]

Landis, Hill, Ready, and Bennett, all follow-up car agents, where among the nine agents involved in the drinking incident of 11/22/63. For his part, Landis stayed out until 5 AM and had to report for duty 8 AM.[4] Perhaps that is why some of the agents wore sunglasses that day.

---

1. Landis' report dated 11/27/63: 18 H 758-759.
2. Landis' detailed report dated 11/30/63: 18 H 751-757.
3. HSCA Report, pp. 89, 606 (referencing Landis's interview, February 17, 1979 outside contact report, JFK Document 014571.
4. 18 H 687.

U. E. BAUGHMAN

U. E. Baughman was made the Chief of the Secret Service on, of all days, November 22: "I remember with absolute clarity the details of that call which was to change my life, give it its final shape. The date was November 22, 1948."[1] In the 1962 book, *What Does a Secret Service Agent Do?*, Secret Service headquarters is depicted with a photo of Ike Eisenhower and an "I miss Ike" sticker. Common protocol, to this day, is to have the current office holder's photo up on the wall.

FBI Director J. Edgar Hoover's bizarre statements that the Mafia did not exist were surprisingly reflected in Baughman's comments to the media: "I will say emphatically that there is no Mafia in this country and no national crime syndicate. Why don't those who talk about the Mafia name its leader or leaders? There has been no mafia in this country for at least forty years. Now about a national crime syndicate: I say there is no such thing, and I say it not simply as a personal judgment but on the basis of talks with other enforcement officials."[2] No wonder JFK got rid

1. *Secret Service Chief* by U.E. Baughman (1962), page 30.
2. *Washington Post*, 7/26/61.

of Baughman. A 2012 book about Agent Charlie Gittens, written with several agents' input, also confirms that Baughman was fired over these remarks.[3] I'm sure the Attorney General, RFK, appreciated the Chief's wisdom, no doubt originating from Hoover. Was this a "parting shot" by Baughman, directed at JFK and RFK?

Baughman wrote a book called *Secret Service Chief* in 1962. Baughman appeared on *What's My Line* on 11/27/55.[4] Baughman was also on the game show *To Tell The Truth* on 4/9/57,[5] as well as *The Jack Paar Show* on 9/10/62.[6]

As one knows from my previous books *Survivor's Guilt* and *The Not-So-Secret Service*, the former Chief was critical of the Secret Service in the aftermath of the assassination and admitted things that the agency probably wished he did not regarding the Secret Service being the boss of the president when it comes to security and the fact that buildings normally were cleared and checked on all parade routes, among other items.

Baughman passed away 11/6/78.

---

3. *Out From The Shadow: The Story of Charles L Gittens Who Broke The Color Barrier In The United States Secret Service* by Maurice Butler, (2012), pages 80 and 91.
4. https://en.wikipedia.org/wiki/U._E._Baughman
5. https://www.youtube.com/watch?v=5Ek41o3aahk
6. http://www.imdb.com/title/tt3602002/?ref_=nm_flmg_slf_1

32

JAMES MASTROVITO

MIKE MASTROVITO

James "Mike" Mastrovito, who passed away 11/24/2006, was quite an enigma – according to his obituary: "He retired in 2004 after a career of some 50 years in law enforcement and intelligence, as an employee of the FBI from June 1958 until June 1959; U.S. Secret Service from July 1959 until July 1979. At the time of his retirement from Secret Service he was special agent in charge of the Intelligence Division at Secret Service Headquarters in Washington, DC. He had served in this Division continuously since 1964. He retired again in 2004 after working as an independent contractor with the CIA and had resided in foreign countries for 20 years prior to his 2004 retirement." As Mastrovito later wrote on his blog from 5/27/05: "On April 1, 1997, I was interviewed telephonically by a representative of the Assassination Records Review Board (ARRB), concerning my years with the U. S Secret Service Intelligence Division, when I was the custodian of the Kennedy Assassination file. The report of this conversation is noted in the ARRB file number MD 261, pages 1892 and 1893." Quoting from the ARRB interview: "From 1960 to 1962, Mastrovito was on the White House Detail. In the summer of 1962, Mastrovito was in the USSS field office in Charleston, West Virginia. After the assassination, he was called to headquarters. He became a Deputy in the Intelligence Division (formerly Protective Research Section PRS) for 10 years before becoming the director of the Intelligence Division a few years before he retired.[1] He worked with Walter Young, who replaced Robert Bouck. According to Mastrovito, Bouck moved out of PRS in the reorganization of the Intelligence Division after 1963.

When Mastrovito took charge of the JFK Assassination file, it consisted of 5 or 6 file cabinets of material. After Mastrovito finished "culling" irrelevant material, the collection was down to one five-draw file cabinet. Mastrovito guessed that his purging of extraneous material took place around 1970. He said that the extraneous material consisted of records of 2000-3000 "mental cases" who called the Secret Service after the Kennedy assassination to claim responsibility for the shooting. Mastrovito offered that Robert Blakey questioned him about this destruction of documents and threatened legal action. Mastrovito pointed out that Chief Rowley's August 1965 memo directed him to remove irrelevant material. Blakey had obtained index cards from the Secret Service for what were then called "White House cases" and/or CO-2 cases. These cares had been sent to the Warren Commission in a card index file. From these cares, Warren Commission members had requested specific Secret Service reports. Blakey had also sought specific files based on his examination of these index cards.

Apparently, Mastrovito had destroyed some files that Blakey had wanted to see. Mastrovito decided which files to keep and which files to destroy." Mastrovito later commented: "In regard to my "culling" of the files, further explanation may be helpful. A CO-2 number was assigned to the assassination as soon as it occurred and until the Warren Commission issued its final report, all information and material pertaining to the assassination in any way was given this sole number. Thus, much extraneous information, such as tips and "confessions" by mental cases was placed in this file. The "culling" did not destroy all of these reports. Those "culled" were given separate file numbers and many of these cases were eventually destroyed in accordance with the official retention and destruction schedule of the Secret Service. Professor Blakey did request certain files of persons whom had been given the original assassination number but were subsequently given separate numbers and had been destroyed, and I recall explaining to his staff in detail why these files no longer existed as I had made the decision that they did not belong in the JFK Assassination File."

---

1. Mastrovito's position as head of the Intelligence Branch of the Secret Service is duly noted in former agent Mike Endicott's book *Walking With Presidents* (2008), page 202.

Once again, back to the ARRB interview: "I asked Mastrovito if he had viewed or obtained any artifacts while he was in charge of the assassination file. Mastrovito replied that he had received a piece of President Kennedy's brain. Mastrovito offered that this item was contained in a vial with a label on it identifying its contents. The vial was the size of a prescription bottle. Mostrovito did not remember if it was glass or plastic. The vial was from the Air Force [sic] Institute of Pathology. [Armed Forces Institute of Pathology] Mastrovito said this vial from the AFIP lab came into his possession "about 3 or 4 years later." i.e. after the assassination. (Later Mastrovito said it was about "1969 or 1970") The label said the vial had been sent from the autopsy at Bethesda; there was no other explanation with it. Mastrovito said he could not see what was special about the portion in the vial. I asked Mastrovito who gave him the vial, and he replied that his supervisor, Walter Young (first Chief of the Intelligence Division), gave it to him when he (Young) resigned from the Secret Service. Young had apparently received it from someone at AFIP. Mastrovito offered that Walter Young died last year. Mastrovito said he destroyed the vial and its contents in a machine that destroys food." Mastrovito later commented: "I have been asked several times about my decision to destroy the piece of the President's brain. I make no apologies for this decision. In view of what is being offered for sale on e-Bay these days, I believe I made the correct one."

I contacted Mastrovito's residence while he was still living in 2005. The former agent did not wish to be interviewed and, as noted above, passed away later on the next year. However, I was pleasantly surprised by being contacted out of the blue by Mastrovito's daughter Michele Beard in 2012. She wrote the following on 4/22/12: "I was going through some of his boxes … he told me the "brain" story after he retired completely from work the year before he died. I came across some documents in boxes last night that may or may not be sensitive. One is a copy, with a cover letter, of the doctor's notes/reports from Parkland in Dallas to the head doctor in Bethesda the day after the assassination.… What do you think? Should I turn these over to the Secret Service? I really don't know if there are already copies of these that are public information.… I have a lot of photos that I am sure you would find interesting.… I found a file called "Kennedy Shooting Photos and Evidence Photos." Most are stamped on the back as being made and developed by the Dallas Police Department. I can scan some for you later."

However, when I wrote back expressing interest, she never responded back and ceased contact with me.

BOB NEWBRAND

A s I wrote in *The Not-So-Secret Service*, agent Bob Newbrand was most certainly a mole or "dirty" agent. Author Anthony Summers wrote, "... the Secret Service ... was not uncontroversial during the Nixon presidency ... The service allowed itself to be used for political and private purposes, such as spying on Nixon rivals like Edward Kennedy and George McGovern, or surveilling his own brother Donald." The *New York Times* would write of Nixon's "perversion of the Secret Service." Former White House deputy counsel Edward Morgan has claimed that Nixon tried to convert the Secret Service into his personal "secret police." John Erlichman recalled, "I was concerned about it. The Secret Service turned the president down very seldom. They were very willing to please."[1]

Probably the agent most "willing to please" Nixon was agent Robert Newbrand. Newbrand guarded Chief Justice Earl Warren during the Warren Commission investigation along with fellow agent Elmer Moore, as former agent Rufus Youngblood told me. Bob Newbrand also had guarded JFK, as Gerald Blaine confirmed. Mamie Eisenhower even attended

---

1. *The Arrogance of Power: The Secret World of Richard Nixon*, p. 247.

Newbrand's wedding![2] Interesting background, to say the least. However, there is more to tell.

From excerpts from a 9/7/72 Oval Office conversation between President Nixon, Bob Haldeman, and Alexander Butterfield:

> Haldeman: I told Alex [Butterfield] to tell Rowley that Newbrand was to be put in charge of the detail. That I'm having Alex do.
>
> President Nixon: Yeah.
>
> Haldeman: So that it's a routine – he handles, deals with the Secret Service.
>
> Haldeman: [with Nixon acknowledging] He really will. *And he has come to me twice and absolutely, sincerely said, "With what you've done for me and what the President's done for me, I just want you to know, if you want someone killed, if you want anything else done, anyway, any direction–"*

As I noted in my last book, on Nov. 9, 1963, Miami Police tape-record a conversation in which an extreme right-wing political organizer accurately predicts the assassination of President John F. Kennedy just as it was to happen 13 days later. The man said the President would be killed by shots fired "from an office building with a high-powered rifle." Yet, Bob Newbrand, the local Secret Service spokesman, said: "I know for sure we didn't put him (Joseph Milteer) under surveillance. *We were never that much involved with that.* If anybody made a threat we wouldn't put him under surveillance, we'd lock him up!" Clearly, the Secret Service dropped the ball in a major way here. In addition, Newbrand is dead wrong. As I reported in chapter two of my first book, SAIC of PRS (the intelligence branch) Robert Bouck told me that he was aware of the Milteer threat before the assassination, as Secret Service documents also confirm. With this in mind, it is striking that, of all people, it is Newbrand who is called to "put out the fire," so to speak. From JFK to Teddy, he was there.[3]

Newbrand is now deceased.

---

2. UPI wire photo dated 10/13/54.

3. Clint Hill whitewashes the whole Bob Newbrand matter in his book *Five Presidents* (pages 388-391): http://www.ctka.net/2016/book-review-five-presidents/five-presidents-by-clint-hill-with-lisa-mccubbin-a-review.html

34

TOM SHIPMAN

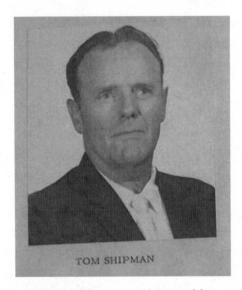

TOM SHIPMAN

The world at large would not even know of former agent Thomas B. Shipman if not for my early reporting in 1997, my first book *Survivor's Guilt*, and my third book *The Not-So-Secret Service*. "October 14, 1963: Died of a heart attack while on a presidential protective assignment at Camp David, Maryland": so reads the official "obituary" for the former agent at the Association of Former Agents of the United States Secret Service (AFAUSSS) website. Out of literally thousands of former agents, officials and personnel who have come and gone from the agency since 1865, only 36 unfortunate souls have passed away in the line of duty ... and the only one from the JFK era-and who died at Camp David, of all places – was Shipman.

Shipman was one of President Kennedy's driver agents and one cannot help sincerely wondering if destiny and fate would have been much better for JFK had Shipman, and not William Greer, taken the wheel of the limousine on 11/22/63. Apparently, I am not the only one pondering this situation. Many fellow authors and researchers, as well as Shipman's surviving family, also wonder about this.

New information was gleaned from unsolicited contacts from Shipman's family in 2015. Christine Jones, Shipman's niece, wrote to me on 10/3/15:

"Thank you for your coverage of Tom Shipman, my uncle. I just discovered your site and thought that you may find the following information helpful.

Jacqueline was my mother's older sister and went by "Jackie." She grew up in Pittsburgh, and her maiden name was Maglaughlin. Her parents lived at 7004 Meade Place in Pittsburgh until her mother, Marion E. Maglaughlin died in July of 1975.

Uncle Tom and Aunt Jackie had a daughter named Laura, who was approximately five years old when her dad died. Jackie and Laura later moved to Colorado where Laura still lives and works under the name Laura Shipman-Hamblin. Jackie was Tom's second wife. Laura knew Tom's children from his first marriage, and I guess that they are in their 60's or 70's.

Tom and my mother were going to meet for dinner the day that JFK came to Dallas. (My mom and dad moved to Texas in 1950 and Dallas was our home.) Prior to the scheduled dinner with my mom, Tom expressed concern to her that JFK refused to use the protective bubble for the car to ensure his safety. During their phone conversation, Tom said that he was prepared to pull quickly out of the motorcade and do whatever was necessary to protect JFK if anything was to happen.

When my mom received the call that Tom had died, she was shocked. According to Aunt Jackie, Tom had received a clean bill of health for his annual physical the month before his death. Aunt Jackie told my mom that after Tom had eaten lunch at Camp David, he told others that he did not feel well and went to take a nap. Sometime during the nap, he suffered a heart attack. The fact that no autopsy was ordered, and that Aunt Jackie was encouraged to bury Tom quickly, seemed strange.

Aunt Jackie and my parents are deceased now so I can only share what I remember my mom telling me about Uncle Tom's death. I hope that this information is helpful to your ongoing research."

On 10/6/15, I had a nice conversation with Laura Shipman, Tom Shipman's youngest daughter. She corroborated and did not dispute anything her cousin Christine Jones (her father's niece) had to say; no wet blankets. She also said her older sister always criticized Greer. Their father has a box of items that she was going to look through and scan for me, as well. In addition, her brother said her dad thought that JFK would be killed one day! It is true that Tom Shipman knew of JFK's upcoming Dallas trip, had planned to be part of it, and arranged a dinner meeting with his sister in law Josephine who lived in Dallas since 1950. Josephine was

Christine Jones' mother. One more thing – she also views it as suspicious that her father was quickly buried and corroborates Christine that her mother was *urged* to bury him quickly! She also said that, when her father passed away, Kennedy's personal physician, Dr. George Burkley, took care of everything.

Shipman's grandson, John Thomas, wrote to me on 10/27/17:

> My grandfather, Thomas Shipman was a good and honorable man. I was always told how proud he was that he protected the President of the United States and that he would have sacrificed his life to save the President. If John Kennedy's assassination was planned by anyone within the Secret Service I cannot imagine that he would have ignored it, I believe that he would have taken active steps to prevent it. However, I am probably not an objective commentator on this matter.

35

LEM JOHNS

LEM JOHNS

Regarding the JFK assassination, former agent Thomas Lemuel "Lem" Johns stated, "The first two [shots] sounded like they were on the side of me towards the grassy knoll."[1] In a February 1999 *Newsday* article written by Michael Dorman, Johns said, "If you get the tie [JFK was wearing] nicked by a different bullet, you've got a second gunman – simple as that. I've never thought that was out of the question." On the 2013 DVD, *Lem Johns: Secret Service Man*, the former agent said, "I thought that's where it [the shots] was coming from" and that "the sound came from the right. I just assumed that that's where the shooting was taking place from that location." Johns told the HSCA: "... I was running towards LBJ's car, which was now some distance away from us and picking up speed. I was left on the street with no way to get back in our car. A passing car with White House photographers in it came by and one of them recognized me. He said 'Hey, there's Lem Johns. Let's give him a ride.' They stopped and picked me up and we drove to the Trade Mart ..."[2] This further debunks the notion that Johns was the agent of unknown

1. HSCA interview with Johns, 8/8/78: RIF# 180-10074-10079.
2. HSCA interview with Johns, 8/8/78: RIF# 180-10074-10079.

repute in Dealey Plaza. We can discard the notion that "Lem" Johns was the agent: Johns told me on 2/11/04 that he "ran right to the first convertible" and was only on the street very briefly: "Time enough to catch a ride."[3] In fact, on the 2013 DVD *Lem Johns: Secret Service Man*, Johns is equally adamant in his refutation of the notion that he was the "agent" on the knoll. "Absolutely not," Johns stated, adding that he stood in the street to hitch a ride for a minute or less and did not go to the knoll.

Like Youngblood, Johns was originally a JFK agent until his reassignment to Vice President LBJ.[4] Johns retired from the Secret Service in May 1975 after 21 years to work as a Special Assistant to HEW Secretary, and former LBJ aide, Joseph Califano. At the time of his HSCA interview, Johns had a son who was on the Secret Service White House Detail, protecting President Jimmy Carter. Johns told the author on 2/11/04 that his son Jeff served Presidents Carter and Reagan during his time on the WHD. In fact, Johns' son was in charge of the Amy Carter Detail, while his grandson Michael has served Bush and Obama. The agent also added that Bob Camp, an agent sent to Dallas from the Columbia, SC office immediately after the assassination, had a son on the WHD protecting President George W. Bush.

President Nixon saw to the retirement or dismissal of the top five Secret Service officials – Chief James J. Rowley: replaced by H. Stuart Knight, former SAIC of the V.P. LBJ Detail[5]; Deputy Director Rufus W. Youngblood[6]; ASAIC of White House Detail William L. "Bill" Duncan, who was the advance man for JFK's Fort Worth stop 11/21-11/22/63[7]; SAIC of WHD Robert H. "Bob" Taylor, who dated back to Nixon's Vice Presidential days[8]; and Assistant Director Thomas L. "Lem" Johns.[9]

Johns passed away 5/10/14.

---

3. See also Michael T. Griffith's article titled, "*The Man Who Wasn't There, Was There.*"

4. Interestingly, Johns rose to become assistant Secret Service director in charge of all the agency's protective operations.

5. HSCA testimony of Rowley, 9/78 (audiotape); Author's interview with Rowley, 9/27/92; Author's interviews with Knight, 10/22/92 & 2/8/94; See also *The Secret Service: The Hidden History of an Enigmatic Agency* by Philip Melanson (2002), pp. 105, 186 & 221, and *New York Times*, 10/23/73.

6. *Confessions of an Ex-Secret Service agent*, p. 45. Author's interviews with Youngblood, 10/22/94 & 2/8/94 (same dates as Knight) See also *The Arrogance of Power: The Secret World of Richard Nixon* by Anthony Summers, page 247, and *Washington Post*, 10/19/71.

7. A. Dale Wunderlich, a PRS agent who went to Dallas after the assassination re: the investigation, and William L. Duncan now are leaders of an established executive protection firm as of 2003 (although Duncan appear to have left the company around 2001). Both gentlemen sat for videotaped oral histories in 2005 for the Sixth Floor Museum; Rush (Venker), p. 58; see also *Fort Worth Press*, 11/22/63 – captioned photo of Duncan.

8. Rush (Venker), pp. 56-58, 149; *Protecting the President* by Dennis McCarthy, pages 198, 201-202; *The Secret Service: The Hidden History of an Enigmatic Agency* by Philip Melanson (2002), pages 105 and 221; see also *The Flying White House*, pages 260-261.

9. New revelations from his 2013 DVD *Lem Johns: Secret Service Man*; author's interview with Johns.

36

DICK KEISER

After serving in the Army counter intelligence corps and the Federal Bureau of Narcotics, Keiser joined the Secret Service in the St. Louis field office. When JFK was assassinated, Keiser was at a graduation ceremony in his position as a rookie agent. Soon, he was sent to Washington to guard Jackie Kennedy then, after 10 months, he guarded LBJ's Lynda Bird. Keiser would go on to become the SAIC of PPD for Presidents Nixon, Ford, and Carter. [1]

Not long after Keiser had replaced Bob Taylor as SAIC, the Secret Service uncovered a plot to kill President Nixon. It was Keiser himself who told Nixon he had to cancel the New Orleans motorcade. Keiser was not on the 9/5/75 California trip where Lynette Alice (Squeaky) Fromme, a member of the Charles Manson family, tried to assassinate President Ford because he had come down with a severe attack of hiccups.[2]

Keiser bore a resemblance to President Ford, so much so that the press would often begin snapping photos of him, thinking he was the president. Keiser said of Ford: "I found him to be very gregarious, pleasant. My contacts with him led me to believe that he was very self-confident. He was very happy with who he was, and I'll tell you why. I think that getting into the stories a little earlier, when Mrs. Ford had her surgery at Bethesda, cancer surgery, there was a photograph of President Ford and I coming out of Bethesda Hospital and it was just us – the two of us. Some reporters looked at that – "Look how Keiser looks like Jerry Ford. Keiser's a decoy." Obviously the Secret Service has assigned a decoy to Jerry Ford. I was there before he came and stayed after he left, but nonetheless that came out in the *Washington Post*... I always respected him a great deal; still do."[3] As the *Pittsburgh Press* reported: "Keiser says he'll never tell all about his days in the White House by writing a book, as other agents have done. "In my time as an agent, I don't remember any time when a conversation was hushed or stilled or a partition raised between me and (government officials) – not necessarily because of me, Dick Keiser, but me as a Secret Service agent. That's a very special trust."[4]

Keiser said this of Nixon: "I'm not a professional analyst, but during the height of Watergate, the last several months, he spent a lot of time in San Clemente or Key Biscayne. And an interesting relationship that I saw was between he and Bebe Rebozo. Bebe could play President Nixon like a piano. I'm not comfortable putting this out, but what would be normal – President Nixon would call for a car. He'd say, "Bring the car around, Bebe and I are going to take a ride." We'd bring the car around and I'd say, "Where would you like to go?" He'd say, "I just want to be back in an hour." Which meant he didn't care – about thirty minutes wandering, turn around and come back. Now, there would be times in that car when he and Bebe would sit there for an hour and wouldn't say a word. There would be other times and they would sit and talk continuously. I don't know how Bebe knew that – how to do that. On the houseboat that Bebe had, on Key Biscayne, the same thing. They'd go for a cruise and President Nixon sometimes would go up on the flying bridge and sit by himself and Bebe would be down. Other times, they would be together. I don't know how Bebe was able to sense that relationship. It was mysterious to me.

Again, it would not be uncommon for the President to say, "Keiser," President Nixon never called anybody that I remember by first name. Haldeman, Erlichman, more privately he may call him Bob, something like that. But always out, it was, "Hey, Bull." And he'd say, "Get the music on the radio, you know what I like, see what you can find." And we'd say, "Yes, sir." We find something. "That's fine, that's great. I like that a lot. That's good music. Now, listen you, when the news comes on, you turn that radio off. Do you hear me?" I said, "Yes, sir." He said, "I mean it, not one word." "Yes, sir." So therefore, I think he had isolated himself from the news."[5]

In 1979, Keiser became the SAIC of the Washington field office. In 1981, he became the assistant director of inspection. In 1982, he left the Secret Service to work as chief of security for the Atari Corporation. In 1985, he went to work as a security consultant. Then, in 1987, Keiser

3. Gerald Ford Foundation oral history, 11/15/2010.
4. *Pittsburgh Press*, 6/23/87.
5 Gerald Ford Foundation oral history, 11/15/2010.

came to my hometown (literally to where my mom worked!) as head of corporate security for the USX Tower in Pittsburgh, PA.[6]

---

6. *Pittsburgh Press*, 6/23/87.

DAVID CARPENTER

J ust as SAIC Dick Keiser resembled one of the presidents he protected (Ford), SAIC of PPD David Carpenter bore somewhat of a resemblance, especially from a distance, to President Clinton. A syndicated Associated Press story from 7/15/98 said that he was "a tall gray-haired agent often mistaken for Clinton." Carpenter spent 26 years in the Secret Service, a large part of it protecting Presidents Nixon thru Clinton on PPD. Carpenter later served from 1998-2002 as Assistant Secretary for Diplomatic Security and Director of the Office of Foreign Missions for the State Department. In 2002, Carpenter became Vice President of Global Security at PepsiCo, Inc., retiring in 2015.

Carpenter appears on the National Geographic special (later a DVD) *Inside the U.S. Secret Service* from 2004. Carpenter also introduced former SAIC Clint Hill to President Clinton on 5/19/94 on the day Jacqueline Kennedy Onassis passed away.[1]

---

1. *Mrs. Kennedy and Me* by Clint Hill and Lisa McCubbin (2012), pages 337-340.

LARRY COCKELL

Larry Cockell was the first African-American agent to head the Presidential Protective Division (1998-2000) and was also the highest-ranking African American in Secret Service history when he became the Deputy Director in June 2000, serving until January 2002. Cockell is well known for protecting President Clinton, having appeared countless times in newspaper photos and on television, albeit incidentally. The *New York Times* reported on 7/18/98: "In public, Mr. Clinton and Mr. Cockell appear to have a warm relationship, physically affectionate, bantering, sometimes playful, with the President often resting a hand on his shoulder or whispering in his ear. The job calls on Mr. Cockell to be as close to Mr. Clinton as possible, whenever possible.… That closeness to the President is why Kenneth W. Starr, the independent counsel investigating Mr. Clinton, wants to question Mr. Cockell."

The *New York Times* later reported on 12/11/2001: "Larry L. Cockell, the deputy director of the Secret Service and former agent in charge of President Bill Clinton's protective detail, will retire in January to become chief of security for AOL Time Warner, the Secret Service announced today. Mr. Cockell, the highest-ranking African-American in Secret Service history, gained notoriety when he was subpoenaed to testify before the grand jury investigating the Monica Lewinsky matter in 1998. Investigators from the independent counsel's office summoned Mr. Cockell to testify about what he might have seen or heard when he accompanied Mr. Clinton to a deposition taken in January 1998, for the lawsuit filed by Paula Jones."

Like David Carpenter, Cockell also appears on the National Geographic special (later a DVD) *Inside the U.S. Secret Service* from 2004. In 2001, he received the Meritorious Presidential Rank Award for Government Service and was named recipient of the Government Leadership Award for Diversity by the Business Women's Network.[1]

---

1. http://www.slu.edu/readstory/more/4340

39

RON PONTIUS

RON PONTIUS

Former agent Ron Pontius was on the Texas trip when JFK was assassinated (but he was not in Dallas) and he protected President Ford when Sara Jane Moore took a shot at the president on 9/22/75. Author Ron Kessler's account of Sara Jane Moore and her assassination attempt on Gerald Ford in his two Secret Service books is completely and totally without fact. Author Geri Spieler wrote the definitive book on the 9/22/75 assassination attempt called *Taking Aim at the President: The Remarkable Story of the Woman Who Shot at Gerald Ford* (Palgrave Macmillan, 2008). *It is infinitely better and more accurate.*[1]

On Page 50 of Kessler's book, he wrote that Oliver Sipple, a disabled former U.S. Marine and Vietnam veteran pushed Sara Jane Moore's arm as she aimed her gun and shot at President Ford. He also wrote that the bullet flew several feet over the president's head and Secret Service agents Ron Pontius and Jack Merchant pushed Moore to the sidewalk and arrested her. Sipple did grab Moore's arm, but not until after she got off her first shot, which missed Ford's head by only six inches. Sara Jane's own gun

---

1. See also 1/24/2010 blog entry for author Geri Spieler.

had been confiscated the day before, and she bought the .38 she used that day the same morning not knowing the sight was off.[2]

As the crowd gathered to see Ford, no one was looking at Sara Jane Moore. As President Ford emerged, he stood still for a moment deciding whether to cross the street so that he could shake hands with people lined up on the north side of the street.[3] After her first shot, people realized something had happened and Sipple, being a Marine and a hero, lunged at Moore and fouled a second, potentially deadly, shot.

Another factual error in Kessler's account refers to Agents Pontius and Merchant. Kessler said they tackled Moore to the sidewalk and arrested her. Agent's Pontius and Merchant were assigned to guard Pres. Ford and were standing with Ford across the street from Moore. They did not leave Ford's side. In fact, they grabbed the president and pushed him into the limousine and sped away.[4]

SFPD Officer Tim Hettrich is the law enforcement officer who subdued Moore. Hettrich was assigned to crowd detail and was stationed on the sidewalk near Moore. Hettrich pulled the gun from her and handed it over to Secret Service agent Dotson Reeves, who grabbed Moore from the sidewalk.[5]

2. *San Francisco Chronicle*, Sept. 24, 1975.
3. President Gerald Ford in a telephone interview with author Geri Spieler, December 12, 2003.
4. United States of American v. Sara Jane Moore, CR 75-729 SC (U.S. District Court, Northern District of California) Sept. 23, 1975, William Whittaker.
5. In an interview author Geri Spieler had with SFPD Officer Timothy Hettrich, assigned to crowd control for Pres. Ford's San Francisco visit.

40

ROBERT TAYLOR

Taylor protected five presidents during his tenure. Taylor received two government medals during his 23 years in the Secret Service, one for the logistical coordination of Vice President Hubert Humphrey's trip to Vietnam and another for protecting Vice President Richard Nixon during riots in Caracas, Venezuela. During his Secret Service career Taylor worked in Washington, Kansas City, Memphis and on assignments throughout the world. He served Presidents Truman, Eisenhower, Kennedy, Johnson and Nixon. Taylor was special agent in charge of the White House details for Johnson and Nixon.[1]

He retired from the Secret Service in 1973 due to a knee injury. From 1974 to 1978 he was responsible for the protection of the Rockefeller family. In 1979 he returned to Washington to head his own security consulting firm.[2]

President Johnson, reminiscing about his trip to Australia, mentioned Taylor: "I remember Bob Taylor standing there and letting the Cadillac run over his foot in order to protect his President from harm."[3] An April 17, 1972 memo from President Nixon to aide Bob Haldeman following the Canadian trip gives a clue as to Nixon's feelings about Taylor: "The

1. *New York Times*, 3/14/81.
2. *UPI*, 3/13/81;
3. LBJ remarks to the Secret Service, 11/23/68.

situation in Canada was intolerable," Nixon wrote. "[Robert H.] Taylor insisted on sitting on the jump seat where he could have just as easily sat in the front seat because there were only two in the front seat. The jump seats were constructed in such a way that they bent completely back on both Pat (Nixon) and me so that in her case she had to put her legs over on the other side, and I, of course, was totally uncomfortable all the way." Looking forward to a trip to the Soviet Union, he wanted better arrangements. He did not want "some interpreter or some Secret Service man sitting on my lap."[4] Taylor was let go as SAIC of PPD due to run-ins with Nixon aide Bob Haldeman on 2/9/73, despite official denials.[5]

Former agent Dennis McCarthy, who, like Taylor, Clint Hill, and many other agents of the 1960's-1970's, also served five presidents, said this of Taylor: "Well over six feet tall and darkly handsome, Taylor looked like the public's image of a Secret Service agent. Everyone on the White House detail respected him, but he had a lightning temper and wasn't one to ingratiate himself with anyone, including the President, the White House staff, and the Secret Service hierarchy."[6]

Taylor passed away 3/12/81 at the age of 54.

---

4. *The Arrogance of Power: The Secret World of Richard Nixon*, p. 434.
5 *The Morning Record* (CT), 2/14/73; Rush (Venker), pp. 56-58, 149; *Protecting the President* by Dennis McCarthy, pages 198, 201-202; *The Secret Service: The Hidden History of an Enigmatic Agency* by Philip Melanson (2002), pages 105 and 221; see also *The Flying White House*, pp. 260-261.
6. *Protecting the President* by Dennis McCarthy, page 60.

41

WADE RODHAM

WADE RODHAM

Agent Don Cox, who served on the Clinton detail in the 1990's, wrote to me in an e-mail dated 9/21/2008:"Hillary's uncle (Rodham) was also an agent and riding in the [Vice President] Nixon vehicle that came under attack in Caracas." Yes, you read that right: agent Wade Rodham was Hillary Clinton's uncle, a fact not mentioned in any book or article written by or about the Clintons![1] Researcher Mark Henderson wrote to me on 10/26/17: "Yeah Vince found this out in 1992 when doing deep level research on Bill Clinton and Hillary Rodham Clinton. I was pretty impressed – I have never heard HRC mention him ever. He was with VP Nixon in Caracas on 5/13/1958 was in front passenger's seat when it came under attack."

Hugh Simpson Rodham was Hillary Rodham Clinton's grandfather.[2] Her grandfather's brother was Wade Rodham, Sr. Agent Wade Rodham, Jr., was Wade Senior's son.[3] Technically, this would make Wade Hillary's first cousin (once removed – same generation as her father, Hugh Ellsworth Rodham, born in 1911, the year before Wade, Jr.). However, many people understandably think of this connection as an uncle or great un-

1. See chapter 3 of my book *The Not-So-Secret Service* (2017).
2. http://www.findagrave.com/cgi-bin/fg.cgi?page=gr&GRid=22300674
3. http://us-census.mooseroots.com/l/293502910/Wade-J-Rodham

cle (or "kinda uncle," to use the vernacular), thus the reason why several people refer to Wade Jr. – like Wade Sr. – as her (great) uncle. Like Wade Junior and Senior, many of the Rodham's, from the great grandfather on down, came from Scranton (Lackawanna County), PA – including Hugh Rodham Senior (grandfather); Hugh Rodham II (father) ; Hugh Senior's 11 siblings, including Wade Senior; and, of course, Wade Junior.

A relative of Wade's, Maureen McKivigan Crawford, wrote to me on 3/27/16: *"Wade is actually my Great Uncle Wade. We spent many Christmas days at his farm in Virginia. I was just a kid when we used to visit but my dad would spend hours holed up with Uncle Wade. Dad was a high school history teacher in DC so he loved Uncle Wade's stories. Honestly back in those days [the] Secret Service actually respected the people they protected so not much gossip. He was still friends with Jackie Kennedy and they would visit. He never mentioned his niece Hillary."* John Pulawski wrote to me on 3/17/16: "Her Uncle was a Secret Service agent during the Kennedy Administration. I knew her brother when he ran for the Senate in Florida and learned what a complex background they had. Wade had an interesting influence on Hillary – I suspect her Janus methods especially. I have heard that in her seduction of poor innocent William Jefferson Clinton, she used talk of Uncle Wade to make a great impression upon him. In 1988 I was a key Dukakis campaign worker, and in the early 90's I had an environmental radio program in Miami, so I got involved, or tried to get involved, in numerous Democratic campaigns. Meeting with Hugh [Rodham, Hillary's brother], I was less than impressed. Like Hillary, he felt entitled to the Senate seat because of his importance related to whom he knows. I had mentioned my having met JFK as an infant, and Bobby in the third grade, and how hard I worked for Ted in the 1980 campaign, and he came back with how his Uncle was protecting JFK, but 11-22 was not his fault."

Secret Service agent Wade J. Rodham was the Special Agent in Charge of the Kennedy residence in Middleburg (ATOKA), VA. Wade Rodham (without the Hillary connection, of course) is mentioned – with regard to pulling his gun out to protect Nixon – in Rufus Youngblood's book,[4] *Six Crises* by Richard Nixon himself[5], and *The Secret Service Story* by Michael Dorman.[6]

Wade Rodham received the Exceptional Civilian Service Award for protecting then-Vice President Nixon in Caracas, Venezuela (5/13/58). Rodham passed away in March 1983.

---

4. *20 Years in the Secret Service,* pages 70-71
5. Page 216.
6. Pages 143-145

42

JACK READY

JACK READY

Ready was assigned to the Secret Service White House Detail in the spring of 1961, with temporary assignments at Hyannis port and Palm Beach. Ready was on the WHD from 1961 to 1968. From 1968 to 1978, Ready worked out of the San Diego office, and had served on the V.P. Agnew Detail, the Dr. Kissinger Detail, and, curiously, the Watergate and White House Tapes Detail. During the HSCA era, Ready was the ASAIC of the USSS Liaison Division (Win Lawson was the SAIC). By 1978, Agent Ready was ASAIC of the Nixon Protective Division.[1] Interestingly, for the 1993 film *In the Line of Fire*, the famous Altgens photo of the shooting was used. The producers edited out Ready's head in the photo and superimposed Clint Eastwood's in its place.

You see, for most people, Ready will always be infamous for being the agent on the follow-up car who was assigned to JFK's side of the limousine, just as fellow agent Clint Hill rode on the opposite running board and was assigned to Jackie Kennedy's side of the limousine. After the assassination, Ready submitted a report dealing with the shooting itself. He wrote, "There appeared to be no spectators on the right side of the

1. 3/1/78 HSCA interview with Ready; 12/14/77 letter from Secret Service Legal Counsel Robert O. Goff to the HSCA's G. Robert Blakey, RIF #180-10112-10218.

road [Elm Street]." All those people lining the street on Ready's side of Elm, clearly evident in the Zapruder film, must have been photographic anomalies. Also, both Shift Leader Emory Roberts, the commander of the agents in the follow-up car, and Ready claimed the President was traveling at 20-25 mph, and that there was about 20-25 feet separating the two cars. In complete contradiction, all evidence confirms that the cars were only five feet apart when the shooting commenced, after which the limousine slowed from an original speed of 11.2 mph. In fact, in Ready's first report, he stated that the follow-up car slowed, but in his next report, he "corrected" the record to read that the limousine slowed. Actually, both vehicles slowed down once the shooting began. I believe all of this obfuscation was done to try to cover up both Roberts' and Ready's inaction.

I phoned Ready on 6/13/05 after the former agent had previously ignored a letter from the author in 2004. As mentioned in chapter one of *Survivor's Guilt*, Ready said, "Not on the phone. I don't know you from Adam. Can you see my point?"

Jack Ready made a huge mistake on the fateful day, hesitating to react to the gunfire because he thought they were firecrackers. He was also one of nine agents who stayed out late and drank the night before. That said, no one could say Ready did not have guts.

John David Ready was born Aug. 12, 1927, in Springfield, Mass. He joined the Navy at the end of World War II and served again at the beginning of the Korean War. In 1954, he received a bachelor's degree in political science from American International College in Springfield. He joined the Secret Service in 1960 and was assigned to the White House the next year. After serving Kennedy, he worked on President Lyndon B. Johnson's Detail and later, during Richard M. Nixon's administration, for Vice President Spiro T. Agnew. Ready then was assigned to protect Kissinger, who served as Nixon's national security adviser and secretary of state. Ready accompanied Kissinger on his secret trip to China in 1971 in preparation for Nixon's historic visit the following year. Ready retired in 1981.[2]

Ready died on 2/24/2014.

---

2. *Washington Post*, 3/29/14.

43

HOWARD K. NORTON

Norton is a heretofore unknown PRS employee of the Secret Service who worked on JFK's Florida trip, as well as on his proposed trip to Austin scheduled for 11/23/63 and who ended up photographing the bloody limousine on 11/23/63 along with James K. "Jack" Fox.[1] According to former PRS Agent Dale Wunderlich, "Howard K. Norton was the first "Security Technician" that was hired by the USSS. He was retired from the Air Force where I believe that he was a Sergeant Major in OSI. He was never a Special Agent but was extremely knowledgeable in the field of electronics and electronic countermeasures. In fact, I was told by a friend of his that he was one of the technicians that discovered the resonance cavity that the Russians planted in the U.S. seal that was given to the U. S. Ambassador to Moscow, Russia. Regarding the makeup of the advance team in Palm Beach for the opening of the Ambassador's residence … Howard and I were the only two on the advance from PRS. Howard was primarily responsible for oversight of the tech-

---

1. IF#154-10002-10420: Survey Report re: Palm Beach, FL trip 11/18/63; RIF# 1541000110033 re: shift report for Austin, TX trip; CD 80, page 3 [also found on p. 430 of *Murder In Dealey Plaza*; see also HSCA RIF# 180-10102-10212: 3-page chronology of the presidential limousine & Charles Taylor's March 1976 Affidavit to the Church Committee].

nical sweeps, which I assisted him with, and I was also involved in doing backgrounds on employees, CO-2 cases and contractors that were doing some repairs to the kitchen floor at the Ambassador's residence. CO-2 cases were individuals who were of record with the Protective Research Division of the USSS."[2]

There is a reason why there is no photo of Norton. None are known to exist. You see, as anyone knows from reading chapter two of my book *Survivor's Guilt*, even agents themselves were overcome with amnesia when asked about him (other than Wunderlich, of course). Agent Jerry O'Rourke, on the Texas trip, responded to the question of his familiarity (or lack thereof) with Norton in typical fashion: "No, I do not recall anyone by the name. He could have been in PRS (Protective Research Division), now called Intelligence Division and I wouldn't have known him at the time as I was on the White House Division, now called Presidential Protective Division. Much later, I served, for a short time, at PRS and I don't recall him. Today, the retired agent's association are very active and had he retired or served for at least one year (the requirements to belong to the retired agents), I would have heard of him and/or he would be listed on our web site."

Yet Norton was on both the Florida *and* Texas trips, as was fellow PRS agent Glen Bennett, in what I think is an obvious role: a covert monitor of mortal threats to the president that the agency knew of and covered up after the fact, as they did the presence of Norton and the true role of Bennett. The author wrote to Secret Service Public Affairs Assistant Director George M. Rogers on 7/5/05 asking for tenure dates for Howard K. Norton (Mr. Rogers previously helped the author on other inquiries). In the same message, the author matter-of-factly mentioned Norton's presence on the Austin leg of the Texas trip. Rogers' reply, dated 7/15/05, was surprising: "Dear Mr. Palamara: A search was conducted in response to your electronic message received on July 5, 2005, requesting tenure dates for former Secret Service employee Howard K. Norton... *We were unable to locate any reference that provided information regarding the length of time [Norton] spent with the Secret Service* [emphasis added]." It should also be noted that Rogers did not comment on or dispute the issue of Norton's participation on the ill-fated Texas tour.

To date, over 10 years later, I have been unsuccessful in finding Norton, nor have I come across a photo of him or any information if he is alive or dead.

---

2. E-mail to author 10/9/99.

44

GEORGE HICKEY

W hile I attempted (and, quite often, succeeded) to find, contact and interview each and every Secret Service agent connected to the protection of President Kennedy, there was one agent I left alone: George Hickey. Why did I do this? This man was haunted since the 1970's by researcher and author Howard Donahue (later the author of *Mortal Error* in 1992) and, since I felt he was one of the good guys, I did not wish to bother him any more than he already was. Truth be told, if I thought he had something to offer and/or was a bad guy, I would have no reservation in contacting him. But, alas, I chose to not bother him. Donahue passed away in 1999. His "story" was picked up by author Colin McLaren for the book and Reelz documentary *The Smoking Gun* in 2013, while *Mortal Error* was reissued by Bonar Menninger, the actual writer of Donahue's book. Both Donahue and McLaren believe Agent Hickey accidentally shot JFK, a theory I think is totally ridiculous. I spoke to and corresponded with Donahue and I corresponded with McLaren (and I am briefly mentioned in his book, as well). Nice guys, but the theory is out to lunch.

Agent Sam Kinney revealed to me that Hickey "loved JFK probably more than he should have" and, Kinney revealed, it was Hickey who found the coconut in the famous PT-109 saga during WWII, and gave it to Lieutenant John F. Kennedy![1] Kinney later clarified for the author, "He's the one who turned [the coconut] over to Kennedy. Nobody knew that 'til George Hickey was probably an agent for 2 or 3 years."[2] The *Baltimore Sun* reported on 8/23/96: "Mr. Kennedy cleared the way for Mr. Hickey to be assigned to the president's personal protection detail in July 1963, four months before the murder in Dallas. Mr. Hickey was 40 at the time." The author's article in the May 1992 issue of *Third Decade* magazine totally undermines the thesis in the 1992 book entitled *Mortal Error*, in which it is alleged that Agent Hickey accidentally shot JFK. Even before that book's publication the author discovered contradictions through correspondence with Howard Donahue. The author also uncovered contradictions inherent in the thesis itself, and the Bronson film[3] totally refutes the book's main thrust, as does a popular 2013 Internet article.[4] The author decided not to contact Hickey due to the fallout he received from this book and his severely declining health at the time.

Agent Kinney told the author, "I tried to squelch that book. George Hickey was a very good friend of mine ... it's ruined George Hickey. I talked to the publisher of the book for 45 minutes on the phone ... the last time I talked to George Hickey he called me and said 'Thanks a lot, Sam, for helping me.'"[5] Hickey did try to sue over the allegations in Menninger and Donahue's book, but the judge in Maryland found that he had waited too long to file. However, Hickey did win an out-of-court settlement.[6]

Hickey passed away in 2011.

---

1. Author's interview with Sam Kinney, 10/19/92.

2. Author's interview with Kinney, 3/4/94.

3. This is a spectator who filmed the assassination, Charles Bronson, not the famous actor of the same name!

4. http://www.philly.com/philly/news/Shooting_holes_in_theory_that_a_Secret_Service_agent_killed_President_Kennedy.html

5. Author's interview with Kinney, 3/4/94. *Mortal Error*, pp. 252-253 (letter to St. Martins Publishers from 1991 or 1992 and Publishers call to Kinney in response) – "I was driving the car at the time and I can assure you that there was not a gun fired from the U.S.S.S. follow-up car."

6. *Baltimore Sun* (2/3/98) ran a story which read: "Lawsuit is settled in favor of former Secret Service agent; Book claimed man accidentally fired bullet that killed Kennedy: A retired U.S. Secret Service agent has been paid an undisclosed sum of money by the publishers of a book that claimed he fired the bullet that killed President John F. Kennedy, an allegation that prompted the agent to sue. The obscure book, *Mortal Error: The Shot That Killed JFK*, claimed that George W. Hickey Jr. slipped during the confusion on Nov. 22, 1963, and accidentally pulled the trigger of his high-powered AR-15 rifle. Kennedy, according to Missouri-based author Bonar Menninger, was hit in the head by the bullet. Hickey, who lives in Abingdon, filed a libel suit in U.S. District Court in Baltimore. He has received a confidential monetary settlement in the case, according to attorneys representing Hickey and St. Martin's Press, which published the book."

45

HENRY RYBKA

HANK RYBKA

L ike Agent Don Lawton, Rybka was ordered to stay back at the Dallas airport by Shift Leader Emory Roberts, despite both agents taking turns jogging beside the limousine as it departed (Lawton relieved Rybka, thus causing some initial confusion for later researchers, this author included).[1] Rybka was "mistakenly" placed in the follow-up car in reports by Roberts afterwards, while Lawton, who lamented to the author about the agency not letting agents on the rear of the limousine, was given the opportunity to ride on the running board of the follow-up car by Agent Paul Landis, yet chose not to. Agent Rybka was "mistakenly" placed in the follow-up car in three separate reports on or after 11/22/63: two by Emory P. Roberts dated 11/22/63 (a later report, #3, "corrects" the error), and the Final Survey Report by Winston Lawson, who also "corrects" the error, although Rybka is not even mentioned in the Preliminary Survey Report.[2]

While it is hard to get a handle on what this means, the timing of these "errors" is significant. Lawson's Preliminary Survey report, dated 11/19/63, states that SA Lawton and SA Warner will "Remain at airport

---

1. See https://www.youtube.com/watch?v=mCHGNvTvqU0 and https://www.youtube.com/watch?v=gGeE0FZUv94
2. CD 3 Exhibits.

to set up return"; this is mentioned twice (with no mention of Rybka anywhere to be found). Also, while Agent Donald Lawton spells out in his report what his instructions were that day, "to remain at the airport to effect security for the President's departure," Rybka does not do the same in his. In addition, Agent William Patterson mentions only Lawton, not Rybka, with regard to securing Air Force One and Two, while Agent John J. "Muggsy" O'Leary explicitly states what his instructions were, including "remain [ing] at the airport until the President's motorcade returned for departure for Austin, Texas. SA Don Lawton remained at Love Field with me." No mention of Rybka.[3] On 11/30/63, 8 days after the assassination, ASAIC Kellerman finally writes in his second report, "SA's Lawton ... and Rybka ... remained at the airport, to effect security at the plane during our absence."[4] Sam Kinney told the author on 3/4/94 that Rybka was deceased but was not specific as to cause or time of death. In a letter to the author dated 1/15/04, Jerry O'Rourke wrote that Rybka's death was "long ago." Winston Lawson wrote the author: "Hank Rybka was a driver and died on Dec [ember] 25, 1975!! – don't know when he retired."[5]

It is important not to dismiss Rybka or any of the White House Garage Detail agents as mere "drivers." They received the same training and were gun-carrying protective agents. In fact, as we know, a member of this detail, George Hickey, manned the AR-15 rifle in the follow-up car in Dallas.

Agent Henry Rybka (right) jogs with the limo directly behind agent Don Lawton in this still frame from motion picture footage from Love Field shown for the first time in 2013:

---

3. Agent reports, CD 3 Exhibits.
4. CD 3 Exhibits.
5. Letter to author dated 1/20/04.

46

ELMER MOORE

E lmer was born March 17, 1909, in San Jose, California, and grew up in Palo Alto, California. He received his BS in 1934 at the University of San Francisco. In 1941, he was awarded his BA, with distinction, in Police Science at San Jose State College. Elmer began his law enforcement career in 1939 with the Santa Clara County Sheriff's Office. He was appointed a Special Agent in the US Secret Service in 1942. From 1943 to 1945, he served in the US Coast Guard Intelligence. In 1945, he returned to the US Secret Service and served his country and 7 presidents, until his retirement in 1976.

Secret Service Agent Elmer W. Moore should be viewed with deep suspicion. Moore, who told reporter Earl Golz that he was in San Francisco on 11/22/63[1], played a crucial and completely overlooked part in various aspects of the case:

    1. Moore guarded Chief Justice Earl Warren.[2]

---

1. *Dallas Morning News*, 8/27/78. That said, according to a Secret Service Memorandum, 8/10/64 Sorrels to Kelley, Moore was temporarily assigned to Dallas from San Francisco, CA office of the Secret Service from 11/30-12/13/63 (14 days) to investigate the JFK assassination. Interestingly, as mentioned above, Deputy Chief Paul Paterni was the SAIC of the San Francisco office during part of the Truman and Eisenhower era.

2. *20 Years in the Secret Service*, p. 170.

2. As author David Scheim duly noted[3], Moore was involved in Jack Ruby's canned alibi: Ruby said, "Does this conflict with my story and yours in great length?" Moore replied, "Substantially the same, Jack, as well as I remember." Ruby goes on to state, "I may have left out a few things. Mr. Moore remembers probably more … ."[4]

3. On 12/4/63, Moore questions Ruby "regarding his whereabouts and movements" on 11/21/63, the day before the assassination.[5]

4. On 12/3/63, Moore interviews Ruby's roommate, George Senator.[6]

5. Secret Service Report 491: On 12/2-12/5/63, Moore, along with fellow agents Arthur Blake & William Carter, began a series of interviews with the employees of the Texas School Book Depository over a four-day period. Three of the witnesses interviewed, Harold Norman, Bonnie Ray Williams, & Charles Givens, gave totally new evidence to Moore & company that conflicted dramatically with earlier statements made by each of them to the FBI. As Patricia Lambert put it, these new stories "ultimately influenced the Warren Commission's reconstruction of events in Dallas on November 22, 1963."[7] Even the Warren Commission's star witness, Howard Brennan, was influenced by contact with the Secret Service. On the night of the assassination, Brennan could not identify Oswald in a police lineup as the man he claimed to have seen in the sixth floor window of the Texas School Book Depository.[8] Several days later, Brennan was visited by a Secret Service agent who asked him, "You said you couldn't make a positive identification. … Did you do that for security reasons personally or couldn't you?"[9] Brennan apparently took the hint, and when the FBI visited him about two weeks later on 12/17/63, Brennan told them, "he was sure that the person firing the rifle was Oswald."[10]

6. Parkland doctors: On or around 12/11/63, Moore and another agent, Roger C. Warner, interviewed the Dallas physicians who treated JFK.[11] As the 12/18/63 *St. Louis Post-Dispatch* wrote, "Secret Service gets revision of Kennedy wound – after visit by agents, doctors say shot was from rear. [The Secret Service] obtained a reversal of their original view that the bullet in his neck entered from the front. The investigators did so by showing the surgeons a document described as an autopsy report from

---

3. *Contract on America* by David Scheim (1991), pp.186-189, 290, 570.
4. 5 H 185, 194, 207 – Ruby's complete testimony can be found 5H 181-213.
5. CE2399; Scheim, p. 290.
6. 23 H 459-461; see also Seth Kantor's *The Ruby Cover-up* (1992), p. 121.
7. Lengthy article by Patricia (Billings) Lambert written in the late 1970's obtained via Jim Lesar & the AARC.
8. WR145; 24 H 203; 3 H 148.
9. 3 H 148.
10. WR 145.
11. See *Murder In Dealey Plaza*, pp. 115, 165, 256, and especially 272.

the United States Naval Hospital at Bethesda. The surgeons changed their original view to conform with the report they were shown."[12]

7. Moore told graduate student James Gouchenaur that he "felt remorse for the way he (Moore) had badgered Dr. Malcolm Perry into changing his testimony to the effect that there was not, after all, an entrance wound in the front of the president's neck."[13] Furthermore, Gouchenaur quoted Moore as saying that Kennedy was a traitor for giving things away to the Russians; that it was a shame people had to die, but maybe it was a good thing; that the Secret Service personnel had to go along with the way the assassination was being investigated: "I did everything I was told, we all did everything we were told, or we'd get our heads cut off."[14]

8. According to Gouchenaur, Moore was the "liaison between the staff of the Warren Commission and the Secret Service.[15] As Chief Justice Earl Warren himself said to Jack Ruby, "You know that Mr. Moore is a member of the Secret Service, and he has been a liaison officer with our staff since the Commission was formed."[16]

9. *Dallas Morning News* reporter Earl Golz wrote, "All but one of Sorrels' six Dallas agents in 1963 submitted reports of their whereabouts the day of the assassination: Elmer Moore, the agent who did not submit a report, said he was in San Francisco and did not return to Dallas to join the investigation until a week later."[17] That said, two other agents from the Dallas office, Mike Howard and the late Charles Kunkel (deceased 6/27/92[18]), also did not submit reports. Howard claimed in a lecture in Feb. 1999 that he was at the Hotel Texas cleaning up when the shooting occurred and that Kunkel was in Washington, D.C on an unspecified investigation at the time. Howard and Kunkel's whereabouts remain unverified.

Moore died 12/4/2001.[19]

---

12. See also 2 H 39, 41; *Best Evidence*, pp. 156,166-167, 196, & 286.
13. HSCA 6/1/77 interview transcript RIF#180-10109-10310; SEE ALSO CD 379; 3 H 363, 364, 387; 6 H 6,7, 17, 27, 44, 50-51, 57,63, & 75.
14. During the ARRB's 9/18/96 interview of Floyd Boring, the agent said:" ... Mr. Boring was asked whether he was acquainted with SA Elmer Moore, and he indicated that he knew him quite well, and said he was still living in Seattle. Mr. Boring was asked to read and comment on several pages of the HSCA 6/1/77 interview transcript of its interview with former graduate student James Gouchenaur, in which Gochenaur recounted a very long conversation he reportedly had with SA Elmer Moore in 1970 ... Mr. Boring said that it would be just like SA Moore to give such a lengthy interview, but that he doubted very much whether agent Moore had really said those things, since he himself had never heard agent Moore say anything like that, nor had he heard any other Secret Service agents say anything like that."
15. HSCA 6/1/77 interview transcript RIF#180-10109-10310.
16. 5 H 210.
17. *Dallas Morning News*, 8/27/78 and Golz notes, AARC.
18. *Austin American-Statesman*, 6/29/92.
19. *Seattle Post Intelligencer*, Dec. 14, 2001.

47

HARVEY HENDERSON

Agent Henderson should be a familiar name for anyone who has read either my book *Survivor's Guilt* or former agent Abraham Bolden's *The Echo from Dealey Plaza*. As Bolden told me, "I was personally told by Harvey Henderson, 'You're a nigger. You were born a nigger. You're going to die a nigger. So act like a nigger.'"[1] Former agent Walt Coughlin wrote, "Harvey (The Birmingham Baron) Henderson had left the Detail when I arrived [6/62] but I recall he was there thru most of the 1950's."[2] Walt later added, "Harvey Henderson he [Bolden] is probably rite (sic) about." In contrast, former agent Gerald Blaine, who claims to have been on Bolden's temporary shift at the White House, wrote the author on 6/12/05: "I don't remember anybody on the detail that was racist. Merit was perceived by a person's actions, their demeanor, reliability, dependability and professional credibility – not race! Harvey was not even on the shift that Bolden was during his thirty day stay. Even though Harvey Henderson was from Mississippi, I never heard of him discriminating nor demeaning anyone because of race." Blaine's best friend, Clint Hill, later said, "Now there were certain individuals in the service, I won't deny that, who were very, very bigoted. Most of them came from Missis-

1. Author's interview/correspondence with Bolden, 9/15 & 9/16/93.
2. Undated letter to author received 2/21/04.

sippi or Alabama or somewhere in the South. Sometimes we had problems with them. They didn't want to work with a black agent."[3] What's more, Phil Strother, a former agent who happens to be African American, served on the LBJ detail with Hill and Blaine, said that "I was referred to as 'Johnson's nigger' ... he heard them use the N-word plenty of times... maybe five guys out of 30 accepted me. The bulk of them worked with me out of necessity. There was no camaraderie, no socializing" with most. He was excluded from parties and informal gatherings, and he grew so accustomed to hearing racist language, he says, he sometimes felt invisible." Strother also related how "a white supervisor was sent with Strother to recruit at historically black Southern colleges, but he complained, "I don't know why we have to go to this nigger school anyway."[4]

Secret Service agent Abraham Bolden stated that it was "a matter widely known in the Service" that some unauthorized person had used Secret Service credentials in Dallas on 11/22/63 (again, perhaps the greatest smoking gun in the entire case). Accordingly, all Special Agents were required to surrender their identification documents for "an unprecedented Service-wide check."[5] Bolden further added, "Do you know what happened to Harvey Henderson? I heard that he had been relieved of his Detail by President Kennedy himself ... Harvey had made some threats like, 'We'll get you' ... I understand that he told the President 'I'll get you', or something to that effect ... (it was) no secret that Kennedy wanted him removed from the detail ... Harvey was a quick-tempered guy who couldn't take the heat ... Where is Harvey Henderson at? I think that you would do well if you could find out where Harvey Henderson was on November 22. Can you track him down?" In reference to the illicit Secret Service credentials present in Dealey Plaza on 11/22/63,[6] Mr. Bolden said, in reference to Harvey Henderson, "that's the first thing that crossed my mind – he would have the nerve, the guts, the anger, the craziness, the instability ... I'm not saying he was in Dallas, but I'm saying that ... it would be something to look at." In the book, Martin Luther King, Jr.: the FBI File,[7] it is revealed that information regarding a plot to kill Martin Luther King was

---

3. Butler, Maurice. *Out From The Shadow: The Story of Charles L Gittens Who Broke The Color Barrier In The United States Secret Service.* KY: Xlibris, 2012, pp. 125-126.

4. *Washington Post*, 1/7/2001.

5. *A Citizen's Dissent*, Mark Lane (New York: Holt, Rhinehart & Winston, 1968), p. 193; AARC files on Bolden provided by researcher Bill Adams; Author's interview/correspondence with Bolden, 9/15 & 9/16/93.

6. Agent Marty Venker later said, "... they'd [the Secret Service] given him phony ID's so he could work undercover at demonstrations." (*Confessions of an Ex-Secret Service Agent*, p. 246).

7. pp. 366-367.

furnished to Henderson, the ASAIC of the Birmingham Secret Service field office, on 3/11/65, over three years before MLK's murder.

Henderson died in early 1994.[8]

---

8. Agent "Lem" Johns, after serving on the WHD, became the SAIC of the Birmingham, Alabama office, while Henderson was his deputy. After retiring from the Secret Service, Johns became Special Assistant to LBJ aide Joseph Califano! [RIF# 180-10074-10079: 8/8/78 HSCA interview with Johns].

48

CHARLIE GITTENS

Agent Charlie Gittens was the first African-American in the Secret Service, joining the Secret Service in 1956. Gittens started out at the Charlotte, NC field office, then transferred to the New York field office. In 1963 he was a member of a security detail assigned to guard President Kennedy during a weekend at Hyannisport. The president sank into his favorite rocking chair, glanced Gittens's way and said: "Come here, Charlie." "Of course, I responded," Gittens recalled. "No sooner had I done so when this little dog rushes past me and jumps into his lap. That was Charlie, of course. The President's dog. President Kennedy just laughed his head off."[1]

Later on, Gittens transferred to the Puerto Rico office, then came a most prestigious assignment: a promotion as SAIC of the Washington field office in 1971, the second most important Secret Service office in the United States. Located at the seat of government, the Washington office received most of the "protective intelligence" cases of abusive mail, often with threats to the President.

He retired in 1979, then worked for the Department of Justice, where he investigated war criminals who were living in the United States.[2] "He

---

1. *Telegraph UK*, 8/10/2011.
2. *Los Angeles Times*, 8/10/11.

was a great agent," said Mark Sullivan, director of the Secret Service. "When you talk to people who worked with him, the one thing I hear is that he was just a regular guy.... A lot of agents, black and white, have benefited from the things he has done. He led by example, and he set the standards for all of us to follow."[3]

Gittens passed away on 7/27/2011. An excellent book on his life story is entitled *Out From The Shadow: The Story of Charles L Gittens Who Broke The Color Barrier In The United States Secret Service* by Maurice Butler from 2012.

---

3. *Washington Post*, 8/10/2011.

49

HARRY NEAL

Harry Neal retired as a top Secret Service official – Assistant Director in 1957, after 31 years with the agency – and started a second career as an author, writing 31 books. Beginning at the Secret Service as a stenographer, Mr. Neal sometimes accompanied agents. In a 1931 raid on counterfeiters, he retrieved a negative of a $10 bill from a furnace. It was the only evidence seized and it won a conviction, earning Mr. Neal a promotion to agent.[1]

During World War II, he helped direct the shipment of the Constitution, Declaration of Independence and other special documents from Washington to Fort Knox, Ky., for safekeeping. He also helped write the law that made the Secret Service a permanent agency.

As an agent, he wrote articles on counterfeit money, then gradually expanded his work to short stories and nonfiction articles for popular magazines like *Collier's, The Saturday Evening Post, Cosmopolitan, Changing Times* and *Esquire*. Although he wrote about the Secret Service, he had a variety of other book topics: the Salvation Army, kites, political parties, maps, the Industrial Revolution, time, writing techniques, the telescope and the Smithsonian Institution.

---

1. *New York Times*, 6/16/93.

Many of his books were for young people and were about careers in engineering, banking, foreign service, medical research, conservation and aviation. In all, his works sold more than 500,000 copies.[2]

He served as the president of the Association of Former Agents of the United States Secret Service (AFAUSSS) and editor of their newsletter *The Pipeline*. He was awarded the Treasury Department's Albert Gallatin Award and Exceptional Civilian Service Medal.[3]

Neal passed away at the age of 87 on 6/14/93.

2.*New York Times*, 6/16/93.

3. *Washington Post*, 6/15/93.

50

TIM MCCARTHY

Like Jerry Parr, agent Tim McCarthy is, by any standard, a true hero of the Secret Service. He literally took a bullet fired by John Hinckley, Jr. that was meant for President Reagan on 3/30/81. He later received a special letter from President Reagan expressing his heart-felt thanks. Reagan wrote, "There will always be the special gratitude I feel for your extraordinary heroism on that one cold day in March. It is a gratitude words could never convey."[1]

Tim McCarthy has served as Chief of the Orland Park, Illinois Police Department since May of 1994. He retired from the United States Secret Service in October of 1993 after 22 years of service. His career included eight years assigned to the Presidential Protective Division in Washington D.C. and 14 years as a criminal investigator in the Chicago Division. McCarthy also served as a special agent in charge of the Chicago Division from 1989 until his retirement in 1993.[2]

"It was, hopefully, going to be a routine movement day, as we called it, to the Washington Hilton Hotel," McCarthy told CBS' *The Early Show* co-anchor Rene Syler on 6/11/2004. "The advance work had been done

1. http://law2.umkc.edu/faculty/projects/ftrials/hinckley/mccarthy.htm
2. http://www.orland-park.il.us/index.aspx?nid=141

by Special Agent Bill Green. He spent a week on it, setting up the security. "We arrived at the Hilton Hotel. The president gave a speech to (the Construction Trades Council). We left and were leaving the hotel, walking in a formation around the president, as is the standard protocol, when we just about got to the armored car, and as you recall, President Reagan had only been president for 60 days. There was no information that he would work a rope line or anything like that. So we were prepared to go to the car. Just before the president got to the car, John Hinckley pushed himself forward and fired six rounds in about one and a half seconds."

McCarthy told CNN on 3/31/2013: "In the Secret Service," he continued, "we're trained to cover and evacuate the president. And to cover the president, you have to get as large as you can, rather than hitting the deck. So I have to say people have asked me, and I said quite frankly, it probably had little to do with bravery and an awful lot to do with the reaction based upon the training. It was a heck of a team effort out there that day. It was people like Ray Shaddick and Jerry Parr, pushing the president into the car, other agents going to John Hinckley and helping subdue him, to help save the life of the president that day."

51

RAY SHADDICK

A s with agents Jerry Parr and Tim McCarthy, Shift Leader Ray Shaddick was one of the heroes of 3/30/81 when President Reagan barely survived an assassination attempt by John Hinckley, Jr. Reminiscing about that incredible day, Shaddick said: "As we're coming out, Jerry is on his left side and I am on his right side," he said. "We were about 10 feet from the fully armored car coming out of that exit, when he shoots six rounds off in less than two seconds. He just followed the President and he didn't care what got in the way ... Jerry grabs [Reagan] by the shoulders and starts moving him inside the car. As soon as his head gets down ... I came in right behind and hit him in the small of the back and drove him across the car. He went flying across the car and, as he was trying to break his fall, he was shoved in and he got hit under the left arm. I remember when I closed the door and looking at him. He wasn't grimacing. He was just ashen looking, like, 'What the hell happened.' Jerry starts talking to him and he says, 'You guys really hurt me when you put me in the car. He said my ribs are really hurting, I'm having a hard time breathing." After they made the decision to go to the hospital and upon arrival, Shaddick said: "The President says, "I'm okay. I'm okay. I'll walk in," Shaddick said. "He wasn't okay.... So he starts walking in and he gets to 30/40 feet to the entrance of the emergency room. As soon as he gets there he collapses. Jerry's on one side of him, I'm on the other side of him. We carry him in and put him on the gurney."[1]

Shaddick later became SAIC of PPD for the final years of Reagan's term and the first two years of George H.W. Bush's presidency. Retiring from the Secret Service in 1998, Shaddick became head of corporate security for CNN for 10 years.

---

1. http://patch.com/georgia/sandysprings/memories-are-vivid-for-ex-secret-service-agent-now-li7bf2695d91

52

JOHN BARLETTA

F ormer agent John Barletta wrote to me on 11/18/11: "What a world of difference from protecting Jimmy Carter to Ronald Reagan. That being said, I would have taken the bullet for President Carter just as I would have for President Reagan. It is the job- protecting the presidency no matter who holds the office." Barletta, also the author of the poignant 2005 book *Riding With Reagan*, is best known as the agent who protected President Reagan on horseback both when Reagan was president and for many years afterward. Barletta became a family friend and shared his memories of the former president and the struggle Reagan had with Altzheimer's disease both in his book and in various media appearances.

Barletta, who protected Reagan for 17 years and became a family friend, said he first became concerned when Reagan began forgetting how to saddle his beloved El Alamein, a towering white stallion. Then, Reagan's masterful technique in the saddle failed. "He knew how to ride, he knew his equipment, but he was having trouble," Barletta said. Reagan would come up with a piece of equipment in his hand and ask, "What am I supposed to do with this?" Barletta feared for Reagan's safety, and he had to tell the former president that their rides were over. The task left Barletta in tears. They never talked of horses again.

In time, Reagan's cherished Saturday trips to the golf course became a challenge, said Barletta, who would accompany him there. "He would say, 'John, where are we going?' I would say, 'The Los Angeles Country Club.' He would say, 'What are we going to do there?' I would say, 'You're going to have lunch with some friends and play some golf, ' " Barletta recalled. "A minute later, he would ask me the same question."[1]

John Barletta retired from the Secret Service in 1997 after 23 years of dedicated service. He was commissioned into the Secret Service in 1974 and assigned to the Boston Field Office. In 1978, he was transferred to the Presidential Protective Division at the White House to protect Presidents Carter and Reagan. John was assigned to the Candidate Nominee Protective Division; the Dignitary Protective Division; and the Liaison Division.

---

1. *Cincinnati Enquirer*, 6/11/2004.

CARMINE MOTTO

Agent Carmine Motto, the brother of fellow agent Robert Motto, was Renowneded for his undercover work catching counterfeiters and the like. He was also an author of some repute, writing *Undercover* (1971) and *In Crime's Way: A Generation of Secret Service Adventures* (1999). Motto completed over sixty years in the field of law enforcement, much of his career devoted to being the U.S. Secret Service's recognized expert in undercover operations. He also served in the New York State Police, the U. S. Treasury Office of Law Enforcement, as Deputy Commissioner of Public Safety, and as police commissioner in New York.

In *Undercover*, Motto's classic guide to the trade, Motto cautions that the initial meeting is crucial. "The most important time during the whole undercover case is the first five seconds when the suspect is introduced to the agent," he wrote. "It is these first few seconds when the suspect makes a personal judgment and decides whether or not he wants to do business." "Both my dad and my uncle were very, very low-key people," said Robert Motto's niece, Irene Kaufman. "I think that's what helped them both be very successful undercover agents."

Both Carmine and his brother Robert passed away in 2002.

DENNIS MCCARTHY

Agent Dennis McCarthy, something of a hero on 3/30/81 for subduing assassin John Hinckley, Jr., became *persona non grata* after publishing his 1985 book *Protecting the President.* With its tawdry tales of presidential voyeurism and foul language, as well as perhaps too in-depth stories of agency doings, *Protecting the President* became something of an embarrassment, as former agent's Robert Snow, Darwin Horn and Walt Coughlin conveyed to myself. McCarthy (no relation to Tim McCarthy) served on the White House Detail during the LBJ and Nixon days and, all told, served in the Secret Service from 1964-1984. McCarthy received the Medal of Valor for subduing Hinckley that fateful day,[1] yet the Secret Service was not pleased with his book.

The 1995 Discovery Channel documentary *Inside The Secret Service* contains evidence of the agency's dissatisfaction with McCarthy. An actor portraying an assassin is shown reading his book as if searching for tips on

---

1. *Protecting the President* by Dennis McCarthy (1985), page 270.

how to achieve success, while a photo of the heroes of 3/30/81 is shown (the same one that appears in McCarthy's own book) but with Dennis McCarthy edited out.

As *People* magazine reported, "He joined the Secret Service in 1964 and four years later was assigned to the White House detail guarding President Lyndon Johnson. McCarthy and the other agents could hardly stand Johnson, who treated them like servants. Compared to LBJ, Richard Nixon was a delight to work with. "He was courteous and at times even friendly," McCarthy recalls. He describes the time in 1970 when a fire broke out at Nixon's San Clemente home. McCarthy was so busy putting out the fire, spraying the dining room wall with a hose, that he lost track of the Chief Executive. "Who's got the fucking President?!" he yelled. "I'm right here; everything's fine," Nixon answered calmly. When Nixon surveyed the damage – mostly caused by McCarthy's hosing – the President said, "Oh, Pat's going to be pissed off when she sees this..."

McCarthy describes Henry Kissinger as "a real pain," citing a trip to Acapulco in 1977 with the former Secretary of State and his wife, Nancy. Though there were signs posted warning of sharks in the bay, Nancy said she wanted to bathe, so Henry asked the agents to stand in the water and guard against the sharks. "Dr. Kissinger," McCarthy says he replied, "if you're concerned about sharks, my suggestion is that you don't swim." He explained that battling sharks in the sea was not in the Secret Service agents' job description, but, he solemnly assured Kissinger, "if the sharks come up on this beach, my agents will fight them."[2]

McCarthy passed away in 1993.

---

2. *People Magazine*, 10/28/85.

JOE PETRO

A gent Joe Petro was the Assistant Special Agent in Charge (ASAIC) of the Presidential Protective Division (PPD) during the Reagan era and the author of the book *Standing Next to History* from 2005. Petro served from 1971 to 1993 and guarded Vice President Ford, Vice President Dan Quayle (in which he was the SAIC), and the aforementioned President Reagan, among others. When I wrote to Petro's immediate boss, SAIC Robert DeProspero, he expressed nothing but positive feelings for his deputy, stating that he was also his ambassador to the president's staff.

Petro attended Temple University on a football scholarship. He was drafted by the Cleveland Browns in 1966. But he left football to enroll in the U.S. Navy Officer Candidate School, Newport, R.I., where he graduated with distinction in 1967. He entered active military duty with the Navy at Pensacola Naval Air Station, Florida, and served a tour of duty in Vietnam. He holds the Bronze Star with combat V and the Navy, Marine Corps Combat Action Ribbon. He left the Navy as a lieutenant.[1]

Offering insight into his work with the president at the White House, Petro said Reagan "so respected that space that it reflected how he conducted himself. He never took off his suit jacket. One of the most memorable moments I had in the Secret Service was when President Reagan met General Secretary Mikhail Gorbachev for the first time face to face. The only people in the room were President Reagan, Gorbachev, myself and a KGB counterpart. It was an amazing moment in history. It was the turning point in Soviet and U.S. relations. It ended the cold war and the Soviet Union. I was lucky to have been there."[2]

Petro left the Secret Service in 1993 to become head of security for Citigroup.

1. *The Morning Call*, 3/12/98.
2. *The Morning Call*, 3/12/98.

MARTY VENKER

Without question, agent Marty Venker was one of the most colorful agents ever. He became a DJ after leaving the Secret Service and wrote a witty, funny and controversial book in 1988 with writer George Rush called *Confessions of An Ex-Secret Service Agent*. Venker protected Presidents Nixon, Ford and Carter and also protected Nixon after his fall from grace. Venker served from 1971 to 1981.

Venker's book is a real gem. Personally, I get a kick out of Marty Venker: he is a lot like one of his evident heroes, Brooks Keller (the wild former agent chronicled briefly in both his book and Dennis McCarthy's). Venker's book, actually written by George Rush, is a funny yet informative chronicle of a square peg in a round hole – Venker, the wild child, trying to conform to rigid, structured, pressure-packed duty as a Special Agent. The lack of an index will frustrate you (at least in the paperback), but there are many nice nuggets and anecdotes to be found here.

The *Chicago Tribune* reported: "Rush met Venker after he'd left the Secret Service and become a disc jockey at several New York dance clubs, those huge halls that throb and shudder with galaxies of strobe lights, sound systems capable of making ears bleed and an aura of exhilarant, evanescent escape. He started at a swingers club for $50 a night and progressed to a former sheet metal factory that had been transformed into a sprawling spot called the Kamikaze; one of the bartenders was a cocky aspiring actor who went by Bruno, but who would be more widely known as Bruce Willis.

It was more satisfying than following Jimmy and Rosalynn Carter on moonlit walks at Camp David, accompanying Imelda Marcos on a shopping spree or watching a drunken Anastasio Somoza, the former Nicaraguan dictator, crawl on his hands and knees across the lobby of the Waldorf Towers after a night on the town with prostitutes. After Rush made Venker the subject of an article in *Rolling Stone* magazine, a book contract and movie deal followed. The hook, of course, was the bizarre juxtaposition of night-crawling punk deejay and Secret Service agent."[1]

Venker passed away 5/8/2013.[2] Former agent Gordon Heddell said of Marty: "I met Marty Venker for the first time on a Monday morning, on September 28, 1971. Marty was the kind of guy in whom you could instinctively sense qualities of genius combined with an amazingly likable personality. What I didn't know about Marty on that Monday morning was just how memorable, and how special a friend he would become. In many ways Marty and I became inseparable. A great deal of what I learned about being a good criminal investigator." Former agent John Giuffre had this to say about Marty: "Have fond memories of "Venkie" when we worked together for the United States Secret Service in Springfield, Ill., 1972 to 1976. Marty was one of the most productive agents on the job. Besides being a fine agent, he was a friend and also a very funny guy. He was transferred to New York because he was a good agent and they needed the help of a number of top notch people. I was sorry to see him leave because he was a great asset to the organization."[3]

---

1. *Chicago Tribune*, 10/19/88.
2. http://observer.com/2015/06/saluting-a-secret-service-agent-turned-dj/
3. http://www.tributes.com/obituary/show/Martin-J.-Venker-95873675

57

FRANK WILSON

Secret Service Chief Frank Wilson is a legend. While working for the Treasury Department's Intelligence Unit in 1928, Wilson was assigned to go after the famous mobster Al Capone. As it turned out, Capone could be prosecuted under a 1927 ruling by the Supreme Court which declared that any income from criminal activities must be subjected to income taxes. Wilson would spend the next three years gathering information on Capone's financial dealings including tracking down mob accountants and bookkeepers. Becoming aware of Wilson's investigation, a nervous Capone ordered five gunmen to murder Wilson. Federal authorities were informed of the contract and, after urgings from former mentor Johnny Torrio, Capone reluctantly canceled the hit. As a result of Wilson's investigation, which revealed millions of dollars in unreported income, Capone was eventually sentenced to 11 years of imprisonment.[1]

If that weren't enough, Wilson was part of the team investigating the Lindbergh kidnapping. Some sources indicate that Wilson had insisted on tracking the serial numbers on the gold certificates used as ransom money (which ultimately led to the arrest and conviction of Bruno Richard Hauptmann).[2]

1. https://en.wikipedia.org/wiki/Frank_J._Wilson
2. *Get Capone: The Secret Plot That Captured America's Most Wanted Gangster* by Jonathan Eig (2010), p. 372

Wilson was named Chief of the Secret Service, serving from 1937-1946. While he was Chief of the U.S. Secret Service, Wilson was devoted to curbing counterfeiting. The amount of counterfeit currency rose to an all-time high during the Great Depression. To curb counterfeiting, Wilson launched a "Know Your Money" campaign. As part of this campaign, a booklet and video was produced and distributed to students, bankers, and storekeepers that demonstrated how to identify counterfeit currency. By 1943, annual losses from counterfeits had dropped 97% from the 1936 level. Wilson also changed many of the protocols for Presidential Protection, many of which are still in place today.

Wilson also wrote the 1965 book *Special Agent: A Quarter-Century with the Treasury Department and the Secret Service.* Wilson was also interviewed 6/25/64 by William Manchester for his book on the JFK assassination entitled *The Death of a President.*

Wilson passed away 6/22/70.

58

GEORGE DRESCHER

Agent George Drescher was the Special Agent in Charge (SAIC) of the White House Detail from 4/12/45 to 5/3/46. Interestingly, his nephew Earl L. Drescher became the deputy chief of the Executive Protective Service in the late 1970's. Drescher was a witness to a fairly famous incident involving President Truman at the Potsdam conference. Fellow agent Floyd Boring stated the following:

> Well, of course, the Potsdam trip [7/17-8/2/45] was unique in itself. We landed, I think, in Brussels as I recall, and they had a left-handed drive car there. I was driving that thing, and it was unusual for me. Actually we were driving across bridges, you know, that were pontoon bridges, and I guess you may have heard this story. I don't know whether you've heard it or not. We were waiting outside; I was waiting near the car. They had a colonel riding back and forth with the President, you know, just as company, and [George C.] Drescher – that was one of his last trips over there – got into the car. This guy, the colonel, says to President Truman, "Listen, I know you're alone over here; your wife hasn't arrived yet," and he said, "If you need anything like, you know, I'll be glad to arrange it for you." And he [the President] said, "Hold it; don't say anything more." He said, "I love my wife, and my wife is my sweetheart." He said, "I don't want to do that kind of stuff." And he said, "I don't want you to ever say that again to me." That's about the way he ended it."[1]

---

1. Floyd Boring Truman Library oral history, 9/21/88.

Drescher was also mentioned in James Rowley's 9/20/88 Truman Library oral history (Rowley replaced Drescher).

FDR and Truman Assistant White House Press Secretary Eben Ayers wrote on 5/30/45: "As soon as President Truman came into the White House, a new and strange group of secret service agents appeared, headed by one, George Drescher, a big, somewhat rough, individual, far from the gentlemanly type of [Mike] Reilly [the previous SAIC]. Drescher, it seems, had at one time been at the White House some years ago but had moved out, and the story was that he had been waiting for his revenge. The chief of the Secret Service is Frank Wilson, who is cordially disliked by most of the men, at least those of the White House detail. The story is that Wilson disliked President Roosevelt intensely and was hoping for his defeat in the election last year. He formed a detail, headed by Drescher, which was to take over [Thomas] Dewey upon his election. When he was defeated, of course, that plan fell through. Drescher, however, was assigned to the vice president, Truman, and so came into the White House with him. In the first days of the administration he made himself conspicuous, and there was general knowledge that he was expecting to take over. Reilly, however, got – so he told me during that period – assurance that he was to remain."

"When the president planned to go to Kansas City to get his mother and bring her back to Washington, Reilly went ahead, as customary in these cases, to make arrangements there. One story was that he got drunk or failed to show up. Mike told me today that after he had been there a few days, he received word from Washington to return. He got on the telephone and communicated with a friend here who told him that twelve members of his old detail were being transferred to posts in the field – other assignments in other cities. So Mike tendered his resignation. Mike told me that some of the men who had been brought in were men whom he had refused to have on the detail when he was in charge of it. He did not feel that they were suitable for the important and responsible job of guarding the life of the president. They are, in many cases, obviously inexperienced and know little of what to do, and Drescher … is not the type that should be in this post."[2] Ouch.

Ayers may have a point. Drescher took part in an oral history for the Herbert Hoover Library on 6/1/67 in which he ridiculed former SAIC Edmund Starling: "[Col. Edmund] Starling [SAIC of WHD during the 1930's] wrote a book. He was a phony. He was the biggest phony in the

2. *Truman in the White House: The Diary of Eben A. Ayers* (1991), pages 35-36.

world, the way he used to parade." Interestingly, Drescher also said: "Anybody in God's world could take a maximum silencer and put it on a rifle and knock off any President.... Don't let them put a parade on a narrow street with buildings all around you. Keep them in the wide open spaces." Keep in mind, this was said only a few years after the JFK assassination.

Drescher was on the White House detail during the Coolidge and Hoover eras.

Drescher died 1/21/77.

59

ROBERT BOUCK

The *Washington Post* reported on 5/8/2004: "Robert Inman Bouck epitomized discretion. He knew the ins and outs of the White House like few people do. He kept secrets, personal and political, without a qualm. It was the code of the Secret Service, Bouck's employer for 30 years. "A lot of things he did, I didn't know he was doing," said his wife of 67 years, Marjorie Bouck. "Some things he would talk about, but he would not talk about the private lives of the presidents at all, he really didn't. He didn't even tell us," said James Bouck, one of his sons.

He protected six presidents, from Franklin D. Roosevelt to Richard M. Nixon, but he had a special affection for President John F. Kennedy and his family, and the assassination "just devastated him," said his wife. The subsequent years were "the worst couple years of his life," she added.

Bouck, who died of congestive heart failure April 27 [2004] at age 89, was the special agent in charge of the protective research division at the time and was in Washington on Nov. 22, 1963. Upon hearing the news, he immediately removed a secret reel-to-reel tape recording system that he had installed at Kennedy's request in July 1962. Kennedy left the machine running when he left the room during the Cuban missile crisis. The tapes, a television documentary later reported, recorded members of the Joint Chiefs of Staff cursing what they considered the president's weak-minded proposal to blockade Cuba without invading it.

Bouck also oversaw the chain of evidence from Kennedy's assassination after it arrived in Washington. He testified before the Warren Commission and a congressional investigative committee that he turned over boxes of evidence to Kennedy's personal secretary, Evelyn Lincoln, at the National Archives. At the time, he said that one of the containers held remains of Kennedy's brain. The brain was discovered to be missing some years later, and because of this discrepancy, Bouck's name still turns up on conspiracy-theory Web sites.

As important as the Kennedys were to him, Bouck had an enviable career before 1960. A Michigan farm boy, he studied police science at Michigan State, married his college sweetheart and joined the Secret Service in 1939[1]. He was rejected for active duty in the Army during World War II because of high blood pressure. Yet he traveled the world as an advance man for President Dwight D. Eisenhower and then accompanied him on the official trips to Europe, China, India, Pakistan, Africa and South America. He was a member of the U.S. delegation to the Potsdam Conference in 1945, where Allied leaders determined the future of postwar Europe. He was at the Allied Commission on Reparations in Europe in 1945 and was at the Geneva Convention in 1955.

Bouck also completed the advance trip to arrange for Eisenhower's 1960 trip to the Soviet Union, which was canceled after an American U-2 spy plane was shot down over Russia. In 1957, he was described as the "electronics ace" of the Secret Service in an article in the *Washington Post*, a description that a former colleague endorses. "He knew the mechanical gadgets, the electronic devices you use to supplement human intelligence," said H. Stuart Knight, the director of the Secret Service from 1973 to 1981, who called Bouck a mentor whom he admired for his character, professionalism and integrity. "He was head of training when I went there. He was an example you aspire to emulate. That's part of the culture of the Secret Service. "He was a leader."

Bouck was on a presidential trip to Moscow when Soviet leader Nikita Khrushchev greeted a throng of visitors. Bouck did not want to shake Khrushchev's hand, so he kept moving to the back of the crowd. Khrushchev spotted him, pursued him, and finally thrust his hand between two people, forcing Bouck to acknowledge the host. Another time, Bouck was at a meeting at Winston Churchill's home when the British prime minister and famous amateur painter interrupted the proceedings to call for

1. Another news article noted: "On Sept. 5, 1939, Mr. Bouck entered the United States Secret Service as one of the first two agents with college degrees in police administration." The other was Gerald Behn, also from Michigan State University.

his paints and a ladder. He climbed up to one of his pieces and dabbed a bit of paint on a hanging painting. Bouck also told his family about a time in Bermuda when Churchill, worried that the ocean was too chilly for swimming, asked a well-known aide to dip his top hat to test the water's temperature.

After 30 years of protecting presidents, Bouck retired in 1969. He had a second and third career with the Federal Reserve and with central banks of several foreign countries. But there's little doubt how Bouck defined himself. One of the few mementos that Bouck kept, his son said, was a receipt, signed by Robert Kennedy, for the president's Cartier watch that he returned to the family after the assassination."

On 9/27/92, Bouck confirmed to me that having agents on the back of the limousine depended on factors independent of any alleged Presidential "requests": "Many times there were agents on his car." On 4/30/96, the ARRB's Doug Horne questioned Bouck: "Did you ever hear the President personally say that he didn't want agents to stand on the running boards on his car, or did you hear that from other agents?" Bouck: "I never heard the President say that personally." The former agent also told the ARRB that JFK was the "most congenial" of all the presidents he had observed (Bouck served from FDR to LBJ). Bouck also told me had known about JFK's sordid private life, as well as the Joseph Milteer threat, and others, prior to 11/22/63. The failure to disseminate and act upon this threat information apparently had dire consequences for Bouck's career. As the HSCA's Mr. Matthews stated, "The Chief of the intelligence branch of the Secret Service [Bouck] testified before this committee that he was removed from his position for what he interpreted as the failure of his mission."[2]

Bouck told the ARRB on 5/2/96 that he believed there was a conspiracy involved in the death of JFK; although he thought Oswald was the lone shooter.[3]

---

2. 3 HSCA 358.

3. See also *High Treason*, 1998 edition, p. 433. Although Bouck does not offer an opinion on the matter during his JFK Library Oral history, dated 6/25/76, Bouck echoed the above sentiments to the author, among other things, on 9/27/92.

60

ROGER WARNER

Agent Roger C. Warner, who passed away 6/4/16 at the age of 80, was quite an interesting character, to put it mildly. Warner served in the Secret Service and the CIA, as well as serving in the U.S. Army briefly. A 1957 MSU graduate, Warner served three years for the US Bureau of Narcotics, 20 years in the Secret Service, and 12 years in the CIA.[1] Warner was an agent on the Texas trip when JFK was assassinated. It was his very first presidential protective assignment![2] Warner later accompanied Robert Oswald to his brother's funeral.[3] In addition, according to fellow agent Jim Hardin, Warner served on the Treasury Secretary John Connally detail (Connally, a victim of the shooting that day in Dallas, went on to become the boss of the Secret Service during the Nixon era). Warner also served in the Washington, D.C. (as a supervisor) and Jacksonville, Florida field offices. He also served on Vice President Hubert Humphrey's detail (with fellow agents Walt Coughlin, Glen Weaver and others).

Colleagues had high praise for Warner. Fellow agent Rad Jones said: "Roger was a true professional and outstanding example of a Secret Service agent." Agent Jim McCully said of Roger: "I learned a good deal from him. He was one of my favorite people in the Secret Service." Agent Rog-

---

1. Roger Warner, Facebook profile.
2. HSCA interview with Roger Warner, 5/25/78 [RIF# 180-10093-10026].
3. *Four Days in November* (2008) by Vince Bugliosi, page 508.

er Counts said: "Greatly enjoyed working with him for many years and many places." Agent Paul Kelly said: "Roger was a true patriot who served his country faithfully and in ways that many will never know. He was a friend to all and a mentor to many." Agent Gary Strnad said: "Roger was a true professional and represented the USSS with class. It was my pleasure to work for him at the 1972 Miami Republican convention; wherein, he backed me up during a confrontation with the local press!"

Agent Roger Warner stated in his report that, while at Love Field during the forming of the motorcade, "I undertook duties to aid SA Lawson … in lining up cars for the motorcade, passing out numbers for the automobiles, and other general duties … "[4] Warner also mentioned in his report that, " … Mrs. Kennedy had requested no photographs or persons be allowed near the area where she would board Air Force One … "[5] This alleged "request" came approximately "ten minutes" before Jackie and the body of JFK arrived at the airport. Since it was the Secret Service who prevented the media from taking pictures of the bloody limousine just a short time before, it appears strongly that it was an agent (or agents) who actually made this request.[6] If this was really Jackie's request, why was official White House photographer Cecil Stoughton allowed to take numerous photos of this very area at that same time?[7] Stoughton probably made these photos on the sly, unknown to the agents. Warner even wrote that, "… no photographs were taken … "[8] Evidently, the Secret Service did not want any compromising photos taken that day, such as the uncleaned limousine with a bullet hole in the windshield and dented chrome; or the identities of the agents carrying the coffin containing JFK's body. In fact, Agent Clint Hill revealed in his report dated 11/30/63: "[calling from Parkland Hospital] I requested that no press be admitted to the area in which Air Force One was to be placed."[9] Agent Warner questioned another suspect in the assassination on 11/22/63, Donald Wayne House, a man that bore an uncanny resemblance to Lee Harvey Oswald. House was mentioned by the media before Oswald came into the picture and

---

4. 25H 786-7 CE 2554.

5. 25 H 787.

6. 18 H 801-802. Newcomb interview with DPD Stavis Ellis, early 1970's.

7. See Stoughton photos in *Best Evidence* and Richard Trask's *That Day in Dallas*.

8. DPD Bobby Joe Dale told author Larry Sneed: "… there was a DPS trooper taking pictures, and the Secret Service hollered at him to get his camera out of there [*No More Silence*, page 137]."Airman first class aircraft mechanic William E. Sale wrote: "One photographer took a picture as JFK's copper colored coffin was being carried up the rear steps. A Secret Service agent pointed at him and a group of Dallas police chased him along the warehouse roof." [Undated Sale letter, approximately 1988].

9. CD 3 Exhibits.

his arrest even made the television airwaves. Nothing ever came of the investigation of Mr. House.[10] Warner was also present, along with Agent Patterson, when Oswald was in surgery at Parkland Hospital after Ruby shot him.[11] It was Warner who picked up JFK's watch from Parkland Hospital on 11/26/63, which prompts the question: Why didn't Agent Greer obtain this item during his return trip to Trauma Room One while the body of JFK was being taken to Love Field?[12] Greer told the HSCA on 2/28/78: "When the doctors pronounced President Kennedy dead [he] was handed the President's clothing, wallet and watch, which he took back to Washington. He directed agent Rybka at Andrews Air Force Base to put the shopping bag in his locker at the White House. A few days later he returned Kennedy's watch and wallet to Ken O'Donnell." However, Dallas agent Roger Warner's report, and Commission Document 3, tell a different story regarding JFK's watch. It went to Parkland Head of Security O.P. Wright, then to Warner, then off to Washington, D.C. Although seemingly trivial, why would Greer be in such conflict with the others (who are corroborated) on this matter? Agent Warner may also be one of the two agents mentioned in a *St. Louis Post-Dispatch* article who effected a radical revision of the Parkland Doctors' views on the wounds. Agent Warner interviewed Ruby employee, stripper Karen Carlin, on 11/24/63. His report reads in part: "She stated to me that she was under the impression that Lee Harvey Oswald, Jack Ruby, and other individuals unknown to her were involved in a plot to assassinate President Kennedy and that she would be killed if she gave any information to the authorities." Karen Carlin came out of hiding in October of 1992, after living under an assumed name. She confirmed the contents of her Secret Service interview with Warner and added that Ruby was definitely in on a conspiracy to silence Oswald.[13]

---

10. 25 H 787; NBC 11/22/63; SA Mike Howard notified Warner re: Mr. House.
11. 20 H 445.
12. 21 H 230.
13. 26 H 509; *Kennedy Contract* by John Davis (Harper Mass Market Paperbacks, 1993).

LARRY BUENDORF

While working for the Secret Service, Larry Buendorf was special agent in charge of the protective division (1983-93) assigned to former President Gerald and Mrs. Ford. Buendorf also was special agent in charge of the Secret Service Omaha Field Office (1982-83); the Denver Field Office (1977-82); and was a member of the presidential protective division (1972-77), during which time he provided protection to President's Nixon, Ford and Carter. Buendorf was previously a member of the Chicago Field Office (1970-72).

For his role in preventing the assassination attempt on President Ford, Buendorf was awarded the U.S. Treasury Meritorious Service Award and the United States Secret Service Valor Award. Buendorf successfully thwarted the assassination attempt by Lynette "Squeaky" Fromme against President Ford in Sacramento, Calif., on September 5, 1975.

TIM MCINTYRE/LARRY NEWMAN/ TONY SHERMAN/JOE PAOLELLA

William T. McIntyre   LARRY NEWMAN   TONY SHERMAN   JOE PAOLELLA

T hese four agents are part of what I call the "Seymour Hersh Four": the four former Kennedy detail Secret Service agents who spoke to Pulitzer Prize winning author Seymour Hersh about President Kennedy's private life. I spoke to these men, as well, but I focused on the protection afforded JFK (or lack thereof). A look at each one is in order now.

During the course of a 3/25/78 HSCA interview, fellow Agent Ernest Aragon painted an unflattering picture of the Secret Service in general, and McIntyre in particular. The interview summary states, "Aragon was more than mildly critical of the performance of the Secret Service in the area of Presidential Protection. He said that most agents, including some of the White House Detail, were less than proficient in their duties. 'I did not consider the protection of the President a statutory obligation; I considered it a personal one', he said. Alone, of all the agents interviewed thus far by the writer [James Kelly, HSCA investigator and former Secret Service agent], former SA Aragon seemed to feel that the Secret Service was not always doing its best to protect the President. He recalled how on the November 18th, 1963 visit he went to the Americana Hotel were President Kennedy was giving a speech. In the lobby he saw SA McIntyre standing alone. He went to pass the time of day with him and McIntyre allegedly said, 'What am I supposed to do? I don't know what to do.' Aragon[1] said he was in the

---

1. Apparently, Aragon was scheduled to testify before the full Committee, along with Thomas Kelley and Chief Rowley; this is duly noted in Chief Counsel G. Robert Blakey's 9/19/78 Agenda Memo that contains a brief biography for Aragon and a slot for the agent to testify, sandwiched between Kelley (listed as the first witness) and Rowley (listed as the third, after Aragon, the second). For some unknown reason, Aragon did not testify, instead giving the above-mentioned staff interview

process of explaining his functions to him when SA Coughlin came up. He suggested to Coughlin that he instruct him on his duties." Coughlin wrote the author on 4/28/05: "Don't remember. Could have happened!" McIntyre was one of the agents protecting JFK on the follow-up car in Dallas. Not surprisingly, the ARRB reported during their 9/18/96 interview with Floyd Boring: "When shown the HSCA interview summary of its interview with Miami field office SA Ernest Aragon (specifically, Aragon's allegations of Secret Service security lapses), he said he would not agree with that statement, and expressed the opinion that SA Aragon may not have known what he was talking about." McIntyre, positioned behind SA Hill on the driver's side running board, took the time to share a hearty laugh with Hill just a few blocks before the assassination, causing both men to look away from their posts. Although some may consider this a minor infraction, this indicates the level of vigilance of the agency that day.[2]

More troubling are the revelations McIntyre and three of his Secret Service colleagues shared with author Seymour Hersh in 1997,[3]and, soon after, on ABC television,[4]concerning JFK's private life (and, indirectly, Emory Roberts) ... but not for the reason the reader might think: a disturbing and alarming mindset was demonstrated by these men concerning the president they were sworn to protect. As McIntyre put it, "His shift supervisor, the highly respected Emory Roberts, took him aside and warned ... that 'you're going to see a lot of shit around here. Stuff with the President. Just forget about it. Keep it to yourself. Don't even talk to your wife' ... Roberts was nervous about it. Emory would say, McIntyre recalled with a laugh, 'How in the hell do you know what's going on? He could be hurt in there. What if one bites him' in a sensitive area? Roberts 'talked about it a lot', McIntyre said. 'Bites' ... In McIntyre's view, a public scandal about Kennedy's incessant womanizing was inevitable. 'It would have had to come out in the next year or so. In the campaign, maybe.' McIntyre said he and some of his colleagues ... felt abused by their service on behalf of President Kennedy ... McIntyre said he eventually realized that he had compromised his law enforcement beliefs to the point where he wondered whether it was 'time to get out of there. I was disappointed by what I saw.'" McIntyre repeated the Roberts story on ABC (without naming Emory), with this comment included: "Pros-

and a deposition on 7/27/78. Perhaps this was because, unlike Kelley and Rowley, Aragon was critical of the Secret Service.

2. Film clip shown during author's appearance on *The Men Who Killed Kennedy*, 2003.

3. For Hersh's book *The Dark Side of Camelot* (1997).

4. *Dangerous World: The Kennedy Years*, 12/4/97, ABC, hosted by Peter Jennings (also a home video and on You Tube).

titution-that's illegal. A procurement is illegal. And if you have a procurer with prostitutes paraded in front of you, then, as a sworn law enforcement officer, you're asking yourself, 'well, what do they think of us'?" McIntyre felt this way after having only spent a brief time with JFK before the assassination: he joined the WHD in the fall of 1963.[5] Fellow former agent Gerald Blaine confirmed to the author on 6/10/05 that McIntyre was indeed "brand new" and lacked experience. In addition, these feelings of anger and impotence, especially by Roberts and McIntyre, loom large in the context of the actions and inactions of the Secret Service on 11/22/63.

Soon after the airing of the aforementioned television program, Bill Clinton's Secret Service Director Lewis C. Merletti wrote a letter to 3,200 current and 500 former agents reminding them not to talk about "any aspect of the personal lives of our protectees." He further reminded the agents to recall their commission book oath, "to be worthy of trust and confidence." Merletti said this "confidence ... should continue forever."[6] After all, this is the Secret Service's motto: Worthy of Trust and Confidence.[7] In fact, the Former Secret Service Agents' association censured all four of the agents who spoke to Hersh for talking about President Kennedy's private life.[8] Fellow agent J. Frank Yeager, also a Texas trip veteran, wrote, "I cannot speak for McIntyre. I personally don't believe that the President's personal life should be public information."[9] Former agent Walt Coughlin weighed in on the situation: "It was their rite [sic] to say it but I wish they had not. I would never say anything bad (of a personal nature) against a protectee. We are there by law, not as a guest!"[10] Coughlin later wrote the author, "[Tony] Sherman and [Larry] Newman got crossways with AFAUSSS for "talking about personal incidents" of JFK[.] Also Joe Paolella and Tim McIntyre."[11]

Author Ronald Kessler quotes agents Larry Newman and Tony Sherman, as well as three new agents, Charles Taylor, Robert Lutz and an anonymous agent, about Kennedy's sordid private life.[12] To demonstrate some true hypocrisy, Lutz was on the record in 1998 as stating that he was "stunned, shocked, and ashamed" at the revelations about JFK's sor-

5. Hersh, pp. 240-241.
6. Wire service story picked up by many newspapers and media outlets, an example of which was the *Chattanooga Times* in an article written by Sandra Sobieraj on 12/18/97.
7. *Extreme Careers-Secret Service Agents: Life Protecting the President*, pp. 9 & 55. See also the 2004 National Geographic documentary *Inside the U.S. Secret Service*.
8. *The Arrogance of Power* by Anthony Summers (Penguin: reissue edition), p. 511.
9. Letter to author dated 1/24/04.
10. E-mail to author dated 2/22/04.
11. E-mail to author dated 4/27/05.
12. *In The President's Secret Service* by Ronald Kessler, pp. 11-12.

did private life provided by Newman, Sherman, Paolella, and McIntyre in Seymour Hersh's book.[13] But he goes on to regale Kessler about a gorgeous Swedish Pan Am flight attendant who turned out to be "part of the president's private stock," as an unnamed detail leader (perhaps Roberts) told him. In addition, agent Bill Carter also talked about JFK's sexual escapades in his book *Get Carter*.[14]

An unnamed agent of the era spoke to author Philip Melanson on 1/9/2002 and stated that, while he conceded that President Kennedy was a womanizer, "It was not on the sordid scale of the four agents' claims ..." The retired agent also contests the Hersh agents' claims that Kennedy tarnished the office, and offers, "Kennedy had the most respect for the office of any president I have seen." The agent is questioning the accuracy, scale, and the sheer venom, in his opinion, of the four accounts. He adds angrily, "I've never heard any agent talk about a president that way."[15] Needless to say, this author agrees with this former agent's account to Melanson. So, if these stories have been exaggerated (and even if they haven't), why all the ire? If McIntyre and Roberts felt this way before Dallas, and there's every reason to believe they in fact did, the implications of their subsequent actions, or lack thereof, are frightening.

At least the other three agents, Joseph Paolella, Tony Sherman, and Larry Newman, were not on Kennedy's detail on the Texas trip, though that's no excuse for their ill feelings. As Agent Marty Venker wrote, "God-damn, I was protecting these guys. Once you got your feeling involved, it made it that much harder to step in front of a bullet. You might think, at the last minute, 'How do I feel about this guy?' I'd just as soon not know what he stood for."[16] Agent Dennis McCarthy reflected, "They [Secret Service] are around politicians, often some of the most powerful ones in the world, much of the time and frequently see these men and women at their worst as well as at their best."[17]

Agent Ron Williams wrote, regarding President Clinton, "The primary reason I retired was because I had become disenchanted with the egotistical arrogance of the Clinton staff and because I saw character flaws in Clinton that I had not seen in the five past presidents I had protected since 1970. His attention to image and style but lack of substance and character was evident in private. He was the ultimate con man ... I find myself amazed

---

13. *Reading Eagle*, 10/23/98.
14. Carter, pp. 21-23.
15. *The Secret Service: The Hidden History of an Enigmatic Agency*, pp. 309-310.
16. Rush (Venker), p. 59.
17. *Protecting the President*, p. 31.

that a majority of the American people still are buying this con man ... My intuition in 1992 was right. Bill Clinton lacks substance and character. I just wish the American people felt values, substance, and character were important."[18] How similar were these other agents' feelings about JFK to those of their colleague McIntyre, and presumably, by extension, Roberts? See below. Tony Sherman, who spent two years at the White House with JFK: "I wanted out ... I didn't want a part of it ... I got mad ... I got angry at any president who doesn't treat the White House like I think he should ..."[19] Sherman added, "Seventy to eighty percent of the agents thought it was nuts ... Some of us were brought up the right way. Our mothers and fathers didn't do it. We lived in another world. Suddenly, I'm Joe Agent here. I'm looking at the president of the United States and telling myself, 'This is the White House and we protect the White House.'"[20]

On the ABC special, Sherman related a tale of JFK and prostitutes that occurred during the President's trip to Honolulu, Hawaii, in June of 1963 (incidentally, two clips are shown of this trip, depicting agents running with the limousine on all four corners during the motorcade, motorcycles beside JFK, and SAIC Behn on the trip, among other things). Sherman said, "The Honolulu episode made me angry. It did make me angry ... I'm not a holier-than-thou guy ... but he shouldn't be doing this in public." The agent also added that this debauchery "continued constantly" and was "a regular thing." Larry Newman: "It [JFK's behavior] caused a lot of morale problems with the Secret Service ... you felt impotent and you couldn't do your job. It was frustrating ..."[21] On the ABC special, Newman mentioned JFK's sexual trysts with White House secretaries who were known by the nicknames of "Fiddle" and "Faddle." The agent also said that this facet of JFK made them not want to associate with the man in any way. Joseph Paolella: "[He] acknowledged that the Secret Service's socializing intensified each year of the Kennedy administration, to a point where, by late 1963, a few members of the presidential detail were regularly remaining in bars until the early morning hours."[22]

This is corroborated by what Abraham Bolden told the author, and it also is best exemplified by the drinking incident of 11/21-11/22/63.[23]

18. *Orange County Register*, 10/31/96. "I retired from the United States Secret Service as the Agent in charge of protection for the Los Angeles area immediately after Clinton was elected president in 1992."
19. Hersh, pp. 241-243.
20. *The Atlantic Online*, January 1998.
21. Hersh, p. 230.
22. Hersh, p. 244.
23. Joe Paolella later told the *Boston Globe* (11/22/1997): "There were so many misquotes. He used literary license in what he has done. When the book was sent to me I almost fainted. I was so em-

Agent Tony Sherman also told author Edward Klein, "His womanizing was so routine and common ... that we slipped into the nefarious duty of protecting Kennedy from his wife by alerting him is she was returning to the White House unexpectedly ... Some agents felt that if the President could get away with this kind of stuff, so could they. ... Drinking, partying, and sex became part of traveling with the President."[24] Agent Larry Newman wasn't finished. He spoke at even greater length to author Barbara Leaming about JFK's womanizing several years later.[25] I did contact Newman, Sherman, Paolella, and McIntyre, but did not discuss JFK's womanizing at any length. Floyd Boring stated, "I can't recall – and I was there the entire time during the president's administration and prior to the president's administration – and I know I can never recall at any time the president meeting with any girl. Everything I've ever seen the man do was with a moral attitude ... Never seen the girl [Judith Campbell Exner]. Never heard her name until I read it in the paper ... wouldn't know her [Mary Pinchot Meyer] ... I never at any time had ever seen the president with Frank Sinatra ... at no time was Frank Sinatra at the President's house (!)"[26] Regarding Agent Boring, former agent Larry Newman told the author, "He's been a proponent that JFK wasn't a womanizer."[27] Former ASAIC of the Los Angeles office Darwin David Horn, Sr. wrote the author, "Never saw Marilyn Monroe ... ever."[28]

---

barrassed [if these were misquotes, why did the agents repeat what they said on a major ABC documentary that made it to home video? Why didn't they sue Hersh? Why, indeed] The article continues further: "Another agent, though not a Hersh source, also rebutted the book. Floyd Boring, the number two agent at the White House during the Kennedy administration, said the book's allegations are false. He said that Larry Newman and Paolella, the main sources, had reasons to be vengeful because both were transferred off the prestigious White House assignment after relatively short stints. Boring said Newman badmouthed the president and his brother, Attorney General Robert Kennedy, and Paolella was "a misfit ... we had to unload him after a very short term. These guys are trying to get a little bit of fame as they wander off the scene. They take lot of people down with them," said Boring, now 82, who protected five presidents, from Franklin D. Roosevelt to Lyndon B. Johnson. "These people wait until everybody dies off and then they attack people." Newman, reached at his home in Colorado, stood by his allegations. He said Boring "was never where these things took place. So what he says and what I say are two different things." He declined to explain the reasons for his transfer."
24. *The Kennedy Curse*, pp. 171 & 173.
25. *Mrs. Kennedy: The Missing History of the Kennedy Years* by Barbara Leaming (Free Press, 2002). See especially pp. 61-63, 142, 167, 204, & 252-253 Newman also spoke to author Edward Klein [*Just Jackie: Her Private Years*, p. 374], and is acknowledged for his help in *The Fourth Perimeter* by Tim Green (Warner Books, 2003).
26. Boring's JFK Library oral history, 2/25/76, released 1998. For a picture of Boring right in front of Marilyn Monroe, see p. 217 of Carl Sferrazza Anthony's *The Kennedy White House* (New York: Touchstone, 2001). To be fair, just with regard to Campbell and Meyers, SAIC Behn echoed the same lack of knowledge as Boring [JFK Library oral history, 2/24/76]. See also *The Arrogance of Power*, p. 511.
27. Author's interview with Newman, 2/7/04.
28. E-mail to author dated 1/30/04.

Horn later wrote, "Never saw Marilyn Monroe with him but wouldn't tell you if I had."[29] Horn also wrote, "Never saw JFK and Sinatra together."[30] Finally, former Chief James Rowley stated to the JFK Library in 1976: "I never saw or heard anything [regarding allegations of women and JFK] … I had never heard or saw anything that would indicate any truth to it, because certainly any agent on the detail that saw anything like that naturally would report it. But I hadn't received. … This was all a surprise to me when I read these so-called stories."[31] Agent Tim McIntyre also told the HSCA that he did not believe he was assigned to either the Miami or the Chicago trips for November 1963.[32]

However, like Agent Bennett's "amnesia" noted earlier and as proven by the Secret Service Shift Reports released by the ARRB in the 1990's, McIntyre was on both trips. Again, like Bennett, the author naturally wonders: is there a reason for this amnesia? Were several mortal threats to the President being covertly monitored and was there also a covert security test taking place in those few short days and weeks, and even moments, before the fatal shots rang out in Dealey Plaza on 11/22/63? Did Bennett, McIntyre, and others seek to disassociate themselves from these trips due to this knowledge? Having arrived at the WHD in the fall of 1963 from a two-man office in Spokane, WA, McIntyre was an Inspector during his HSCA interview.[33] I contacted McIntyre on 6/13/05. He had previously been contacted via mail but did not respond. Asked about the Tampa trip of 11/18/63, the former agent said, "I was there on the follow-up car." Regarding the question of agents being on the back of the car, McIntyre said, "I believe so – Zboril was on the back," which is where he was positioned. He also mentioned Don Lawton and Emory Roberts as being on the trip, which they were. Regarding the matter at hand, McIntyre stated, "I can't remember if they were told to be off the car."

For his part, Newman phoned me unexpectedly on 2/12/04 to say that "there was not a directive, per se" from President Kennedy to remove the agents from their positions on the back of his limousine.

Joe Paolella had this to say recently: "After the assassination, I was re-assigned to guard the presidential vehicle after it had been flown back to the White House garage. Several hospital staff members from Bethesda Naval Hospital entered the vehicle to remove scalp, brain tissue and bone

29. E-mail to author dated 2/28/04.
30. E-mail to author dated 2/26/04.
31. James J. Rowley Oral History, JFK Library, 3/29/76.
32. 1/31/78 HSCA interview with McIntyre.
33. 12/14/77 letter from Secret Service Legal Counsel Robert O. Goff to the HSCA's G. Robert Blakey, RIF #180-10112-10218.

matter from the back seat. While waiting for the Bethesda Naval Hospital attendants to arrive, I did notice what appeared to be a bullet-hole in the front windshield of the driver's side. I do not remember if the glass remnants were on the inside of the vehicle or the outside of the windshield. If the glass remnants were on the inside of the car, it would offer some acceptance to the theory that at least one of the shots came from the front of the President's vehicle.

I don't remember anything out of the ordinary regarding my duties prior to the assassination other than several trips to the Kennedy residence in Palm Beach, Florida. I also recall an incident in Chicago involving a suspect who was planning to assassinate the President. However, I was not involved in that investigation and the threat was taken care of by the Chicago office of the Secret Service.

I believe Oswald was the shooter and though I am not a conspiracy buff, I believe if others were involved, I think the Mafia would be the only ones who could have pulled it off without someone later confessing involvement in the President's assassination. In those days, Mafia members had a strict code that did not allow them to confess. It had been said that a New Orleans Mafia Don, Carlos Marcello, was heard to say, "If you cut off the head of the snake (JFK), the tail (RFK), would die." At that time, Robert Kennedy was the Attorney General and was working against the Mafia. Shortly after the assassination, Robert Kennedy was fired and it took another 20-years before the FBI made any headway against the Mafia."[34]

Paolella passed away in September 2017.

---

34. http://janbtucker.com/blog/2014/03/12/joe-paolellas-incredible-life/

SAM KINNEY

The *Palm Beach Post* reported on 11/21/2013:"Susan Kinney Rosser was 15 months old on Nov. 22, 1963, and so has no direct remembrance of that day. Nevertheless, the assassination of John F. Kennedy is part of her family's legacy.... As doctors were pronouncing the death of the president, Kinney now had to get the limousine back to Love Field and loaded onto Air Force One for the trip back to Washington, D.C. "He found a piece of the skull," Rosser said. "It was about the size of a small ashtray. He put it in his pocket until he saw White House doctor Adm. (George) Burkley. Burkley put it into his pocket." And in that moment, Kinney added one more detail to the thousands of unresolved questions about the Kennedy assassination, more fodder for conspiracy theorists to this day. "Nobody ever asked him about it again," Rosser said. "That bothered him." Kinney was deeply shaken by what he considered his failure of responsibility. "That day changed his life. It broke his heart," Rosser said. "He couldn't attend the funeral. He said, 'It was our job to protect the president and we failed.' It affected him, it hurt him, it haunted him."

From the HSCA's 2/26/78 interview summary, we learn the following regarding Kinney's background: "SA Kinney, who was the Secret Service's driver of the Presidential follow-up car at the time of the assassination, first entered the field of law enforcement in 1950, when he was appointed to the Metropolitan Police Department (Washington, D.C.). He was assigned to the White House Police Force in 1958 and was then appointed to the Secret Service in 1960. He has spent his entire career with the Secret Service, from which he is now retired, in the field of Presidential protection."[1]

Interviewed three times between 1992 and 1994, Kinney was a rich source of information. The agent admitted, "We [the Secret Service] didn't do our job," adding that he thinks about the assassination "every night" and has even "dreamed about it;" a classic case of survivor's guilt. Surprisingly, Kinney felt compelled by the work of the critics in this case: "I have several different theories that have crossed my mind."[2] Strangely, Kinney claimed that none of the agents have ever discussed the assassination, although he added, "we have discussed it at some of our conferences."[3]

In regard to Agent Hill, Kinney told the author that, although Hill suffered greatly after the tragedy, his fellow former agents "got him straightened out." Although Kinney revealed that Hill had a heart attack and was close to needing help from mental facilities, he stopped drinking and smoking and put himself back on track. In regard to the notion that JFK ever ordered the agents to do anything, Sam said, "that is absolutely, positively false ... no, no, no, he had nothing to do with that [ordering agents off the rear of the limo] ... No, never – the agents say, 'OK, men, fall back on your posts' ... President Kennedy was one of the easiest presidents to ever protect; Harry S. Truman was a jewel just like John F. Kennedy was ... 99% of the agents would agree ... (JFK) was one of the best presidents ever to control – he trusted every one of us ... I loved the guy. I loved the Kennedy family, I really did."[4] In regard to the infamous quote from William Manchester, whereupon Kennedy allegedly made the remark, "Keep those Ivy League charlatans off the back of the car,"[5] Kinney said, "That is false. I talked to William Manchester; he called me on the book [sic] ...

---

1. RIF # 180-10078-10493.
2. Although Sam had also told the HSCA on 2/26/78 that he found the idea of conspiracy "plausible," this interview summary was not released until several years after the author's interviews.
3. Author's interview with Kinney, 3/4/94.
4. Kinney also told the author: "Kennedy had a very unique memory. If you met Kennedy, he'd know you two years from now, three years from now, or probably never forget you." Kinney reiterated all of this to the author on 4/15/94.
5. Manchester, p. 37.

for the record of history that is false – Kennedy never ordered us to do anything. I am aware of what is being said but that is false."[6] Finally, just to nail down this issue, the author asked Sam if an exception was made on 11/22/63, to which Sam replied, "Not this particular time, no. Not in this case." When asked why there weren't agents on the back of the car in Dealey Plaza, Sam said, "We had just come down Main [Street] where the volume of the crowd was. Emory Roberts says 'OK, guys, fall back' to get on the running board … we had been running for three miles … we were ready to hit the open highway [emphasis added]."

Yet, Ready never got onto the back of the car and none of the agents walked, jogged, or ran next to the rear of the limousine, either. Only when the car stopped briefly twice in the outskirts of town did the agents come near JFK's side of the car and only Agent Hill, taking his own initiative, hopped onto the back of the car for four brief moments in the city proper (and on Jackie's side only). Kinney further stated that agents were posted on the rear of the President's car only when "crowds were on both sides or if there's a potential run out from the crowd." Although not as pronounced as earlier in the motorcade, both these situations existed in Dealey Plaza. All it takes is one assassin, as the Secret Service has found out on numerous occasions. As we know, this isn't the first time Kinney defended the strange actions and inactions of Emory Roberts. Sam also told the author that JFK had nothing to do with the limiting of motorcycles during motorcades, and that Ken O'Donnell did not interfere with the agents: "Nobody ordered anyone around."

Thankfully, Sam told the author he did not speak to Gerald Posner, author of the most recent major attempt to shut the door on the truth, *Case Closed*. Again, on the controversial removal of the bubbletop, Kinney was adamant: "I am the sole responsibility of that … Yes, I was." Asked if Kennedy ordered it to be taken off, Sam said, "that is not true." In regard to SAIC of the Dallas office, Forrest V. Sorrels, who was alleged to have removed the top by Jim Lehrer,[7] Sam was equally adamant: "I knew him [Sorrels] very well – he had nothing to do with it." As far as any regrets over his decision, Sam said, "That's one of my thirty-year concerns – whether I made the right decision or not." Kinney went on to say that "only thing the bubbletop may have prevented. It may have distorted Oswald's sight or possibly a ricochet … it might deflect a bullet." Sam said he took the top off because "we were down there on a political move," meaning a pres-

---

6. Kinney was interviewed by Manchester 2/19/65.
7. *A Bus of My Own*, p. 83

idential trip that was political, as opposed to one that was merely for the public; a matter in some dispute, i.e., between the Connally camp and the O'Donnell faction. Sam said Kennedy "would have survived the first one, probably. The second shot, he was leaning over and he had his back brace on. The second shot hit Connally right in the back. I remember talking to Connally and I've talked to him since then – I said 'Governor, I'm the one who called you a son-of-a-bitch.' He said, 'I wondered who that was but I knew I had to be taken out of there before you got the president out.'[8] Very gracious guy, the Governor; nice people … he ended up our boss [when Connally became the Secretary of the Treasury during the Nixon administration]." Sam stated, "I saw all three shots hit," without acknowledging the known missed shot(s); even Governor Connally and Dave Powers did not acknowledge a missed shot.[9]

In regard to JFK's head wound, the author inquired, "Was the back of Kennedy's head really gone?" To which Kinney responded, "Yeah … He had no brain left – it was blown out. Clint Hill and I unloaded him out of the car. There was nothing left … [it was] the whole back of the head as far as I am concerned. I saw it hit and I saw his hair come out … I had brain matter all over my windshield and left arm, that's how close we were to it … it was the right rear part of his head[10] … because that's the part I saw blow out. I saw hair come out, the piece blow out, then the skin went back in – an explosion in and out."[11] Elaborating further, Sam said, after being told that's where the Parkland doctors saw the wound, "I would say that, too … it involved half his head."

Asked to explain the 1500-gram brain at the autopsy (the upper limit of a normal, undamaged brain), Sam seemed perplexed, saying, "there was brain matter all over the place. Mr. Connally even said he was covered with it." Sam also said, in regard to the *Today* show interview of 11/22/93,[12] "I told them 'I'm going to tell you some things that haven't been in books yet': I brought a piece of the President's skull back in my suit pocket. Now,

---

8. Also – in UPI's *Four Days*, page 25, Kinney is depicted transporting some of JFK's clothing, as well as the gifts he received in Fort Worth, to DPD Chief Jesse Curry's car; Curry is directly behind Kinney; same photo: Secret Service agent George W. Hickey, Jr. is seen holding a hand to the top of his head.

9. Connally: numerous, including 4 H 129; HSCA Report 36-44, 46, 48, 82, 182-183; see also *Who's Who in the JFK Assassination*, pp. 85-87. Powers: 7 H 472-474. *JFK: The Day The Nation Cried*, 1988 VHS/DVD, and *Johnny, We Hardly Knew Ye*, p. 30.

10. Kinney reiterated this to the author on 4/15/94.

11. Author William Manchester stated that Kinney, interviewed 2/19/65, "kept his eyes on the back of the President's head … still keeping his eyes on Kennedy's head [on Elm Street] … [saw] the back of the President's head erupt." [*The Death of a President*, p. 134, 154, 159, and 664].

12. Sam was also credited on Rick Boudreau's *Presidential Limousines* video (1996), although he does not appear on the program itself.

all these books are wondering about this hole, this unbelievable missing part. I got the answer to that but nobody's called me ... I went over that automobile coming home ... I found it on the plane [C-130] in the car and I put a phone patch in to Admiral Burkley[13] who was a very good friend of mine – he was one hell of a man; I've got his picture hanging on my wall along with the president's and I thought just as much of him as I did them." Returning to the skull fragment, Kinney added that it looked "like a piece of a flowerpot, clean as a pin ... like piece of a clay pot – there wasn't blood or hair or anything on it ... I don't know what else it could have been but the back of his head ... mine was a big piece ... I told him [Burkley], 'I may have something that is crucial to the autopsy' ... I gave it [the fragment] to one of his aides [Tommy Mills]." Interestingly, Sam was aware of the separate "Harper" fragment found 11/23/63,[14] as was fellow agent Clint Hill.[15]

In regard to Sam's skull fragment account, the author contacted several members of the 76th Air Transport Squadron, who have never been contacted before by any private researchers, the Warren Commission, or the HSCA. Vincent J. Gullo, Jr. responded in an 8/27/98 letter to the author: "Sam told me that a) he found the piece of the right rear of President Kennedy's skull on the C-130 while en route back to AAFB after the tragedy and b) that one of you guys got sick from seeing the rear of the limousine with all the blood and gore ... do you remember any of these specific events?" Gullo responded,"... I am totally familiar with the facts as you outline them ... [T]his was a bench mark in my life and I have shared my thoughts on this incident with few individuals – mostly federal agents. I am sure you can understand my reluctance to entertain your questions given the sensitivity of the matter even to this date."[16] Gullo did not re-

---

13. Dr. Burkley later stated that he believed there was a conspiracy: 3/18/77 HSCA Memorandum [RIF#180-10086-10295]; *Reasonable Doubt*, p. 49 (1982 interview by Henry Hurt + letters of 10/6/82 and 10/14/82).

14. Kinney had also told the HSCA on 2/26/78 the same thing: "Inside the aircraft [the C-130 transport plane] during flight, the loading sergeant, who had been in the rear compartment where the cars were stored, entered the forward cabin and said, "I can't stand to be back there." SA Kinney gave him his seat and returned to the rear compartment. At this point he discovered in the Presidential limousine (1) a skull fragment under the jump seat where Connally had been seated, and (2) a bullet fragment in the front seat between the driver's and passenger's seat. He remarked that the bullet fragment "looked like it had hit the windshield frame above the windshield." SA Kinney put on a radio patch to Presidential Physician Admiral Burkley to inform him that he had discovered the skull fragment. Chief Petty Officer Tommy Mills, an aide to Burkley, received the message. SA Kinney then announced that he was going to go directly to the White House non-stop. The Washington Field Office learned of this and sent 6 or 7 Park police to escort SA Kinney to the White House Garage. In the garage they were met by FBI agents.'"

15. 2 H 140.

16. See also *The Great Zapruder Film Hoax* by James Fetzer, pp. 27-28.

spond to a follow-up letter. The author could not locate the pilot, Capt. Roland H. Thomason, nor could David J. Conn, Stephen A. Bening, or Frank E. Roberson be found. The author did locate the remaining two, Hershal R. Woosley and Wayne E. Schake, who did not respond to the author's letters. "I believe there was a conspiracy," Kinney told me: "This thing was so well set up – whoever did the shooting – he picked that area where he knew there wouldn't be any men by the car." Sam told the author that PRS agent Glenn A. Bennett was allegedly making his first trip. "I knew him very well. In fact, I knew him before he was even an agent. He's from Harrisburg, Pennsylvania, as a matter of fact … nice guy." Kinney also added that Asst. Press Sec. Mac Kilduff was, like ASAIC Roy H. Kellerman, a third-stringer and making his "first trip – first official debut" without Asst. Press Sec. Andy Hatcher or Press Sec. Pierre Salinger. SAIC Gerald Behn's absence from the Texas trip, leaving ASAIC (#2) Floyd M. Boring to be the agent in charge of the Texas trip, was characterized by Sam: "Jerry Behn doesn't know anything because he wasn't there." Sam added, "I have never been back there. I have been to Dallas, but I've never been back to Dealey Square." This would have been for either the 1985 or the 1991 Association of Former Agents of the Secret Service (AFAUSSS) conference. "I've had no less than 20 offers to write a book but I won't do it," Sam told the author. "This is the old school of Floyd Boring, Jerry Behn, and Clint Hill – all us old-timers won't sell out for any kind of money."

Indeed, even the four agents who spoke to Seymour Hersh did not receive a penny for their troubles. Kinney told the author that Emory Roberts became the "appointment secretary to President Johnson[17] … I was the off-records Secretary … Emory and I worked together during the Johnson Administration at the White House … I was in the protection end all of my career, then all of a sudden I'm appointment secretary.[18] I don't need that. I don't want it. I couldn't take it. I don't like desk jobs." Coincidentally, a Mrs. Juanita Roberts was LBJ's Chief Private Secretary.[19]

---

17. At first, Sam seemed to have trouble with exactly what designation Emory Roberts had in this new role under LBJ: "He became the secretary … no, the press secretary … no, the appointment secretary for Johnson."

18. Again, Kinney seems confused about the exact title he (and Roberts) had during the LBJ years.

19. The author obtained the late Juanita Roberts' LBJ Library oral history: on the surface, there appears to be no overt relation to Emory Roberts. Probably just a coincidence … but a relation of some sort cannot be ruled out as of this writing. Author David Lifton spoke to Mrs. Emory (Betty) Roberts re: the filing of Emory's Secret Service report (*The Third Decade* journal, Jan-March 1992: article by Joel Waggoner). Unfortunately, nothing else is said (no details) and the author was unable to gain further insight from Lifton. See also *Washington Post*, 10/11/73. A further note: Johnson's other secretary, Marie Fehmer, later became the first woman officer of the CIA [*Today* show, 1/12/89: interview with Fehmer].

In regard to Roberts' fellow ATSAIC/ shift leader Stu Stout, Kinney told the author that he died of a heart attack not long after the assassination, a statement confirmed by fellow agents Boring and Scouten, yet confounded by agent Lawson. Kinney added, "He [Stout] was Mamie Eisenhower's first man." Sam Kinney would not give the author a straight answer as to why the motorcade could not have traveled straight down Main Street to Industrial Blvd. The author also attempted to get Kinney to go on the record in writing but was too late. His widow Hazel informed the author that Sam passed away 7/21/97 while they were traveling through Iowa.[20] Former agent Walt Coughlin wrote the author, "Sam Kinney was a hoot. One of my favorites."[21]

---

20. Letter to author dated 11/20/97.
21. E-mail to author dated 5/6/05.

JERRY KIVETT

Jerry Kivett served in Army counter intelligence before joining the Secret Service in 1961. Kivett, an LBJ detail agent who rode in Johnson's Secret Service follow-up car on 11/22/63, stated for the record that "[JFK] was beloved by those agents on the detail and I never heard anyone say that he was difficult to protect."[1] During the Ford era and continuing until his retirement in 1982, Kivett was SAIC of the Atlanta, Georgia office.[2] Most of the agents who served LBJ were extremely close. In fact, Kivett told the author that Rufus Youngblood was "the godfather of one of my children."[3] Regarding the necessary merging of the former JFK WHD with the LBJ detail into one unit after the assassination, Kivett wrote, "I was not aware of any tension between the two details. We merged together well, even though it took a while for us to get used to the White House, just like it did for them to get used to the LBJ Ranch. We were just doing our job."[4] Kivett became the lead agent for Lady Bird Johnson when LBJ became president.

Kivett later wrote to me: "I have already read some of your thoughts and conclusions on the internet and did not necessarily agree with them, but then everyone is entitled to their own opinion."[5]

Kivett passed away 6/26/2010. Former agent Jean Dugger had this to say of Kivett: "Jerry first touched my life when he hired me in Atlanta, GA,

1. Letter to author 12/8/97.
2. 12/29/76 letter from Glenn Bennett to HSCA Robert Blakey; *Within Arm's Length* by Dan Emmett (2014), pages 30-31, 33; correspondence with Dan Emmett.
3. Author's interview with Kivett, 2/7/04. The former agent also confirmed to the author that he was not contacted by the HSCA. Regrettably, Kivett highly recommended the book *Case Closed!*
4. Letter to the author dated 2/28/04.
5. E-mail to author from Kivett, 2/4/06.

beginning my 35+ year career with the Secret Service. It was an honor and a privilege to have worked for him and call him "Boss," and I will be forever grateful for that opportunity. His impact on the Secret Service will always be felt!" Former agent Tom Wells said: "Jerry was a quality person who earned the respect of all who worked with and/or for him. His ability to make decisions on the highest level while maintaining a common sense approach to all situations was an uncommon skill."

65

ANDY BERGER

Andy Berger resigned from the Secret Service in 1981 with an impressive resume: youngest agent, at 32, in charge of the Buffalo, N.Y., field office; cracking down on forgers and counterfeiters from offices in Syracuse, N.Y., Baltimore and Washington; personal detail for presidents Kennedy and Johnson and Vice President Agnew. Berger is best known for his time protecting President Kennedy. He was in Dallas that fateful day, stationed at the Trade Mart.

Berger reported meeting the following persons at Parkland Hospital shortly after the assassination:

> 1. FBI agent Vincent Drain (sent via Hoover); the same agent who would go on to accompany Agent Lawson during the transfer of critical assassination evidence later on that weekend.

> 2. "A doctor friend of Drain's." This unidentified doctor came with the FBI agent.

> 3. An "unidentified CIA agent" who had credentials. Like the FBI man sent by Hoover, how could the CIA agent get to the Dallas hospital so soon after the murder?[1]

---

1. See also *Breaking the Silence* by Bill Sloan (1993), pp. 181-185, *The Man Who Knew Too Much* by Dick

4. An "unidentified FBI agent" who did not have credentials.[2] Berger's report was totally ignored by just about everyone.[3]

Berger drove the hearse containing JFK's body to Love Field after the assassination. During the HSCA era, Berger was the SAIC of the Baltimore, MD field office.[4] In the Fall of 2003, newspaper articles reported at length about Berger's connection to the events of 11/22/63, his wife Dolly, and the fact that Berger was suffering from Altzheimer's disease.[5] While quite lengthy, a few pertinent excerpts deserve attention: "Berger, of Charlotte, was a member of the Secret Service for 20 years, trusted by presidents and their families. But today, he is rapidly losing the memories of those exciting years, and of the quieter moments he shared with his wife, Dolly, and their four children. Alzheimer's is sapping the strength of the man who drove the hearse with a grieving Jacqueline Kennedy to Dallas' Love Field, who flew to Andrews Air Force Base, the man whose shoulders gently helped lift Kennedy's casket from Air Force One. Now it's the job of Andy Berger's family to take care of him ... Andy Berger had witnessed the death of one president and the inauguration of his successor.

Closer than most, he had seen the widow in the bloodied pink suit who had insisted on sitting beside her husband during that hearse ride. Andy Berger didn't say a word. 'He cried and cried and cried,' Dolly Berger said. 'My heart ached for him.' Andy Berger loved Jack Kennedy. They were Catholics, making something of themselves at a time when being Catholic could be a liability ... Yet, even after he moved to Charlotte that year [1981] to work as director of security for North Carolina National Bank, eventually started his own business, then retired, he carried the Secret Service with him. At parties, friends would sit close to Andy Berger and try, after a couple of drinks, to get him to reveal presidential secrets. All struck out, as the phrase 'to the grave' became his trademark ... Andy Berger is there in the pictures on the family room wall: with Lyndon Johnson and his daughter, Luci, with Frank Sinatra, with Dolly and the kids all

Russell (1992), pp. 570-571, and *Who's Who in the JFK Assassination* by Michael Benson (1993), pp. 40-41.
2. The FBI Agent turned out to be J. Doyle Williams [see *Reasonable Doubt* by Henry Hurt (1985), pp. 71-72 (based on Feb. 1983 interview); see also 18 H 795-796 (Berger), 798-799 (Johnsen); 21 H 261 (Price); RIF#18010082-10454: 1/31/78 HSCA interview of SS agent Tim McIntyre; Also: *Bloody Treason* by Noel Twyman (1997), pp. 90, 91, 93, 96, and 110; 5 H 132, 144; 18 H 96 and *Pictures Of The Pain* by Richard Trask (1994), p. 105: photo of Williams; 22 H 841, 910; 23 H 681; 24 H 523; *No More Silence* by Larry Sneed (1998), pp. 130 and 164.
3. 18 H 795.
4. 12/14/77 letter from Secret Service Legal Counsel Robert O. Goff to the HSCA's G. Robert Blakey, RIF #180-10112-10218.
5. *Charlotte Observer*, 11/14/03; *Duluth News Tribune*, 11/22/03.

wearing the polyester prints of the 1970s. He's there in the books about Kennedy and Nov. 22 that line the shelves: driving the hearse in *Johnny We Hardly Knew Ye*, hitting the siren to clear a way through traffic in *The Day Kennedy Was Shot*." (The interviewer asked) Tell me about Kennedy. Was he your favorite? 'Oh yes. It was the way he handled himself.' The day of his assassination? 'We thought, 'Why did it all happen?'"[6]

Berger passed away 6/22/2006.

---

6. *Charlotte Observer*, 11/14/03.

66

SAM SULLIMAN

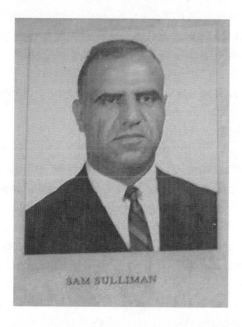

SAM SULLIMAN

S ulliman told me on 2/11/04 that he grew up in Connecticut, went to college, and spent summers in Hyannis port with ex-military colleagues, which led him to Jim Rowley and the Secret Service. Before summer excursions, Sulliman joined the U.S. Army and took part in the Korean War, where his gifted athlete brother was to perish. As for his time in the Secret Service, the former agent said, "I don't regret my time. Experience-wise, you couldn't ask for anything better. The agent was with JFK on the WHD from the Inauguration in January 1961 until Dallas, and continued with LBJ until 1964, when he joined former WHD agent Robert E. Lilley in the Boston office. Sulliman said of Lilley: "He was a big, tall guy. Everyone liked him." Sulliman returned to the WHD in 1966 as an Assistant Shift Leader, then a Shift Leader, and then, in 1968, he looked after Vice President-elect Spiro Agnew. While agent Clint Hill was initially the SAIC of this particular detail, Sulliman would eventually take over for Hill in this capacity. Former agent Darwin Horn wrote, "Sam Sulliman had the Agnew Detail which was one of the best of all time."[1] Sulliman was

---

1. E-mail to author dated 2/28/04.

with Agnew until the Vice President resigned in disgrace and was a member of the WHD until just into the start of President Ford's term, when the agent was promoted to Inspector. Finally, by the time of the HSCA hearings, Sulliman was SAIC of New Haven, CT office.[2] Regarding JFK, Sulliman told me, "He was easy to get along with." Regarding Sam's brother who was killed in North Korea, Kennedy offered his heartfelt condolences, saying to the agent, "I heard about your brother. That's too bad." President Kennedy "invited everyone down to Palm Beach during one Christmas time with their wives and gave gifts to everybody." Sulliman added, "Each man that sits in that office is the most important man in the world. They trust the [Secret] Service."

Describing the Texas trip, Sulliman, who was "on the afternoon shift," mentioned going to Houston on 11/21/63 for the Congressman Albert Thomas testimonial dinner. It was in this city that the agent says that he "saw, for the first time, some anti-Kennedy demonstrations." Regarding the assassination the next day in Dallas, Sulliman said it was "like a shock that you didn't believe happened. You didn't put it all into perspective. It didn't sink in until I was assigned to Arlington Cemetery for the funeral." Mr. Sulliman is now VP of Corporate Development for SERAPH Inc. With regard to the AFAUSSS, Sulliman mentioned Hamilton Brown, the Executive Secretary, as well as Jerry Bechtle, who the agent described as "our regional director. I talked to him the other day. Forty-seven of us guys [former agents] had a meeting." Sulliman also mentioned that he "helped a kid [unnamed] get into the Secret Service – he's been in 13 years now." Finally, the agent said his old Secret Service star, number 101, is encased in a plastic holder now, and that he was part of a small, elite crew back then: "Numbers-wise, there was only about 300 agents then."

2. 12/14/77 letter from Secret Service Legal Counsel Robert O. Goff to the HSCA's G. Robert Blakey, RIF #180-10112-10218.

170

67

JOHN "MUGGSY" O'LEARY

MUGGSEY O'LEARY

O'Leary dates back to JFK's Senate days, when he was a Senate policeman serving as Kennedy's driver and servant of sorts. Kenny O'Donnell called O'Leary, "the President's long-time driver and bodyguard."[1] As author Jim Bishop put it, "O'Leary, a Kennedy idolator, was a member of the Secret Service because John F. Kennedy endorsed the appointment."[2] Author Geoffrey Perret was a bit tougher on the matter: "The President forced the Secret Service to make Muggsy an agent so he could still drive him around Washington."[3] Former agent Walt Coughlin wrote the author: "Muggsy was merely on the SS payroll – He was in his late 60s and former JFK driver – Not expected to be an agent but was a good sounding board for us as he had JFK's ear – Never carried a weapon Thank goodness!!!"[4] O'Leary was posted at the entrance to the Hotel Texas late on the evening of 11/21/63 when he "saw a figure lying on a roof directly across from Kennedy's window, and a policeman scurried off to chase him away."[5] O'Leary later briefly attended the president's autopsy

1. *Johnny, We Hardly Knew Ye*, p. 45.
2. *The Day Kennedy Was Shot* by Jim Bishop, p. 604.
3. *Jack: A Life Like No Other* by Geoffrey Perret (New York: Random House, 2001) p. 290.
4. E-mail to author dated 2/27/04.
5. *The Death of a President* by William Manchester, p. 88.

on the evening of 11/22/63.[6] Interviewed for Manchester's *The Death of a President* on 11/10/64, a picture of O'Leary also appears in Mary Gallagher's book.[7] Unfortunately, while O'Leary mentions in his report that he was "present at the autopsy and the official picture taking of the President's body,"[8] the agent was not called to testify before either the Warren Commission or the HSCA regarding the details of JFK's wounds. Even Manchester reports nothing on the matter.

O'Leary passed away in December 1975.

---

6. CD 3 exhibits; FBI (Sibert & O'Neill) report 11/26/63 [see *Post Mortem*, pp. 532-536] – listed as present at autopsy; 2 H 99; 17 H 614; 18 H 727; 18 H 728-729; 18 H 815; 22 H 97.

7. *The Death of a President*, p. 666; *My Life With Jacqueline Kennedy*.

8. CD 3 Exhibits. Kellerman also states: "SA O'Leary was also in the morgue briefly" in his 11/29/63 report, repeating in his 11/30/63 report that "SA O'Leary remained in the morgue only briefly."

68

THOMAS KELLEY

K elley joined the Secret Service in July 1942, during the FDR era.[1] In the 1970s HSCA presented some biographical data on Kelley: "Inspector Kelley received a B.A. from Providence College and an LL.B. from Georgetown University Law School. He has been the special agent in charge of the Philadelphia field office, an Inspector in the Washington office, the Assistant Director of Protective Intelligence and Investigations in Washington, D.C., and he currently is the Assistant Director of Protective Operations in Washington, D.C. Inspector Kelley is a member of the International Association of Chiefs of Police and he has served as a consultant to several Far Eastern police agencies, as well as consultant to the Dominican Republic on protective matters."[2] Kelley retired from the Secret Service on February 28, 1978.[3] The HSCA also duly noted that Kelley "was assigned to represent the Secret Service in the investigation of President Kennedy's assassination. Inspector Kelley served as Secret Service liaison to the Warren Commission."[4] Kelley represented the Secret Service before both the Warren Commission and the HSCA, as did Chief Rowley. Also like Rowley, he perjured himself in his denial

---

1. 5 H 130; 3 HSCA 346.
2. 3 HSCA 323.
3. 3 HSCA 323 and 346.
4. 3 HSCA 323 and 346.

of the "threat knowledge" he had before 11/22/63.[5] Inspector Kelley was involved in at least four interviews with Oswald,[6] including the interrogation 15 minutes before the accused assassin's fatal encounter with Jack Ruby. In fact, Kelley "... approached Oswald then and, out of the hearing of the others except perhaps one of Captain Fritz's men, said that as a Secret Service agent ... we were therefore very anxious to talk to him to make certain that the correct story was developing as it related to the assassination."[7] This statement is wide open to interpretation – the Secret Service may have assured Oswald of their belief in his innocence and that, if he would just cooperate with them, they would help clear up the matter and, thus, clear his name. Ruby's bullet put an end to that scenario. The agent testified to the HSCA: "[Oswald] indicated to me that he was a Communist but not a Marxist."[8] If anything, Oswald always took great pains to state the opposite. He said he was a Marxist, not a Communist.[9] Kelley described Oswald this way: "He turned out to be the kind, as I say, of the typical assassin, the typical assassin of Presidents, a loner, a man with a history of mental problems, a bitter man, a man who felt himself a failure. In talking to Marina [Lee's wife], he was a very disturbed man."[10]

There are many authors before this one who have argued at length that this thumbnail sketch is wildly inaccurate. Even Marina has equivocated back and forth regarding Lee and his innocence or guilt.[11] Kelley was heavily involved in his agency's first on-site reenactment on 11/27/63, where he would reach the same conclusion as that of the FBI: three shots, three hits, all from the rear, completely ignoring the documented missed shot that the Warren Commission was forced to acknowledge in 1964.[12] Inspector Kelley stayed in Dallas until "probably the first week or ten days of December [1963]."[13] Kelley was also involved with the 5/24/64 reenactment.[14] Although the autopsy photos were officially withheld from the Warren Commission by the agency, Kelley privately displayed a photo to Arlen Specter, allegedly of the back of JFK's body with a hole in it. Perhaps, after seeing this photo, Specter realized the importance of his

---

5. HSCA 335-337, 340, 342, 343.
6. 3 HSCA 325, 455 (referencing Kelley's 7/30/64 Affidavit to the Warren Commission).
7. 24 H 479.
8. 3 HSCA 352.
9. See, for example, the filmed interview of Oswald in New Orleans from August 1963 contained in *The Men Who Killed Kennedy: The Patsy*.
10. 3 HSCA 355.
11. See, for example, *The Men Who Killed Kennedy: The Truth Shall Set You Free* (1995).
12. Kelley's Secret Service report of 11/28/63.
13. 3 HSCA 329.
14. 5 H 129-134.

"single-bullet theory" in convincing the public that Oswald was the sole assassin and all shots came from the Book Depository.[15] Unlike Rowley, who at least hemmed and hawed a bit, Kelley told the House Assassinations Committee flatly that "no agent violated any Secret Service rule" in the drinking incident – a blatant falsehood that went unchallenged by the government.[16] The ARRB reported, "Mr. Boring was shown Inspector Kelley's 2/14/64 memo to Chief Rowley re: HR 9958 [USSS document No. 154-10002-10332], and stated that he had never heard Inspector Kelley speak in that manner of the inadvisability of allowing the FBI sole investigative jurisdiction over future assassination investigations; or of a Seven Days in May scenario [military intelligence coup]; or of a possible venal Director of the FBI bringing about or allowing an assassination under these new investigative guidelines; etc. He seemed somewhat surprised and speechless by the contents of this memo."[17]

---

15. Richard J. Whalen, "Kennedy Assassination," *The Saturday Evening Post*, 1/14/67, p. 69; *Post Mortem*, p. 555; *Murder From Within*, pp. 216 & 255; see also HSCA interview of Agent Bouck 9/6/77: "Prior to the transfer [April, 1965], Bouck said the [autopsy] materials [photos and x-rays] had only been seen ' ... about twice ... ' [Also] believes Tom Kelley may have been present during the inspection by the WC representative who he believes was ' ... possibly the general counsel or a staff attorney [Specter?] ... "Bouck believes the other time the material was viewed was ' ... rather early, when someone from Secret Service and possibly MR. Kelley looked to see what was in there.'"
16. HSCA Report, page 235. 3 HSCA 327, 344, 345-346.
17. 9/18/96 ARRB interview of Floyd Boring.

69

WILLIAM CRAIG

William Craig was the first agent of the United States Secret Service killed in the line of duty. Craig was killed on September 3, 1902, when a speeding trolley car rammed into the open horse-drawn carriage carrying President Theodore Roosevelt in Pittsfield, Massachusetts. Also in the car were Massachusetts governor Winthrop M. Crane and presidential assistant George B. Cortelyou. The President received only superficial cuts and bruises. The President said: "The man who was killed was one of whom I was fond and whom I greatly prized for his loyalty and faithfulness."

The *Washington Post* reported on 9/4/1902: "Everywhere yesterday were heard expressions of sorrow at the fate of William Craig, the Secret Service officer, who was the only member of the President's party to receive fatal injuries in the accident at Pittsfield. Scores of officials whose business takes them frequently to the White House had a kind word to say of the officer, who during his term of duty in Washington had made hundreds of friends." The *Chicago Sun Times* reported a century later on 9/2/2002: "Secret Service honors its first hero. Shortly after the third assassination of an American president in 36 years, Chicagoan William Craig was tapped to be one of the first entrusted with the safety of future leaders. A giant of a man at 6 feet 4 inches (1.93 m) tall and 260 pounds,

Craig quickly earned the respect of President Theodore Roosevelt, who was at first wary of having men shadow his every move. But within less than a year of taking over as the president's bodyguard, Craig was killed in the line of duty September 3, 1902, when a trolley hit the carriage in which he and Roosevelt rode. Tuesday, exactly 100 years later, the Secret Service will pay tribute to Craig."

Craig joined the Secret Service in 1900. In September of 1902, President Theodore Roosevelt went on a New England speaking tour. President Roosevelt, Massachusetts Governor Crane, George B. Cortelyou, and William Craig were in a carriage heading from Dalton to Lenox. In Pittsfield, at the foot of Howard's Hill (on what is now South Street), a speeding electric trolley car crashed into the carriage. Agent Craig tried to flag the trolley operator to get him to slow down, and when collision was unavoidable, stood up to protect Roosevelt with his own body.

Craig was thrown under the trolley and run over. Roosevelt was thrown 30 feet and suffered cuts and bruises but was not seriously injured. Cortelyou and Crane were uninjured. One horse was so badly injured that he was put down. The driver of the trolley was sentenced to six months jail time.

The President said of Craig, "He was a sturdy character and tremendously capable in performing his duties. My children thought a great deal of him, as we all did." Also, "I was fond of him. He was faithful and ready, and I regret his death more than I can say." The president referred to Craig as "my shadow."[1]

---

1.   http://www.findagrave.com/cgi-bin/fg.cgi?page=gr&GSln=Craig&GSfn=William&GSby-rel=all&GSdy=1902&GSdyrel=in&GSob=n&GRid=42818974&df=all&

70

GERALD O'ROURKE

Gerald O'Rourke is an interesting character. He was both forthcoming and reluctant to reveal details and thoughts when I spoke to and corresponded with him a number of times. O'Rourke was a Texas trip veteran who also was on the second NY trip and a part of the FL trip that President Kennedy was involved in. The former agent, who came out on the 40th anniversary of the JFK assassination to reveal his conviction that a conspiracy took the life of President Kennedy, was friendly, cordial, and quite informative in response to the author's first letter of inquiry, answering every question in detail. In fact, O'Rourke ended his letter by stating, "If you have other questions please feel free to contact me. Jerry."[1] Taking the hint, the author promptly wrote another letter to O'Rourke but did not receive a reply. The author's second letter asked for information about Bennett's role on the NY, FL, and TX trips. When the author phoned O'Rourke on 2/11/04, obviously all was not well on the other end. When asked about Bennett, the former agent said forcefully, "I don't want to do it. I don't want to do it. I'm afraid for my agency." O'Rourke then abruptly ended the conversation.

Jerry O'Rourke later responded to the question of his familiarity (or lack thereof) with PRS Agent Howard K. Norton in this fashion: "No, I do not recall anyone by the name. He could have been in PRS (Protective Research Division), now called Intelligence Division and I wouldn't have known him at the time as I was on the White House Division, now called

---

1. Letter to author dated 1/15/04, in response to the author's letter dated 1/7/04.

Presidential Protective Division. Much later, I served, for a short time, at PRS and I don't recall him. Today, the retired agent's association are very active and had he retired or served for at least one year, the requirements to belong to the retired agents, I would have heard of him and/or he would be listed on our web site. Is it possible he could have been a political advance man? I do not have a copy of the Warren Commission Report which would have listed him and his activities. Sorry that I could not have been more help!"

Jerry O'Rourke was part of the shift consisting of ATSAIC Arthur L. Godfrey, the shift leader, SA Gerald S. Blaine, SA Kenneth S. Giannoules, SA Paul A. Burns, and SA Robert R. Faison. This group arrived in Fort Worth from Washington, D.C. at 2:15 p.m. on 11/21/63 for duty at the Hotel Texas as part of the 4 p.m. – midnight shift (JFK arrived at 11:50 p.m.) After having helped protect the President during the morning of 11/22/63 in Fort Worth as part of the midnight to 8 a.m. shift, this coterie of agents proceeded on to Austin for JFK's next stop after Dallas.[2]

O'Rourke waited nearly 40 years to break his silence, but it was worth the wait.[3] From the 11/20/03 *Rocky Mountain News*: "Lee Harvey Oswald didn't act alone when he killed President John F. Kennedy, a retired agent said Wednesday, and the president died because Secret Service agents failed at their jobs. 'Officially, the answer to Oswald when somebody asks – because we were ordered to say it – is that the Warren Commission found that he acted alone,' retired agent Jerry O'Rourke said. 'But was there more than one gunman? Yes, personally I believe so. And my personal opinion about Jack Ruby is that he was paid to kill Oswald.'

"O'Rourke grew up in Telluride and attended Western State and Regis colleges, then spent 22 years in the Secret Service. Now retired and back home, he spoke Wednesday to the downtown Grand Junction Rotary Club. O'Rourke said his group of agents, about 10 of them, had protected Kennedy the morning of Nov. 22, 1963, at a breakfast speech in Fort Worth. Then the group left by air for Austin, the next stop planned for the president's Texas tour.

"'We got the word (of the assassination) in the air, and we didn't believe it at first,' he said. 'We were joking. But later, most of the agents had tears in their eyes. Agents believed in Kennedy, and we knew we failed our

2.   Sources-RIF#1541000110104;   1541000110064;   1541000110057;   1541000110050; 1541000110044; 1541000110033; 18 H 779; Air Force One radio tapes/ transcripts; Bill Moyers' interview on A&E 1992; *Death of a President*, p.317.
3. "Ex-agent refuses to toe party line on JFK slaying" By Ellen Miller, Special To The News November 20, 2003. RockyMountainNews.Com.

job in Dallas.' After his White House tour ended during Johnson's presidency, O'Rourke spent a year in the Secret Service intelligence division, which offered him glimpses into the investigation of Kennedy's death.

"Those glimpses, and the accounts of other agents, have convinced O'Rourke that Oswald didn't act alone. He cited several reasons: "Kennedy had a number of enemies, any of whom could have plotted against him. They included Southerners angered by his insistence on civil rights; organized crime; labor unions unhappy with investigations of them by Attorney General Robert F. Kennedy; Cuban dissidents angry over the failed Bay of Pigs invasion; and FBI Director J. Edgar Hoover.

"The shots were impossible to make. O'Rourke learned to shoot as a boy and trained as a marksman in the military. He said his visits to Oswald's perch at the Texas Book Depository convince him that no one could have fired a rifle three times so quickly, hitting the president and Texas Gov. John Connally.

"The trajectory of one of the shots could not have been made from a gunman on the sixth floor of the Texas Book Depository. The shot entered Kennedy's body at his lower back and traveled up, to exit near his throat.

"The circumstances of the autopsy were irregular. Texas law requires autopsies to be done in state, but agents, acting on the orders of White House, took Kennedy's body back to Washington, D.C. The autopsy was performed at Bethesda Naval Medical Center under secrecy that prevails to this day.

"Evidence was destroyed. O'Rourke said that on the day of the assassination, one agent was ordered to clean out the cars used in the motorcade, getting rid of blood and other evidence. The agent told O'Rourke that he found a piece of skull, asked the White House doctor what to do with it, and was told to destroy it.

"Instructions were given to lie. The agent in charge of motorcade protection [presumably Kellerman] told O'Rourke that he was told by the Warren Commission during his testimony that he did not hear a fourth shot and he did not see someone running across the grassy knoll. But the agent insisted that his account was accurate. "Evidence about the shots is in conflict. An open microphone on a motorcycle in the motorcade picked up four shots, not three.

"'In my opinion, Hoover wanted the commission to find that Oswald acted alone,' O'Rourke said. 'The complete file won't be released until 2027, and the reason for that is most of us will be dead by then [emphasis added].'"

Gerald Blaine wrote the author on 6/12/05: "I did not hear Jerry O'Rourke's comments, but I cannot even imagine an agent who went through the whole thing expressing a conspiracy theory, but everyone is entitled to their own thoughts. My study and evaluation over the years, based upon the threat scenarios we had to deal with pointed to Oswald's acting alone." O'Rourke also wrote, "Did President Kennedy order us (agents) off the steps of the limo? To my knowledge President Kennedy never ordered us to leave the limo … President Kennedy was easy to protect as he completely trusted the agents of the Secret Service. We always had to be entirely honest with him and up front so we did not lose his trust … The bubble top was plastic and wasn't even bullet resistant but it is possible it could have deflected the bullet if the bullet was not coming straight on."[4]

However, O'Rourke would not respond to a second letter from the author and did not wish to speak further about the subject when contacted by phone on 2/11/04. That said, O'Rourke did consent to correspond with the author via e-mail on 6/17/05 and 6/18/05.

The former agent wrote, "Keep in mind, some of the former agents you interview are not going to be receptive to you. Most don't mind talking about the assassination but they still are very protective. Also, many continue to have some problems (mental?) dealing with what they feel as a failure on their part … Some of the retired agents have contested my beliefs on the assassination but most of those agents were still in diapers when 11/22/63 came about. I always answer them by stating, 'I was there, were you?' Some of those guys you interviewed are great guys while the others are … [O'Rourke broke off here]." O'Rourke added, "As I told you a couple agents have problems with the assassination, Clint [Hill] being one. He is a good friend of mine but I have not seen him in 25 years … Yes, Clint still has problems with 11/22/63 … Again, there are a lot of "people" (and agents) that disagree with my findings [regarding] Nov. 22nd but they have not done any research … I have visited with several of the agents that were right with JFK, at the time, and plied them with drink [!] When all of the records are completely released we will know [what happened], if [we are] still alive."

---

4. Letter to author dated 1/15/04.

71

GARY BYRNE

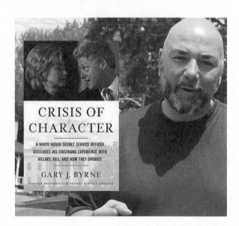

Gary Byrne is a former member of the Uniformed Division (UD) of the Secret Service who wrote a controversial and highly successful book about the Clintons called *Crisis of Character* in 2016. His book contains some unique information from a UD perspective. The AFAUSSS came out in June 2016 forcefully against both Byrne and his book, saying they "strongly denounce" the book, which they add has made security harder by eroding the trust between agents and the people they protect. "There is no place for any self-moralizing narratives, particularly those with an underlying motive," reads the statement from the group's board of directors, which says Byrne has politics and profit on his mind. AFAUSSS rarely issues public statements of any kind.

The book has rankled current and former members of the Secret Service, who don't like anyone airing their business in public. Byrne was a uniformed officer in Bill Clinton's White House. But that's the lowest level of protection within the White House and around the president. "Operationally, one who has the working knowledge of how things are done there would realize that certain of those statements do not coincide with the operational plan," said Jan Gilhooly, AFAUSSS president and a 29-year Secret Service veteran. "One must question the veracity and content of any book which implies that its author played such an integral part of so many [claimed] incidents. Any critique of management by one who has never managed personnel or programs resounds hollow. Additionally, why would an employee wait in excess of ten years after terminating his employment with the Service to make his allegations public?"[1]

To be fair, it must be noted that Byrne is pursuing a lawsuit against Gilhooly and company and adamantly defends his position. He does have a large number of devoted followers, as his book was a number one best-seller for quite a few weeks. On a personal note, I found the book to be compelling, informative and entertaining (and I am a Clinton fan, more or less) and there is no denying Gary's credentials and years of exemplary service to our country. In addition, Gary's co-author gave my third book *The Not-So-Secret Service* a positive review on Amazon, writing the following: "Enjoyed following the trail of well-researched evidence with the sleuth author.... As the co-writer for former Secret Service Officer Gary Byrne, author of *Crisis of Character*, another Secret Service book, Gary and I found the *Not-So Secret Service* a very interesting and well researched read as we continue our own works and research. I enjoyed his tone and how he uses evidence in every instance of his points. He clearly yet neatly goes from commentary to objectivity as he breaks down the lesser known or never before publicly known mysteries of the Secret Service. His work on the Kennedy driver that died of a heart attack prior to the assassination was especially interesting and well researched. This book is also a tribute to many of the Secret Service veterans as well as education at large by keeping history alive."

If that wasn't enough, Gary Byrne himself wrote to me on 8/16/17 on Facebook via his page: "Mr. Palamara!!! I've been trying to look you up and get in contact with you. My daughter and I very much enjoyed your last book! The chapter regarding JFK's driver was especially interesting! It was a story I had never heard and on behalf of so many thank you thank you for bringing so much to light. It was also clear from your book that had you not chased down many of those leads they would have been lost to time."

Byrne is also the author of the 2017 book *Secrets of the Secret Service*. I am mentioned in this book, which I consider quite an honor.

---

1. *Politico*, 6/21/16.

72

KEN GIANNOULES

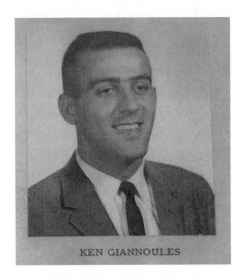

KEN GIANNOULES

Ken Giannoules was the first Greek-American agent to serve on the White House Detail and, at age 23, perhaps the youngest one ever hired. The former agent served from 1959 until 1981, having been a member of the White House Detail during the Eisenhower, Kennedy and Johnson eras. Giannoules was also Chief of Interpol from 1969 to 1974 working directly under Gene Rossides, who served as Assistant U.S. Treasury Secretary at the time, and later served as a publisher of the *National Herald*.[1]

Ken Giannoules is one of the last people to see John F. Kennedy alive. The night before Kennedy was killed, "I was on the midnight shift 11PM-7AM. President Kennedy came in from San Antonio on Air Force One into Fort Worth. I was at lobby to assist his day shift bringing him through the lobby. I put him on the elevator. The elevator doors closed, and he went to his suite. We provided security the rest of the night. That was the last time I saw him. There were no words, there was no reason for words. He went into his suite – we had no reason to go in – the suite was already swept. By the time we got off duty at 7:15AM the next morning, he was still asleep." About five hours later, Kennedy would be dead.[2]

1. *The National Herald*, 10/17/2014.
2. *The National Herald*, 10/17/2014; *Chicago Daily-Herald*, 4/22/2012.

Giannoules later did an oral history for the Sixth Floor Museum on 5/9/2015.[3] The former agent, having ignored two prior letters several years beforehand, told me on 2/11/04: "I don't think I want to participate." One of the more famous photos depicting Giannoules are the ones depicting him walking and jogging beside JFK's limo in Mexico in 1962.

---

3. https://www.youtube.com/watch?v=EuNa-C8WCCM

73

ROBERT FAISON

In the fall of 1963, Special Agent Robert R. Faison was permanently assigned to President John Kennedy's Secret Service protection detail. Abraham Bolden was the first African-American to serve on the White House Detail (June 1961: 30-day temporary assignment before returning to the Chicago field office), while Faison was the first to be permanently assigned. As one of the first black men ever hired as a special agent, he faced challenges being perceived as an equal among peers. He learned that FBI Director J. Edgar Hoover questioned Kennedy on the wisdom of trusting his life to a black man. And for Faison, traveling also proved difficult. The night before Kennedy was assassinated, the protection detail checked into the Hotel Texas in Fort Worth to await Kennedy's arrival from Dallas. A clerk told them they would have to make other arrangements for the Negro. One of the agents informed the hotel clerk that if Faison couldn't stay, the detail wouldn't stay, and if they didn't, neither would Kennedy. The clerk quickly changed his mind.[1]

Bob was the third African-American Special Agent hired by the Secret Service (Charlie Gittens and Abraham Bolden preceded him). Bob

---

1. *Washington Post,* 12/11/2011.

served his country in the US Army, during the war in Korea. He rose to the rank of Warrant Officer and was the youngest 1st Sergeant in a combat infantry company. He was awarded the Bronze Star while in Korea.

Bob was commissioned by the Secret Service in 1962 and was assigned to the Washington Field Office. He was assigned to President Kennedy in October 1963 after serving a thirty-day temporary assignment on the Detail.

Deputy Director of the U.S. Secret Service Keith Prewitt said Bob conducted part of his own background investigation. Prewitt described Bob as an outstanding role model and professional who was always easy to speak to and very good at coaching and mentoring. "He was committed and engaged, but quietly competent," Prewitt said. "He meant a lot to all of us."[2]

Bob passed away 6/28/2011.

---

2. *Roanoke Rapids Daily Herald*, 7/15/2011.

74

FRANK YEAGER

FRANK YEAGER

Agent Frank Yeager was a part of the shift that was specifically assigned to the Austin leg of JFK's Texas trip, which also included William B. Payne (advance agent for Austin, having arrived in Austin 11/12/63), Robert R. Burke (assisted in the advance; specifically, for the LBJ Ranch in Austin City, TX, having arrived in Austin for the LBJ Ranch 11/18/63), Donald Bendickson LBJ Detail), and Gerald Bechtle (LBJ Detail).These agents were augmented by the aforementioned Godfrey, Blaine, Giannoules, Burns, and Faison, as well as by Agents James R. "Jim" Goodenough (LBJ Detail), Michael J. Shannon (LBJ Detail), Robert E. Lockwood (San Antonio Office), and PRS agent Howard K. Norton.[1] Yeager also assisted Payne and Burke with the Austin advance.

The *Asheville (NC) Citizen-Times* reported on 11/20/03: "But for those 40 and older, Kennedy's assassination remains a vivid, painful memory. That's especially true for Frank Yeager, the retired Buncombe County Public Schools superintendent who served in the Secret Service on Kennedy's detail from spring 1962 until the assassination. Yeager typically would have

1.   Sources-RIF#1541000110104;   1541000110064;   1541000110057;   1541000110050; 1541000110044; 1541000110033; 18 H 779; Air Force One radio tapes/ transcripts; Bill Moyers' interview on A&E 1992; Manchester, p. 317.

been in the car behind Kennedy's in the Dallas motorcade that Friday afternoon but instead he was doing advance security work in Austin, Texas.

"He still winces when he talks about receiving the call that the president had been shot and learning 45 minutes later that he was dead. 'It was shock,' Yeager said. 'It was hard to believe. There was extreme sadness, because not only had we lost a president, we'd also lost a person I considered a friend.'

"Growing up in Louisville, Ky., Yeager led a relatively sheltered life, but as a young man he got an itch to work in law enforcement and applied to the Secret Service in 1961. A year later he was traveling the world with Kennedy and his family, when they weren't 'in residence' at the White House.

"Yeager found Kennedy remarkably approachable, a 'super – nice person to work for. He was charming, and he was also sensitive and caring,' Yeager said. 'And he also had a great sense of humor.' One night when Yeager was working the graveyard shift at the White House, stationed at the elevator at ground level, the light came on, and Kennedy emerged in a bathrobe. The president – the most powerful man in the world – just wanted Yeager to have a snapshot of Yeager and Kennedy's aunt that was taken on a recent trip to Ireland. That glimpse of Kennedy points to his larger appeal, Yeager believes.

"'His warmth and caring and his sense of humor and intellect all came out in ways that were real,' Yeager said. 'I think people saw a potential greatness there, and I also think the family – with the two children and the first lady and the type of person she was – that kind of gave us a lift in this country. It was almost too good to be true.'

"That sense of greatness still captivates, Yeager says, because it's so American at its core. 'I think that's what's really lasting about Kennedy – he created a hope that America would be significantly better, particularly for those less advantaged,' Yeager said."

In a letter to the author dated 12/29/03, Yeager wrote, "I did not think that President Kennedy was particularly "difficult" to protect. In fact, I thought that his personality made it easier than some because he was easy to get along with. I can see why some might think that he was more difficult to protect because he was younger than other presidents and had small children who made the Kennedy family much more active than most presidents. With his large extended family, there were many more activities to deal with involving both the extended and immediate family. His popularity also presented unique problems with crowd control."

In answer to my question, "Did President Kennedy ever order the agents off the rear of his limousine?" Yeager responded, "I know of no "order" directly from President Kennedy … I don't know what form or detail that this request was made to the Secret Service … I also do not know who actually made the final decision, but we did not have agents on the rear of the President's car in Dallas. I was doing the advance for President Kennedy in Austin, Texas where he was going next when the President was in Dallas." Yeager also added, "In my opinion, President Johnson did pose more "problems" than President Kennedy because he was much more difficult to deal with on a personal level. He did not try to please anyone that I saw, unless it was his wife, and I am not sure about that." In a follow-up letter, Yeager wrote, "I believe that Oswald was the assassin and that he was alone that day; however [,] I don't know if someone or [some] group put him up to it."[2]

Kennedy's Detail felt a deep loss and carried with them guilt that the Secret Service had, in some way, failed the president, Yeager said. "I was somewhat sheltered from some of the emotion that some of the agents went through," he said. Most agents carried deep thoughts or still do today, if they're alive, and they're not good thoughts, Yeager said.

"You always second guess. Is there something you could've done? And you not only lost the president, but you lost somebody you considered a nice guy, a friend. It was difficult. Some people are still carrying scars from that kind of stuff," he said.

After three months serving under Johnson, working through Christmas in 1963 at his Texas Ranch, Yeager resigned from the service [in March 1964[3]]. To Yeager, Johnson's' confrontational style of leadership was entirely different from Kennedy's warmer approach. "A lot of people were afraid of President Johnson. You didn't want to be on his bad side," Yeager said with a laugh. "Kennedy got things because of his intellect and because of his likeability; President Johnson got things done because people didn't want to cross him."

Yeager said Johnson was difficult to work for. When asked if that was relative to Kennedy, whom Yeager said was easy to work for, he replied: "Difficult, I think, under any circumstance." First Lady Ladybird Johnson, however, was sweet a woman, he said."[4]

---

2. Letter to author dated 1/24/04.
3. *Kentucky New Era*, 11/23/88.
4. *Evansville Courier and Press*, 11/23/2013.

75

ROBERT BURKE

An ex-Army paratroop officer and 1956 Loyola University sociology major, Burke was a member of the Kennedy Detail (joining in around March 1963) and rose to become the ASAIC of PPD in 1973[1] and, later, a Deputy Director with the Secret Service during the time of the assassination attempt on President Reagan in 1981. He was in charge of all security for the 1968 Democratic National Convention in Chicago, his hometown (Burke's brother Kevin was a member of the Chicago field office). Even though the convention itself was a disaster, with much violence in and around the hall, Burke kept all the dignitaries safe.

Burke received the Secret Service's highest honor in June 1968 – the Meritorious Service Award – given in recognition for his brilliant advance security arrangements for Vice President Hubert Humphrey's trip to Vietnam in October to November 1967.[2] Like Gerald Blaine, Burke also went on to become a member of the Overseas Security Advisory Council for the U.S. Department of State, in his capacity as Director of Corporate Service and Security for the Monsanto Company. He even testified on C-Span in 1997.[3]

1. *Five Presidents* by Clint Hill, page 403.
2. *Chicago Tribune*, 8/11/68.
3. *Survivor's Guilt*, page 357.

Burke had assisted Bill Payne in the Austin, Texas advance; specifically, for the LBJ Ranch in Austin City, TX, having arrived in Austin for the LBJ Ranch 11/18/63. Burke had been on JFK's trips to Ireland, Los Angeles, and Chicago, among many others, in 1963.

Former agent Walt Coughlin wrote to me the following: "The reality is the most respected [agents] are those who were good [at] both protection and field work – took lots of transfers and paid the 'full price' i.e. Paul Rundle – Glenn Weaver -Stu Knight – Larry Sheafe – perhaps me! – Bob Newbrand – Bob Burke – (and others) but you get my drift. Most of the protection only guys [such as Art Godfrey and Bob DeProspero] never left D.C. and there was some resentment about that. Never enough to affect friendships but it was there."[4]

---

4. E-mail to author dated 4/26/05.

76

WALT COUGHLIN

WALT COUGHLIN

C oughlin attended DeMatha Catholic High School in Hyattsville, MD. His biography from the school's website reads as follows: "J. Walter (Walt) Coughlin was the first DeMatha athlete to receive ten varsity letters: three for football, three for basketball, three for baseball, and one for golf. He was the starting end on DeMatha's first football teams and was a Scholastic Sports Association All-Prep selection his junior year. He broke his leg in a game during his senior year but completed the game nonetheless. Walt was the starting guard on the basketball team his junior and senior seasons and started at catcher on the baseball team all three years. He was also named All-Prep (by the SSA) in baseball his senior year. Walt also coached and taught at DeMatha in the late 1950's. After graduation from DeMatha, Walt played freshman football at the University of Maryland before being drafted into the service. He was voted on the All-Army football and baseball teams in 1955 and played semi-pro football until 1959. He later received two meritorious awards during a distinguished career with the U. S. Secret Service. He currently is president of J. Walter Coughlin & Associates, an international security consulting firm, headquartered in Dallas, Texas."

Coughlin detailed his entire Secret Service career in a letter: "2-61 thru 3-77 – Charleston, W.Va. – Counterfeit Detail NYC – White House – 6-62 – 12-64 – VP Detail 12-64 to 1-69 – ASAIC Louisville, Ky. – SAIC Omaha, Neb – SAIC Dallas – transferred to Foreign Dignitary Division, D.C., to process out of SS for medical retirement ([due to] ulcers)."[1] From Coughlin's Cushing Memorial Library (Texas A & M University) oral history, 4/19/86: "When I got out of college, in retrospect, I probably would have wanted to go to law school. But I didn't have any money. I had friends who were in the FBI. They were talking about some of the restraints that Mr. Hoover was putting on them at the time. I didn't think that I was that kind of a free spirit in some of those kind of things. I didn't think I would have lasted. Then I heard about the Secret Service. I was not familiar with it. There was the appeal of the White House, the travel, and so on. So I applied and was fortunate enough to be selected."

Coughlin added, "I had the opportunity on three occasions to go to Vietnam. The first would be in 1965.[2] The second was the inauguration of President [Nguyen Van] Thieu and Vice President [Nguyen Cao] Ky, which, I guess from memory, was 1966. And one time after that in late 1967 … I was not in the military at the time. I was there on all three occasions with Vice President [Hubert Horatio] Humphrey who was sent there on a political mission by President Johnson. My mission there was, as a member of the Secret Service, to protect Mr. Humphrey … we used the element of surprise with no scheduling … we worked within the confines of the military in a very secret manner, but it was still a very risky operation … from the standpoint of general protection, the policy in protection of the president is organization, scheduling, [and] logistics. Within all the confines of a smooth operation, you hopefully have real good security. You have good intelligence gathering. You have good communication between different police organizations: motorcade routes, intersection control, ticket control, access control, ushers, and everything right down to where everyone sits and when they're supposed to be in their seats. So basically what you do as a Secret Service agent is to organize as best you can down to the scheduled minute, sometimes the second, particularly for television purposes. Under that umbrella of organization comes good security." During the same oral history interview,[3] Coughlin had some

---

1. E-mail to author dated 2/29/04.
2. Other agents involved with Humphrey's protection included Glenn Weaver (the SAIC of his detail), Rufus Youngblood, Bob Taylor, Bill Livingood, & Bob Burke (Youngblood, pp. 199-210).
3. Cushing Memorial Library and Archives, Texas A & M University, J. Walter Coughlin oral history, 4/19/86.

other interesting things to say: "I'm not that convinced that our intelligence apparatus in Vietnam was that effective at all. I knew a lot of CIA guys that were there. They were really frustrated by it all because you were dealing with the Asiatic mind which in and of itself seems to be rather secretive. Even some of the South Vietnamese forces were sympathetic to the North. You never really knew who your friends were [emphasis added]." The former agent had many thought-provoking things to say about the war in Vietnam, including, "In retrospect, I think we went in there with good intentions. I think we got bogged down in a land war in Asia, which history has told us never to do. It got so political in the end that all of those mistakes just contributed to our downfall. The Americans are very impatient people. For the Asiatics, time means nothing to them. They'll just outwait you ... I think if we went in there to win it, we should have won it. And the only way we were going to do that was to bomb 'em back to the Stone Ages as Curtis Lemay suggested. He was an Air Force general. He should know something about it ... [t]he only way we ever beat the Japanese was bomb them.

Coughlin said that President Kennedy was "very friendly, very funny." Walt later added, "Kennedy and Humphrey were both very nice."[4] The former agent described standing on post at the White House as "usually very boring." Regarding the President's relationship with Frank Sinatra, Coughlin responded, "Sinatra was around a lot as was all the 'Rat Pack', Sammy Davis, Peter Lawford (JFK bro-in-law) and Joey (forget his last name) [Bishop]. I know what Sinatra's rep is but he was always very nice to us. Liked the ladies, had a good time but I truly liked him as a human being. (He was very generous). The kind of person Sinatra was – he was on the BOD [Board of Directors] of Budweiser – one day he saw a Humphrey staff man drinking a Schlitz and said, 'give me your home address because every week for the next year a case of Bud will be delivered to your home so you will stop drinking that shi – y Schlitz.' And it happened!"[5] JFK made a trip to California in March 1962, which was the famous occasion when he canceled plans to stay at Sinatra's home at Palm Springs and, to Sinatra's rage and frustration, went to Bing Crosby's place instead. The official excuse was that the Secret Service thought the Crosby place was more secure. The story ever since has been that either the President or RFK, or both, had simply realized that Sinatra's mob connections compromised him too much for the President to continue to associate open-

---

4. E-mail to author dated 5/6/05.
5. E-mail to author dated 2/26/04.

ly with him.[6] Regarding this trip, Coughlin wrote, "[I] was on that trip but I have no idea why the switch." Former agent Frank Stoner wrote, "I saw Sinatra with JFK on many times. The first time was at JFK's Inaugural Ball. That night he was very close with the Pres. I can't remember if he sat in the Press Box. He was at the White House on several occasions and was always very upbeat with all he came in contact with."[7] In addition to helping advance the Miami (11/18/63) and San Antonio (11/21/63) trips, Walt told the author that he "did the advance to Berlin [June 1963]."

When I asked Coughlin, "Did the assassination affect you guys more because you were so close to JFK?" he said, "Probably so because (only speaking for myself) we failed our mission."[8] Regarding the transition from JFK to LBJ, Coughlin wrote, "Transition was very difficult – firstly we were all very despondent and we really liked JFK and it was mutual. LBJ was anything but friendly and he did not want anything to do with us. Also – the culture shock was significant: from Hyannis Port, Palm Beach and Palm Springs to the dirty ranch and cattle guards of south Texas was a real setback."[9] Coughlin later wrote, "LBJ was a first class prick ... Norman Edwards took his BS – The agents would not – Norman was a good driver and person."[10] The author wrote to Coughlin: "I get the strong feeling that the Secret Service is like the Marines: once an agent, always an agent, and that every (former) agent is your brother. There seems to be a special bond and a lot of guys are still good friends (and even attend your conferences!)." The former agent responded, "Yes – we are quasi-military. We went thru a lot together and remain close forever. We saw the good, the bad and the ugly and keep it to ourselves to protect the current agents."[11] In fact, Coughlin helped produce the AFAUSS book, *Looking Back and Seeing the Future: The United States Secret Service 1865-1990.*[12]

---

6. This was also discussed in an e-mail exchange between the author and Anthony Summers on 2/26/04.
7. E-mail to author dated 2/26/04.
8. E-mail to author dated 2/24/04.
9. E-mail to author dated 2/26/04.
10. E-mails to author dated 4/27/05 & 5/6/05.
11. E-mail to author dated 2/27/04.
12. E-mail to author dated 2/28/04.

77

JERRY DOLAN

J erry Dolan worked as a Secret Service agent from 1961 to 1964, guarding Kennedy and his family. "The concern about him was very intense," Dolan recalled recently. "There were a lot of mentally ill people who came around to try to see the president." Some were women who would come to the capital city with "some really hot ideas" about what they were going to do with the young and handsome chief executive, according to Dolan. Others, he said, intended to kill the president. The potential assassins included a man who showed up at the East Gate of the White House with two straight-edged razor blades in his vest pocket and another who had wired himself as a bomb. The man with the razor blades told Dolan and another agent he was from Mars and it was time for him to return to the planet – with the president. The man who was a walking bomb had placed sticks of dynamite in the pockets of a hunting vest and wired them to a flip switch he wore in the middle of his chest. When he was caught by the Secret Service, he said he did not like the president because he was a Roman Catholic. Thanks to Secret Service agents, Kennedy was largely unaware of many of the threats to his life, according to

Dolan. "We wouldn't tell him that somebody was trying to shoot him or that we caught somebody trying to break into his quarters," Dolan said. "We just couldn't lay that on him. He had enough to worry about trying to run the country." There was an incident in 1962, though, that made Kennedy more cautious. An agent was seriously hurt when he blocked the president from injury as a crowd rushed eagerly toward him during a Rose Garden appearance. "The president apologized afterwards and said he would never place us in a situation like that again," Dolan said. "I think that was the first time he realized that maybe there was a danger involved."

Dolan joined the Secret Service at age 28, after three years as a park police officer and patrolman in St. Paul. He soon found there were many hardships to be endured along with the advantages of the duty. His family did not have a permanent home, and he could not spend much time with them. In addition the work schedule was hectic. One time Dolan had worked into the morning and then was told to pack his bag and report to Andrews Air Force Base. He soon found himself flying to a breakfast meeting in Ohio, a dedication ceremony in Wyoming, and then a dinner reception in Seattle. That night it was time for him to report again for his regular shift. Dolan recalls that a White House doctor gave him two pills the agents called "zingers" to help him get through the night. In the three years Dolan worked for the Service, his hair changed from black to gray.

He became a familiar figure to the Kennedy family. Called "Agent Dolan Jerry" by the president's son, John-John, Dolan, like the other agents, received Christmas and birthday presents from the Kennedys and often found himself in casual conversation with the president. "He was a very thoughtful, a super-intelligent man who had the kindest feelings for everyone around him and everyone working with him," Dolan said.

In late November of 1963, as Kennedy departed on a speechmaking tour of Texas, Dolan did not accompany him as he had expected.[1] Instead he went on leave to Omaha, Neb., to be with his wife, Josephine, for the birth of their third son. Dolan was eating lunch with several federal agents in a downtown Omaha restaurant when a US marshal came to tell him that Kennedy had been shot. Dolan immediately flew to Washington, DC, to resume his duties. He guarded the president's young widow and her two children from then until April 1964, when Jacqueline Kennedy moved to New York City.

1. When asked if he recalled Dolan, former agent Walt Coughlin responded: "Vaguely but cannot put a face on him." [E-mail to the author dated 2/29/04] Coughlin later wrote that he did indeed remember working with Dolan [E-mail to the author dated 5/5/05].

Now a lieutenant in charge of the police department's canine unit, Dolan recently mused about his absence from Dallas on that November day 25 years ago. "If I had been there, maybe it would have been different," he said. "I was charged with the protection of this man, my whole training was towards his protection, and I had had personal contact with the man over a period of months. Then to have happen to him exactly what I was trying to prevent, well, it's still an emotional thing for me. I have been to Dallas, been to the area where it happened and looked at it. And I still dream about it. I guess I have some real guilt feelings because I am a master marksman with my right hand and an expert with my left. And this would have been an easy right-hand shot to where he was in the window. There was nobody facing that window. I would have been the only one on that side of the car. There is no doubt in my mind I could have hit him, or at least put enough rounds in the area so he wouldn't have gotten off a second shot."[2]

From the *St. Paul Pioneer Press*, August 13, 1993: "For nearly 30 years, Jerry Dolan was haunted by the moment that two bullets slammed into then President John F. Kennedy as his motorcade drove through Dallas. Dolan, who died Tuesday, was a young Secret Service agent in 1963, but he wasn't in Dallas the day Kennedy died. He was at home with his wife for the birth of their third son. Funeral services will be held this weekend for Dolan, who died while vacationing in northern Minnesota. He had been on medical leave from the police department since December, and suffered from a heart ailment. He was 62. A native of St. Paul, Dolan joined the army after high school and served in Japan and Korea during the Korean War. When he returned to the US he enrolled in college and graduated in 1958 with a degree in sociology."[3] Dolan was appointed Temporary Patrolman on March 20, 1961; was appointed Patrolman on April 24, 1961; resigned to join the U.S. Secret Service on June 30, 1961; returned as Provisional Patrolman on March 30, 1964; was certified as Patrolman on November 2, 1964; was promoted to Sergeant on September 30, 1967; was promoted to Lieutenant on November 27, 1971; and died on August 10, 1993, while still employed by the police department.[4]

Dolan appeared on Minnesota television in 1988.[5]

---

2. Condensed from the *St. Paul Pioneer Press Dispatch*, Sunday, November 20, 1988.
3. Condensed from the *St. Paul Pioneer Press*, Friday, August 13, 1993.
4. http://www.spphs.org/history/hanggi/hanggi2.php
5. https://www.youtube.com/watch?v=gINf96HLS-w

78

FRANK SLOCUM

From the *Honolulu Advertiser*, 11/22/03, on the 40th anniversary of Kennedy's death: "Tragedy Still Sore Spot For Ex-Agent: November never fails to stir up Frank Slocum's worst memories. Even after 40 years, he can't escape them. They don't bother him as much as they do other retired U.S. Secret Service agents. But they can set his upper lip to quivering, and if he doesn't stomp them back, he'll cry. Slocum, who once headed up the Honolulu office of the Secret Service, protected five presidents during his 20-year career. And while Slocum wasn't in the doomed presidential motorcade in Dallas that morning – he was in Los Angeles working criminal cases – he was there that afternoon, standing on the sixth floor of the Texas school book depository ... Slocum had protected Kennedy on other assignments. He liked him. All the agents liked him. 'He was very personable,' Slocum says ... The emotional measure of their loss could not really be weighed by the Secret Service agents until days later.

"Those agents assigned to remain in Texas, Slocum among them, huddled around a television set in a Johnson City motel to watch the Kennedy funeral. 'We had lost a popular president,' he says. 'We were feeling maybe it could have been avoided. Did we do something wrong?' ... In the aftermath, Slocum and another agent wrote a thick manual on presidential route security. Among their suggestions: no open windows ... 'Was there something we could have done?' Slocum says again, and not for the last time. 'I don't know if there was.'"[1]

In a letter to the author dated 1/16/04, Slocum wrote, "I spent three years at the White House with Ike but was not assigned to the WH Detail during the JFK Administration. I only had short times with him when he visited the Los Angeles Office area plus the special assignment in Florida for the vacation and greeting the Cuban POWs in 1962. I didn't arrive in Dallas the day of the assassination until that afternoon ... My times with JFK I found him to be extremely intelligent with a terrific memory including names of all the agents and a good sense of humor. As to how he will be treated by history, we will just have to wait and see. Unfortunately, we didn't have him with us long."

Former agent Darwin David Horn, Sr., the ASAIC of the Los Angeles office during the JFK era, wrote the author: "Frank Slocum was one of the best partners that I ever had and is still a great friend. He lives in Honolulu and we talk often."[2] Horn later wrote, "He is one of my favorite people. We worked a lot together in L.A. [Los Angeles]. A great partner. Whenever we got together as partners things were going to happen. We talk every week or so now."[3]

1. *Honolulu Advertiser*, 11/22/03.
2. E-mail to author dated 1/30/04.
3. E-mail to author dated 3/1/04.

79

CHARLES KUNKEL/MIKE HOWARD

CHARLIE KUNKEL   MIKE HOWARD

S erving as both her interpreters and her captors, the agents threatened Marina with deportation in subtle (and not-so subtle) ways if
she didn't tow the "official" line that her husband, Lee Harvey Oswald, was the lone-nut assassin of JFK. The *New York Times* of 12/8/63
reported,

> Secret Service agents suggested to her that it might be safer and
> easier for her to return to the Soviet Union than to try to live in
> the United States. This distressed her.... She is now secluded from
> Oswald's relatives as well as from the public.

While Marina originally denied that Oswald had a revolver, a rifle-
scope, or even a rifle, all this would change soon enough after the questioning by these agents.[1] Russian-speaking agent Leon Gopadze, Marina's
interpreter, translated Marina's letter in the following way, in contradiction to the above account: "I am very, very grateful to the Secret Service
agents who treated me so well and took such good care of me. Although
some of the letters which I received accused these wonderful people of
preventing me from seeing others, I am free to do anything I want ... "[2]
Perhaps a tad flowery and overdone. In addition, Gopadze, responsible
for translating Marina's many FBI interviews and her first Warren Com-

---

1. Secret Service interview, Warren Commission document 344, pages 23 & 43; WR 128; 1 H 492; see
also *Cover-Up* by Stewart Galanor (1998), p. 92.
2. 18 H 642.

mission appearance[3], was first introduced to Marina by the Secret Service as "Mr. Lee," the very same name Lee Harvey Oswald had used when rooming at a boardinghouse away from his wife in 1963.[4]

Perhaps Oswald's mother, Marguerite, summed up the situation best: "Mrs. Oswald claimed at certain points that her son was an American espionage agent. She claimed at other points that, if her son shot the President, he was part of a conspiracy involving Marina, Ruth Paine, two Secret Service agents, and a 'high government official' who she refused to identify."[5] As author Fred Newcomb reported,[6] "Secret Service agents Howard and Kunkel made certain claims to gain the confidence of the Oswald family. When Howard interviewed Robert Oswald on Nov. 23, 1963, he asserted that personal details of the family would be of special interest to Mrs. Kennedy. Robert thought this meant that Howard was close to Mrs. Kennedy.[7]

Also on November 23rd, Kunkel told Oswald's mother, Marguerite, that he was sure Oswald killed the President. Marguerite objected. Howard replied that Kunkel was upset because he had guarded Mrs. Kennedy[8] ... Marguerite came to be 'deathly afraid' of both Kunkel and Howard. On May 12, 1964, she told the FBI in Fort Worth she not only refused to allow Kunkel in her home but did not want anything further to do with them both.[9] Marguerite stated, 'I have had documents stolen from me. I have had newspaper clippings stolen from my hand by the Secret Service.'[10] Marguerite also said: '... I thought that we have a plot in our own government and that there is a high official involved. And I am thinking that probably these Secret Service men are a part of it.'"

It's funny how Marguerite picks out Howard and Kunkel over all the agents who guarded her and her family. "On December 4, 1963, Special Agent James M. Howard, assigned to the Dallas, Texas office, and who assisted in the advance arrangements at Fort Worth, Texas,[11] advised that he was on duty at the Texas Hotel from the time the President arrived until 4:00 a.m. on November 22, 1963; that he was representing the Dallas

---

3. 5 H 588; see also *The Warren Omission* by Walt Brown (1996), p. 238.
4. 23 H 385.
5. *The Secret Service Story* by Michael Dorman, p. 213; 1 H 169-170.
6. *Murder From Within*, pp. 291-292.
7. CD 75, p. 356; *Lee: A Portrait of Lee Harvey Oswald by His Brother* by Robert L. Oswald (New York: Coward-McCann, 1967), p. 149.
8. CD 1066, pp. 532, 533, 539; 1 H 169.
9. CD 1066, pp. 532, 533.
10. 1 H 129.
11. The Secret Service's Final Survey Report for the Fort Worth leg of the Texas tour lists Agent's Bill Duncan, Ned Hall, and Howard as assisting in the advance arrangements. However, Howard is listed as "James M. Harwood."

Office and had occasion to meet and to talk to many of the Special Agents accompanying the President from Washington in the lobby, at the President's suite and in the Agents' rooms. He stated that at no time did he ever see any Special Agent of this Service in an intoxicated condition; that he himself was not at the Press Club [how about the Cellar?]. This Special Agent's remarks are worthy of comment, as it is known that he does not drink intoxicants of any kind, and it is believed that any remarks by him would be unbiased [!]."[12] So, where was Dallas agent Howard at 12:30 p.m. on 11/22/63? Why did he wait until a 1999 lecture to state his location at that specific time? Allegedly he was cleaning President Kennedy's room at the Hotel Texas in Fort Worth.[13] He did not mention exactly where he was during the assassination to either the *Fresno Bee* or the *Houston Post*, in 1993; his only known pre-1999 interviews. During the period of his 12/4/63 statement, Howard was temporarily assigned to Lynda Bird Johnson's detail (from 12/1/63-1/24/64). Howard, along with his partner Kunkel, allegedly on an unspecified assignment on 11/22/63 in Washington D.C. (another 1999 Howard statement), were the only Dallas office agents connected to the Dallas trip not to have reports made available to the Warren Commission. Howard became a member of the White House Detail 4 months later, on 3/29/64.

Mike Howard and his brother Pat also planted the story that a janitor saw Oswald pull the trigger.[14] That said, according to author Harrison Livingstone, "Retired Secret Service agent Mike Howard ... has repeatedly hinted at LBJ's involvement in the plot."[15] As for Kunkel, the agent was involved in the investigation of a very obscure yet deadly threat to JFK's life: one Russell W. McLarry, as the following newspaper account makes clear. From *The New York Times*, 12/20/63:

> A 21-year-old Dallas machinist was arrested by the Secret Service today on charges of threatening to kill President Kennedy. The machinist, Russell W. McLarry, said the threat had been made in jest Nov. 21, the day before Mr. Kennedy was assassinated here. Two women to whom Mr. McLarry allegedly made the statement re-

---

12. 18 H 675.
13. Interestingly, Ira David Wood III reported on page 20 of James Fetzer's *Murder in Dealey Plaza*, "While showering this morning [11/22/63, Hotel Texas, Fort Worth], JFK takes off his Saint Jude and Saint Christopher medals and leaves them hanging on the shower head. When later "sweeping" the room, Secret Service agent Ron Pontius finds the medals and puts them in his pocket, with the intentions of returning them to JFK after the Dallas motorcade. Pontius eventually gives the medals to Marty Underwood who, at last report, still retains them." Not only is there no mention of Agent Howard, Pontius did not refute this account when contacted by the author in October 2000.
14. 25 H 721-722,725: Lane-Rankin correspondence; 25 H 844-850: The Howards' side of the story.
15. *Stunning New Evidence*, 2000 (online publication: Secret Service chapter).

ported it to the police in Arlington, about 15 miles west of here, soon after they heard of the assassination.

At a preliminary hearing in Fort Worth today, the Secret Service agent who apprehended Mr. McLarry testified that the machinist had said he was "proud – no glad" that the President had been killed.

Mr. McLarry attends night classes at the Arlington State College in Arlington as a freshman. The alleged threat was made on the campus to two women students.

Mr. McLarry was alleged to have told the women that he would be working near the Trade Mart the next day and would be waiting with a gun to "get" the President. Works Near Trade Mart

Charles E. Kunkel, of the Dallas office of the Secret Service testified that he had confronted Mr. McLarry with this report and that, in substance, the student had admitted it.

Mr. McLarry works at the Dahlgren Manufacturing Company, which makes lithographic printing equipment in a plant three blocks north of the Trade Mart. President Kennedy was driving to the mart to make a luncheon speech when he was killed, apparently by rifle shots from a sixth-floor window of a downtown Dallas building in the other direction from the mart.

United States Attorney Barefoot Sanders said here today that he had no evidence of any connection between Mr. McLarry and Lee H. Oswald, the alleged assassin ... The authorities said they had found no connection between Mr. McLarry and anti-Kennedy leaflets that appeared on the Arlington campus the day before the assassination. The leaflets bore the heading: "Wanted for Treason."

Mr. McLarry was interviewed by the Secret Service Tuesday night and was arrested this morning. The agency indicated that the case had not been pursued immediately after the assassination because there had been more pressing things to do.[16]

The (Washington D.C.) *Evening Star*, 12/19/63, noted, "The Complaint was signed by Charles E. Kunkel, special agent for the Secret Service."[17]

Newsweek added this important detail to the mix: "McLarry, who is unmarried, lived in the Oak Cliff section of Dallas, where Lee Harvey Oswald, the President's accused assassin, and Jack Ruby, Oswald's killer, also lived."[18] With agent Kunkel now dead and agent Howard incommunicado, it will probably be difficult to unravel these mysteries further.

16. *New York Times*, 12/20/63 p. 19.
17. *Evening Star*, (Washington, D.C.) 12/19/63 [this newspaper article photocopy was found in DNC advance man Jerry Bruno's JFK Library Texas trip files].
18. *Newsweek*, 12/30/63, p. 15 [courtesy of researcher Bill Adams].

These agents were to make sure that Marina Oswald portrayed the "patsy," Lee Harvey Oswald, as a lone nut killer. They were to tie up untidy loose ends ... and two of them cannot be ruled out as the unidentified agent in Dealey Plaza that day. Interestingly, just moments before he died on 1/22/73, former President Johnson asked that Agent Mike Howard come to his room "immediately."[19]

In recent years, former agent Mike Howard has done several media interviews and videotaped presentations. In one such interview, Howard said: "Marguerite was as looney as a fruitcake!" he said.

In his testimony to the Warren Commission, Peter Gregory described Marguerite Oswald "as being not necessarily rational.... She demands public attention."

Of Marguerite and Oswald, he said, "I felt they both craved public recognition or ... attention or publicity or whatever you wish to call it."

Howard tells his stories often especially lately, surrounding the 50th anniversary of the assassination.

His goal is not to change the minds of skeptics, but rather to tell them what he witnessed.

"Look," he tells them in his thick Texas drawl, "I'm just telling you what it was. You can take it or leave it."

"If I can get up and explain that to people and tell them what happened, then I feel like I've done a service, not only for the Secret Service, but for the country."[20]

In another press interview, Howard revealed the following:

> Soon after President John F. Kennedy and his wife departed from their Fort Worth hotel for Dallas that morning, Howard and other agents faced a monumental duty – meticulously collecting the half-used cologne, scraps of paper, bars of soap and even left-behind pieces of thread from the Kennedys' hotel suite into two trash bags.
>
> By the time we got everything into those bags we heard over the TV that there had been a shot fired in Dallas," Howard, 82, recalled Monday afternoon at the Carrollton Senior Center. The retired agent spoke there during an event to commemorate the 50th anniversary of Kennedy's assassination.
>
> Immediately after the shooting, Howard's duties quickly changed. Soon he would be questioning suspects and in time, he would guard the family of Lee Harvey Oswald.

---

19. *LBJ: A Life* by Irwin Unger (John Wiley & Sons, 1999), p. 536. Howard wasn't there, but agents' Ed Noland and Harry Harris rushed in with a portable oxygen machine instead. It was too late: LBJ had passed away.
20. *Dallas Morning News*, 11/22/2013.

But first he had to get to Dallas.

After hearing of the shooting, Howard got into the Tarrant County sheriff's new Ford Crown Victoria. The car could go as fast as 150 mph, which Howard said he thought was "kind of funny – until we got in and took that drive to Dallas."[21]

In yet another press interview, Howard talked about 11/22/63: "Howard said he has had a lot of time to think about that day. He has even asked himself lots of "What if's?" and "How's?" on the procedures and events that led to that tragic moment in American history.

"You think what could have been done or what should have done and what wasn't done and did everybody do what they needed to be doing," Howard said…"(President Kennedy) was really a nice fellow," Howard said. "He liked the agents. He always spoke to us. He spoke to everybody. He was very congenial, a good man to work with."[22]

In another press interview, Howard reveals the dubious side of his personality and why some of the things he says should be taken with a grain of salt: "Of course, any Secret Service agent that ever guarded the Kennedy family is always asked is he ever met Marilyn Monroe.

Howard says certainly … at a pool party.

But that meeting came later when Howard was assigned to protect Lynda Bird Johnson. Miss Johnson happened to be dating a fellow by the name of George Hamilton and there was a pool party on the West Coast. Marilyn Monroe was there. Everyone was watching Elvis Presley's movie *Acapulco*.

"She was wearing a swim suit," Howard said, "and that's as far as I'm going with that."[23]

Marilyn Monroe died in 1962, well over a year before this was even possible to have happened.

More dubious tales from Howard continue, this time with some alarming results: "Secret Service agent Mike Howard had been in charge of security for the Fort Worth leg of the JFK trip. As he told me in 1993, there was coincidentally a "grassy knoll" on the way to the Ft. Worth Airport. These kinds of topography were clear security risks, says Howard, who adds, "We placed two deputies there. This is routine. Sorrels [Forrest Sorrels, the Secret Service agent in charge of the Dallas motorcade] did the same thing in Dallas." Howard was told by the now deceased Sorrels

21. *Dallas Morning News*, 6/3/2013.
22. *McKinney Courier Gazette*, 11/28/2010.
23. http://www.ntxe-news.com/cgi-bin/artman/exec/view.cgi?archive=34&num=56336

that, like Howard, he had placed security people in all the obvious areas. Howard elaborated: "We deputized everybody we could get our hands on – including agents from ATF [the Bureau of Alcohol, Tobacco and Firearms], customs, border patrol, reserve police, deputy sheriffs, etc. The motorcade route in Dallas was crawling with these people, especially in Dealey Plaza and the overpass."

Howard adds that many of these security reinforcements were technically off-duty and wouldn't appear on any "official" listing of posted officers. In addition, many of these agents had the standard ATF IDs, which were virtually identical to Secret Service cards, both being issued by the Treasury Department. Compounding the confusion is the fact that the ATF and Secret Service were often perceived as interchangeable in 1963. Frank Ellsworth, a Dallas ATF agent at the time of the assassination, told me, "In 1963, if you would have asked me if I was a Secret Service agent, I most likely would have answered yes – our roles overlapped that much." Robert Gemberling, the FBI agent in Dallas who investigated Oswald after his arrest, told me that he remembers being told that two Customs Agents who worked at the Post Office building across Dealey Plaza were, in fact, spending their lunch break helping with security in the knoll area.[24]

Finally, Howard gave a videotaped talk on 11/14/2013 that is lambasted with dislikes and negative comments from many viewers – they are not fooled, either.[25] A sampling of the comments: "His narrative is full of untruths and distortions as well as pure speculation."; "This was hard to watch. The facts in the case are at odds with what this former agent says."; "suppose his pension depends on proselytizing and repeating the blatant lies told by the Warren Commission, and other nonsense. Not one witness, not even a team of witnesses – could corroborate his version of the J.D. Tippit slaying for example. Couldn't watch the remaining 20 minutes after that. Sorry to be so harsh, but this is simply hearsay from a vested establishment shill. A library should know better; file under fiction."

24. Gus Russo, *Live by the Sword* (Baltimore: Bancroft, 1998), p. 473.
25. https://www.youtube.com/watch?v=-ZPVS-AkkP0

80

LYNN MEREDITH

LYNN MEREDITH

gent Lynn Meredith, along with fellow agents Bob Foster and Tom Wells, guarded the children of President and Mrs. Kennedy (the so-called "Kiddie Detail"). Serving in the Secret Service from 1951 to 1983, Meredith was definitely one of the good guys. Meredith wrote to me the following regarding his thoughts on the JFK assassination[1]: ""To elaborate a little more on the assassination in Dallas, I have always believed that the following adverse situations all contributed to the unnecessary and unfortunate death of President Kennedy:

(1) No Secret Service agents riding on the rear of the limousine. (2) It was a nice day and the bubble top of the limousine was up and open for better viewing of the occupants [sic – it sounds as if Meredith is describing a partial bubbletop formation here]. (3) The President was wearing a back brace which caused him to immediately return to an upright sitting position after he was struck in the back of the neck by the first bullet [this assumes that JFK was both hit in the back of the neck and that this was caused by the first bullet, matters still in contention 40 plus years later]. (4) The 6th floor window of the Texas [School] Book Depository Building where Oswald was located was open and made for easier shots direct-

---

1. Letter to author dated 3/9/04.

ed at the President. (5) Inadequate security along the entire ten-mile motorcade route from the airport to downtown Dallas that day, particularly in the buildings along the route of travel. (6) Oswald being allowed to enter the Texas Book Depository on the morning of November 22 with a rifle wrapped in paper and not arousing any suspicion by anyone in the building [again, matters hotly contested by the research community]. (7) The motorcade route published several days in advance which allowed Oswald [time] to make plans to assassinate the President. (8) The sorry fact that Oswald's Russian wife, Marina, did not alert the FBI, Dallas police, the Secret Service, or anyone else that Lee Harvey Oswald had fired the same rifle at retired Army General Edwin Walker about six months earlier and had missed by a fraction of an inch. (9) Oswald had been a Sharpshooter in the Marine Corps and got lucky in firing 3 shots at the President, and the President and the Secret Service got unlucky." Meredith continued, "I'm sure there are more reasons to explain the assassination but the above are the main ones in my opinion. Incidentally, the Secret Service, the FBI, and the Warren Commission all remain convinced that Oswald was the lone assassin and it was not a conspiracy of any kind. And that is my unswerving opinion, too. The only bullets fired and recovered came from Oswald's Italian made rifle and there were no shots fired from ground level. "Regarding your question [about his background], I spent 32 years and 5 months in the Secret Service from 1951 to 1983, and 19 of those years were spent in Washington, D.C. on numerous protective assignments."

In a follow-up letter to the author dated 5/22/05, Meredith wrote, "Yes, I am flattered that Mary Gallagher included me in her book, *My Life With Jacqueline Kennedy*, and I actually have several copies of this book. I became well acquainted with Mary Gallagher during the first year of the Kennedy Administration in 1961 when she was the personal secretary to First Lady Jacqueline Kennedy ... Clint Hill ... was a good friend of mine and we were assigned together with the Kennedy family for the better part of four years, but I have had no contact with him since I retired twenty-one years ago ... I continue to be impressed with your interest in political affairs and the Kennedy assassination in particular. You knew, I'm sure, that the Secret Service is convinced that the lone assassin was Lee Harvey Oswald and that it was not a conspiracy. He definitely was the only person who fired any shots at the President!"

Born in Rainier, Ore., Oct. 3, 1923, Lynn was raised in Gaston, Ore., graduating from Gaston Union High School and Pacific University in

Forest Grove, Ore., where he studied music and secondary education. Lynn later studied law at George Washington University. Lynn entered the Navy during World War II in July 1943, graduating from the U.S. Navy Reserve Midshipman School at Northwestern University, Chicago, Ill., and was commissioned Ensign. As a Lieutenant, L.G., he served on a Navy Amphibious Ship, USSLCI (L) 952 from April 1944 until July 1946, and from December 1945 as her Commanding Officer, participating in the Allied forces invasion of France. Returning home upon discharge from the Navy, Lynn taught high school English, Spanish and physical education in Forest Grove and Tillamook, Ore., until 1950.[2]

On June 4, 1951, Lynn accepted a position within the Department of Treasury and the U.S. Secret Service and in December of 1955, he became a special agent within that service. During his years with the Secret Service, Lynn had the honor of protecting many presidents and their families. While in Washington, D.C., Lynn was assigned to protective details for presidents and vice presidents, including Harry Truman, Dwight Eisenhower, Richard Nixon, Gerald Ford, John F. Kennedy, Lyndon B. Johnson and Hubert H. Humphrey. Lynn also was involved in providing for the protection of Jimmy Carter, Ronald Reagan and George H.W. Bush. Lynn was especially close to the John F. Kennedy family, as he was assigned as the head of that protective detail. Lynn was transferred to Great Falls, Mont., with the Secret Service in 1970, where he led the Great Falls field office until his retirement in October 1983.

Lynn Meredith passed away 4/17/2008.[3]

---

2. https://www.youtube.com/watch?v=6-UQc0kCtBE
3. http://www.findagrave.com/cgi-bin/fg.cgi?page=gr&GRid=26180625

81

ROBERT LILLEY

BOB LILLEY

A gent Bob Lilley was a highly respected advance man for the Secret Service. Even before Bob joined the Secret Service, he had quite a background: "Immediately upon graduating Bowdoin [College] he entered the USAir Force serving in Combat Air Police & O.S.I. (Office of Special Investigation) a military investigation unit with duty in Japan, Korea & US implementing counterintelligence & major felony criminal & investigations. While in Japan for 2 yrs. he was O.S.I. Agent liaison for 14 Police Departments. Due to sensitive positions during his tenure he was awarded Top Secret "Q" Clearance Classification dealing with the Atomic Energy Commission and "Crypto" Classification with the Central Intelligence Agency (CIA)."[1]

Bob joined the Secret Service in 1958 and helped protect Presidents Eisenhower thru Reagan, serving on the White House Detail during the Ike and JFK years. In fact, Bob was with President Kennedy from election night until October 1963, a month before Dallas, when he went to the Boston office, rising to SAIC (Bob would later become SAIC of the Kansas City, Missouri, and St. Louis, Missouri field offices). He received

---

1. http://www.legacy.com/obituaries/nwfdailynews/obituary.aspx?pid=177927680

the U.S. Treasury Department's "Superior Performance Award," also the Treasury Department's Special Award for "High Quality Work." In 1971 he became Assistant Special Agent in Charge of the US Treasury Forgery Division. Bob was the Treasury Department's representative on the Federal Executive Board for Government agency heads in Washington, DC. He was considered a top manager for the Secret Service.

When I told this former agent what SAIC Gerald Behn said to me in September 1992, that Kennedy never said a thing about having the agents removed from the limousine (repudiating his own original report), Lilley responded, "Oh, I'm sure he didn't. He was very cooperative with us once he became President. He was extremely cooperative. Basically, 'whatever you guys want is the way it will be.'" In interviews and correspondence on four separate occasions, Lilley reiterated this view. Lilley also refuted the Bishop and Manchester accounts, adding that on a trip with JFK in Caracas, Venezuela, he and "Roy Kellerman rode on the back of the limousine all the way to the Presidential palace" at speeds reaching "50 miles per hour [with the bubbletop on]." Furthermore, Lilley did the advance work for JFK's trip to Naples, Italy in the summer of 1963, in which agents rode on the rear of the limousine.

Fellow agent Don Lawton was especially glowing about Agent Bob Lilley when I spoke to him on 11/15/95: "I thought the world of Bob Lilley – super fantastic guy ... hell of a guy; 'A' number one ... Bob Lilley was one fantastic guy-super agent ... Bob Lilley did the advance up there [Maine, October, 1963] ... tremendous advance agent-great rapport, intelligent." Lawton later wrote the following: "If you spoke with Bob Lilley, as you stated, then you can take whatever information he passed on to you as gospel. I must say, in all candor, of all the people I have met and worked alongside in law enforcement, Bob Lilley stands head and shoulders above all of them. I sincerely mean that."[2]

On 9/27/92, I contacted Lilley, learning that the agent was gone from the White House Detail after October 1963. While revealing that Agent Kellerman was his shift leader ("He was a peach"), and that he "was quite close to Roy and June Kellerman," Lilley was unable to go into further discussion about the events of 11/22/63 at the time. Lilley garnered much respect from former colleagues in correspondence with the author; notably, Don Lawton and Walt Coughlin. During later interviews conducted on 9/21/93 and 6/7/96, I brought up the cancelled Chicago motorcade of 11/2/63. Lilley responded, "I don't know if he (JFK) would cancel

---

2. Letter to author dated 11/22/97.

a motorcade," adding further to the notion that the motorcade was can-celled by the Secret Service for JFK, due to mortal threats. Interesting-ly, Mr. Lilley saw JFK October 19, 1963 at the University of Maine and during the Harvard-Columbia football game, a little over a month before Dallas. In addition, Lilley had been on JFK's 3/23/63 trip to Chicago, a model of proper security in sharp contrast to 11/22/63.[3]

Lilley passed away 2/19/2016.

---

3. RIF #154-10003-10012: Chicago trip 3/23/63 Secret Service survey report.

82

JOHN CAMPION

JOHN CAMPION

Agent John Campion was a respected veteran of the Secret Service, serving from the FDR era until the LBJ days. Martha Bowden, the niece of the late former agent John Campion, wrote to me on 5/5/15:

"My uncle was John Campion, who was a secret service agent for Roosevelt, Truman, Eisenhower, Kennedy and Johnson (in an administrative role for Johnson). His widow, my aunt, is currently 100. He was one of the good guys. He never told us much about what he did – he honored the confidence that was placed in him and was later upset when several agents wrote books or gave interviews that he felt were inappropriate. He was asked many times for interviews or to write a biography but would have none of that. Visiting his widow recently, I asked if she would write his biography and she said no, she would honor John's wishes not to tell stories. John died on July 4, 1983 in Southern Pines, North Carolina – a heart attack while playing golf. He was an avid golfer and played golf with Eisenhower, and played poker with Truman – Truman would sign the dollar bills when he lost. He was also in Warm Springs when Roosevelt died and carried the coffin to the train. He had moved out of the White House detail in 1962 to an administrative role as a step to become the

Director of the Secret Service – his widow had it confirmed from several sources after Kennedy was assassinated. He never got that job but she did tell me that he had to replace several of the White House detail under Johnson because the agents disliked LBJ so much. John never spoke of the assassination. But he did tell me that he had been asked personally by Bobby Kennedy to head up his security detail when Bobby decided to run for President. He said he told him no, because he knew that Bobby would never follow John's instructions on security."

Campion served on the White House Detail during the Roosevelt, Truman, Eisenhower and Kennedy administrations. In October 1962, he moved on to a position in headquarters as Aide to the Assistant Chief for Security, the position he retired from during the LBJ era.

The *Naples (FL) Daily News* reported on 2/27/77:

> He is one of the very few men who have shared the lives and the confidences of five First Families – from Roosevelt, Truman, Eisenhower, Kennedy to Johnson. A man who finds "back-stair" stories and books about the occupants of the White House disgusting and "cheap." Campion and his wife, Georgia Ann, winter in Naples and live in Sea Pines, N.C. He retired from the Secret Service Jan. 1, 1966. The former Secret Service agent is firmly convinced from his first-hand study of ail the Kennedy assassination official films, papers and studies that the Warren Commission was negligent in not mentioning strongly that the assassination may have been a plot organized by the Communists."
>
> Campion pointed out these known facts: "First, Oswald was a defector; he married a Russian woman; he was logged coming out of the Cuban embassy in Mexico; and was seen passing out pro-Castro literature in New Orleans. No one has ever answered the question "where did he (Oswald) get the money to join a Rifle club or money for his guns and ammunition?"
>
> He believes that the evidence pointing to a Communist plot, by the Russians, by the Cuban-Communists or by the Chinese, or any combination of these parties, is too strong to ignore. "Millions of dollars could be saved the taxpayers if a new investigation would make a statement on this possibility now. Ignorance has caused all this furor over the new investigation," Campion said.
>
> Campion, a native of Rhode Island, began his career with the Secret Service after eight years with the Rhode Island state police. His first post was with the New York office where he was detailed for weekend duty at Hyde Park when FDR was in residence. From

this post he went to the White House detail. "I think Roosevelt was a distinguished and an austere man; a man who first impressed you with a sense of the regal, but after you got to know him well, he loved to kid."

Mrs. Roosevelt gave him "the first education in the role that women can play in this great country of ours. I was very much impressed with Mrs. Roosevelt. I admired her in that she could take so much of the burden of the Presidency off him. She was brilliant, sincere and a great humanitarian." He compares "Truman with Abraham Lincoln. A self- made man but a well- read President - one of the best in our history." Campion said, "I get burned up with all this current stuff about Harry S. Truman and his profanity. He was a gentleman!" Mrs. Truman was much like "my own mother. She would always take one last look before you went out the door to see that your tie was straight, your hair combed and that you didn't have a cold."

"Eisenhower was stern on the outside but warm, inside. He did a fine job with the Presidency and labored under handicaps the public never understood. His party submarined him with the Sherman Adams thing." Mrs. Campion remembers Mamie Eisenhower with love as the greatest of the First Ladies. "Mrs. Eisenhower always saw to it that cards or flowers were sent to the families of anyone on the White House staff who might have been ill or hospitalized She invited the wives of agents to the Gettysburg farm, offering them tours of the house."

Campion says, "I can't speak too highly of the Eisenhowers. Kennedy was an entirely different matter. Perhaps my age got to me – here were the First Family younger than I was for the first time." He remembered while working for President Eisenhower during a campaign stop in Des Moines. Kennedy came up to Campion and asked to be introduced to Ike. Ike said 'Sure' and the agent was the first man to introduce Ike to JFK. Was Kennedy a ladies' man? "If he was, I never saw it," Campion declares.

"Although he was like a magnet. We'd have to rope off the pews when he went to Mass – the women coming from Communion would scramble after him, running up to kiss him." Campion thinks that people who have worked in the White House and then write "gossip" features or books are betraying a trust.

"They are either vindictive or out for a quick buck. Most people don't understand the relationship between the agents and members of the First Family. The agents are with the First Family all hours of the day, every day and everywhere. I believe that the primary duty of the agent, after the physical protection, is never make them look bad. Official duty or not, do it! You put the best interest of the Presidency first. After all, any person should be proud to work in the White House. Even if you have just a few little things to do, you do them well."

Campion must have done those many "little" things well as his request for retirement was denied because President Kennedy wanted him to remain on the Presidential detail. The Campion home is full of personal notes, mementos, pictures and awards from his unusual career. Most agents serve a two to four year assignment at the White House. Campion himself originated or modified many of the protective techniques now being used by the Secret Service such as helicopter coverage and the coordination between White House signal corps and local police to set up inner and outer perimeter communications when traveling.

Campion makes about 30 speeches per year to civic groups about his White House service. The former Secret Service agent has traveled millions of miles with the Presidents. He has met Stalin, Khruschev, DeGaulle, Churchill and the Queen of England.

He is a man with valid advice to give to incoming presidents. "The trouble with the White House Staff is they begin looking into the other man's garden. First they put one toe in, then two toes, then the foot and then jump in with both feet thinking they can do the other man's job better than he. That's because the other man may be a little closer to the President. They can't be satisfied unless they are the guy next to the President. What they fail to see is that they are only hurting the man in the chair. The only job in the White House is to see that the President is not hurt – to make him look good. To protect the Presidency." John Campion knew world figures."

Indeed.

83

ROBERT JAMISON

BOB JAMISON

Agent Robert Jamison, who served from 1951 to 1971 and was a member of the White House Detail during the Truman era, and figures into the Joseph Milteer saga.

As the HSCA reported: "The Secret Service failed to follow up fully on a threat in Miami, also in November 1963. On November 9, 1963, an informant for the Miami police, William Somersett, had secretly recorded a conversation with a rightwing extremist named Joseph A. Milteer, who suggested there was a plot in existence to assassinate the President with a high-powered rifle from a tall building. Miami Police intelligence officers met with Secret Service agents on November 12 and provided a transcript of the Somersett recording. It read in part:

> **SOMERSETT:** I think Kennedy is coming here November 18 to make some kind of speech. I don't know what it is, but I imagine it will be on TV.

> **MILTEER:** You can bet your bottom dollar he is going to have a lot to say about the Cubans; there are so many of them here.

> **SOMMERSETT:** Well, he'll have a thousand bodyguards, don't worry about that.

MILTEER: The more bodyguards he has, the easier it is to get him.

SOMERSETT: What?

MILTEER: The more bodyguards he has, the easier it is to get him.

SOMERSETT: Well, how in the hell do you figure would be the best way to get him?

MILTEER: From an office building with a high-powered rifle....

SOMERSETT: They are really going to try to kill him?

MILTEER: Oh, yeah; it is in the working....

SOMERSETT: ... Hitting this Kennedy is going to be a hard proposition. I believe you may have figured out a way to get him, the office building and all that. I don't know how them Secret Service agents cover all them office buildings everywhere he is going. Do you know whether they do that or not?

MILTEER: Well, if they have any suspicion, they do that, of course. But without suspicion, chances are that they wouldn't.

During the meeting at which the Miami Police Department provided this transcript to the Secret Service, it also advised the Secret Service that Milteer had been involved with persons who professed a dislike for President Kennedy and were suspected of having committed violent acts, including the bombing of a Birmingham, Alabama church in which four young girls had been killed. They also reported that Milteer was connected with several radical rightwing organizations and traveled extensively throughout the United States in support of their views.

Although it would have been possible to read Milteer's threats as hollow speculation, the Secret Service did not dismiss them lightly. The case agent in the Miami office forwarded a report and a recording of the Somersett-Milteer conversation to the Protective Research Section. Robert I. Bouck, special agent in charge of PRS, then requested that the Miami office make discreet inquiries about Milteer.

On November 18, 1963, Special Agent Robert Jamison of the Miami Secret Service office, in an interview with Somersett, had him place a telephone call to Milteer at his home in Valdosta, Ga., to verify he was in that city. In addition, Jamison learned that Somersett did not know the identity of any violence-prone associates of Milteer in the Miami area. The November 26 Miami field office report indicated that the information gathered "was furnished the agents making the advance arrangements before the visit of the President ..." PRS then closed the case, and copies of its report were sent to the Chief of Secret Service and to field offices in Atlanta, Philadelphia, Indianapolis, Nashville, Washington, and Miami.

The Milteer threat was ignored by Secret Service personnel in planning the trip to Dallas. PRS Special Agent-in-Charge Bouck, who was notified on November 8 that the President would visit Miami on November 18, told the committee that relevant PRS information would have been supplied to the agents conducting advance preparations for the scheduled trip to Miami, but no effort was made to relay it to Special Agent Winston G. Lawson, who was responsible for preparations for the trip to Dallas, or to Forrest Sorrels, special agent-in-charge of the Dallas office. Nor were Sorrels or any Secret Service agent responsible for intelligence with respect to the Dallas trip informed of the Milteer threat before November 22, 1963.

Following the assassination, Somersett again met with Milteer. Milteer commented that things had gone as he had predicted. Somersett asked if Milteer actually had known in advance of the assassination or had just been guessing. Milteer asserted that he had been certain beforehand about the inevitability of the assassination."[1]

During an HSCA interview with agent Robert J. Jamison, the former agent stated that "the threat of November 18, 1963 was posed by a mobile, unidentified rifleman with a high- powered rifle fitted with a scope."[2]

In addition, an interview with former agent Lubert F. deFreese states that "a threat did surface in connection with the Miami trip ... there was an active threat against the President of which the Secret Service was aware in November 1963 in the period immediately prior to JFK's trip to Miami made by a "group of people."[3]

In addition to this threat information, and separate from the Joseph Milteer threat of 11/9/63, a CO2 PRS file, released to the HSCA on 5/3/78 and available to all of us only now is the specific name of another individual who made a threat against JFK on 11/18/63: John Warrington (Sam Kinney also told me of an unspecified "organized crime" threat pertaining to this same trip).

Jamison admitted during his 2/28/1978 HSCA interview that he was debriefed by Chief Inspector Jackson Krill to not discuss the internal operations of the Secret Service.[4]

1. HSCA Final Report, pages 232-233.
2. HSCA document180- 10074-10394.
3. HSCA document 180-10083-10419.
4. http://www.reopenkennedycase.org/apps/forums/topics/show/13339215-robert-j-jamison-hsca-interview

WARREN "WOODY" TAYLOR

Agent Warren "Woody" Taylor was in the motorcade when President Kennedy was assassinated on 11/22/63 (as a member of the VP LBJ Detail) and he was the Assistant SAIC of PPD when President Ford escaped an assassination attempt on 9/22/75. In fact, Taylor made a statement on the matter:

> At approximately 3:25 P.M. (PDT) as President Ford was departing the St. Francis Hotel and was entering his limousine, a single gunshot was fired in his proximity. Immediately thereafter a white, female, approximately 47 years old, Sara Jane Moore, was arrested by the San Francisco Police Department and the Secret Service. A .38-caliber revolver was taken from Ms. Moore. She was arrested and Moore admitted to the Secret Service that she had fired the shot from a revolver that she said she had purchased earlier today. The affidavit also quoted her as having said that she had seen the President coming out of the hotel and "was surprised that she had so much time.

(Interestingly, Donald H. Rumsfeld, the White House Chief of Staff, later to become President George W. Bush's Secretary of Defense, gave the following account of what had happened: As soon as the shot was heard, two Secret Service agents, Ron Pontius [like Taylor, another Texas trip veteran] and Jack Merchant, pushed the President toward the sidewalk. Mr. Rumsfeld crouched beside them. Within moments, Mr. Rumsfeld recalled later, they all got into the President's limousine and crouched on the floor in the passenger compartment as the car sped through downtown San Francisco at 70 miles an hour. After several minutes, the President and the others seated themselves in the car and Mr. Ford asked that his wife, Betty, be advised that he was all right.)[1]

Warren Woody Taylor gave an oral history to the Sixth Floor Museum on 10/14/05. He stated he was born 3/9/36 in Dayton, KY, joined agency in August 1961, and retired in 1982. He claimed to have heard three shots, all of which originated from 6th floor of Texas School Book Depository. Interestingly, Dallas was the first time – and, obviously, the last time – he was in a motorcade with JFK. From Taylor's Secret Service report, we learn the following detail: "[After the first shot] Out of the corner of my eye and off slightly to the rear of our car, I noticed what now seems to me might have been a short piece of streamer flying in the air close to the ground ... I thought that it was a firecracker going off."[2] This was a missed shot, at least one more than the mandated official count of three, making it possible for Oswald to be the sole assassin. In yet another example of important information blithely ignored by the investigations, this was overlooked until the author noted it back in 1991.[3] Taylor rose to ASAIC of PPD during the Carter era.[4] Taylor was one of the very few still-living agents from the Kennedy/Johnson era I was unable to find due to the commonality of his last name.

---

1. *New York Times*, 9/23/75.
2. 18 H 782.
3. Author Walt Brown credits the author with this discovery in his 1995 volume *Treachery In Dallas*, pages 31, 325-326 (although this information was also revealed in *Mortal Error*, Menninger's book came out a year after this author first reported this overlooked bit of information).
4. http://www.jimmycarterlibrary.gov/documents/diary/1977/d051877t.pdf

LESLIE COFFELT

Leslie Coffelt was an officer of the White House Police, considered to be a member of the Uniformed Division of the Secret Service, who was killed while defending President Harry Truman against an armed attack on November 1, 1950 at Blair House, where the president was living during renovations at the White House. Coffelt is still the only Secret Service member to be killed while defending the President.

Coffelt was wounded during the assassination attempt, which two Puerto Rican nationalists carried out. Though mortally wounded by three bullets, Coffelt returned fire moments later and killed one of the attackers with a single shot to the head. The other was convicted by a federal jury and sentenced to death; Truman commuted the sentence to life imprisonment and the man was released from jail in 1979.

Coffelt was buried in Arlington National Cemetery on November 4, 1950 in Section 17, Site 17719-59. His epitaph reads, "White House Policeman: Who Gave His Life in Defense of the President of the United States During an Assassination Attempt at the Blair House, Washington, D.C." A plaque at the Blair House commemorates Coffelt's sacrifice, heroism, and fidelity to his duty and his country. The day room for the U.S. Secret Service's Uniformed Division at the Blair House is named for Coffelt as well. Very good biographical information and research on Coffelt can be found in the 2005 book by Stephen Hunter and John Bainbridge, Jr. *American Gunfight: The Plot To Kill Harry Truman – And The Shoot-Out That Stopped It.*

86

JOHN MARSHALL

Agent John Marshall served on the White House Detail during the FDR and Truman eras. Before that, he had served with fellow agents Stu Stout and Floyd Boring in the Pennsylvania State Police (Marshall served most of his six and-a-half years in the Pennsylvania State Police with Floyd Boring before entering the Secret Service on 6/30/41 and maintained regular contact with him). [1] During the 2/22/78 House Select Committee on Assassinations (HSCA) interview of Miami Special Agent In Charge John Marshall, former White House Detail agent who conducted all the advance work on President Kennedy's frequent trips to Palm Beach, the former agent had something stunning to relate: "Twice during the interview, Mr. Marshall mentioned that, for all he knew, someone in the Secret Service could possibly have been involved in the assassination. This is not the first time an agent has mentioned the possibility that a conspiracy existed, but it is the first time that an agent has acknowledged the possibility that the Secret Service could have been involved." Marshall also stated that a stick of dynamite was discovered on the motorcade route by the Miami Police Department after JFK's Orange Bowl speech to the Bay of Pigs brigade in 1962.[2] Marshall stated that he and fellow Miami office agent Robert Jamison knew about the Joseph Milteer threat information before Dallas.

1. *Reading Eagle*, 10/7/48.
2. RIF# 180-10074-10393.

During his 9/18/96 ARRB interview, fellow agent Floyd Boring related the following: "When shown the HSCA summary of its interview with Miami SAIC John Marshall (specifically, Marshall's twice expressed opinion that there may have been a Secret Service conspiracy), Mr. Boring expressed surprise at those sentiments and said he had never heard that opinion expressed by SAIC Marshall (a personal friend of his from their previous association as Pennsylvania State Troopers) before."

Marshall served as SAIC of the Miami field office from 1950 until 1971.

87

JACK WARNER

A gent Jack Warner had quite a career. He served on the White House Detail during the Eisenhower and JFK eras (rising to Inspector during the Johnson era), then launched a very long career as a Secret Service spokesman and consultant, becoming Public Affairs Director and top communications official. In fact, Warner was one of the advisors/technical consultants to the 1993 Clint Eastwood blockbuster *In The Line of Fire*. Warner's communications career spanned the 1960's[1], 1970's, 1980's, and 1990's – former Director Stu Knight twice balked at a full interview with me, both times advising that I speak to Jack Warner instead (I never did)!

Warner was interviewed a whopping *four* times by author William Manchester for his massive best-seller *The Death of a President* (6/2/64, 11/18/64, 2/5/65, and 5/12/65, the last date being identical to the date of Blaine's interview). Warner was the agency spokesman during the two attempts on the life of Gerald Ford in 1975 and the attempt on Ronald Reagan in 1981. Warner stated, after the first attempt on President Ford on 9/5/75, "We are not anticipating any dramatic changes in our methods of providing security."[2] Ford was almost assassinated again on 9/22/75.

1. *New York Times*, 11/8/69.
2. *Daytona Beach Morning Journal*, 9/7/75.

Previously, Warner officially denied that the Secret Service was gathering dirt for the Nixon White House on political opponents, yet, as it turned out, that is exactly what happened.[3] Warner also denied agent Abraham Bolden's claim of a Chicago plot to kill Kennedy, as well as offering this rather lame statement after the attempt on President Reagan:

> The Secret Service was at a loss to describe how Hinckley had managed to work his way to the front of the crowd of reporters outside the Hilton, especially since all of the newsmen wore, in full view, necklaces of special cards and credentials. "The onus is on our shoulders," said Secret Service spokesman John Warner.[4]

The first women special agents, transferred from Nixon's old Executive Protection Service (later known as the Uniformed Division) of the Secret Service were hired 12/15/71: University of Wisconsin and Milwaukee native Holly Hufschmidt [a nurse in Vietnam, later infiltrated John Kerry's group VVAW], Beloit College graduate Laurie Anderson from Jersey City, NJ, University of Maryland graduate Phyllis Schantz of Rome, NY [the very first woman Secret Service officer, sworn in 9/15/70], Salt Lake City Utah's Kathryn Clark (originally from Colorado), and present author and Ohio University graduate Sue Baker of Oak Ridge, Tennessee, who spent two weeks at a Summer camp in 1971 with JFK's daughter Caroline. Former Kennedy Detail agent Jack Warner told the press on 11/25/71 that the women were "very talented and kinda cute."

Agent Jack Warner (sunglasses) jogs besides JFK's limo in New Orleans

3. *The Secret Histories: Hidden Truths That Challenged the Past and Changed the World* by John S. Friedman (2005), page 499. See Bob Newbrand, above.
4. *New York Daily News*, March 31, 1981.

88

HAMILTON BROWN

Agent Percy Hamilton "Ham" Brown served in the Army in Germany from 1954-1956. Upon his discharge from the Army he returned to West Virginia and attended Concord College, graduating in 1960. In 1961, "Ham" joined the US Secret Service and was assigned to the Washington Field Office. In 1962 he was assigned to Joseph Kennedy, returning to the White House detail in 1964. He was assigned to Presidents Johnson and Nixon. In 1970, "Ham" transferred to Chicago for eight years, returning to the VP detail under VP's Mondale and Bush. "Ham" retired from the Secret Service in 1981 and became a member of the Association of Former Agents of the US Secret Service (AFAUSSS). He held every elected position except Vice President and was elected to Executive Secretary, a position he held for 17 years.[1]

Ham Brown appears twice in my work. On 9/30/92, I received the infamous call from the then-Executive Secretary of the Association of Former Agents of the United States Secret Service (AFAUSSS),"Percy" Hamilton Brown, angrily telling the author to "cease and desist from contacting any more of my associates … I gave you no authority to do so." As former agent Bob Lilley me, "Who died and made him boss?" Likewise, Sam Kinney told me, "Hey, it's a free country."

---

1. http://www.legacy.com/obituaries/washingtonpost/obituary.aspx?pid=166843821

The other instance involves the work of Gerald Posner. On page 503 of his book *Case Closed,* Gerald Posner writes:

"David Whipple, president of the association of retired intelligence agents, HAMILTON BROWN, WHO HOLDS THE SAME PO-SITION FOR RETIRED SECRET SERVICE AGENTS, and Les Stanford, for Alcohol, Tobacco, and Firearms, were DILIGENT IN FINDING THOSE LONG-RETIRED FROM THEIR RESPEC-TIVE AGENCIES" (emphasis added).[2]

So what's the problem? Well, as someone who has interviewed and corresponded with many retired Secret Service agents (and document-ed each and every contact), I was amazed to find not one specific agent cited in the entire text or endnotes of *Case Closed* as being interviewed/ contacted by Mr. Posner. Knowing full well how Hamilton Brown does not like dealing with the press on controversial topics, my skepticism rose to a high level (examples of Brown's evasiveness are: 1) my attempt to interview Brown at length, 2) *Washington Post* reporter Ann Eisele's un-successful attempt to do the same and 3) Brown's anger at the agents who spoke to myself, Seymour Hersh, and Kenneth Starr.

You see, even though I knew Posner did contact, on his own, one for-mer agent, Floyd M. Boring, a major planner of the Texas trip[3], Boring told me, in no uncertain terms, that he told Posner nothing at all – he merely forwarded him on to Hamilton Brown.

In addition, no other agent I contacted spoke to Posner (including Sam Kinney, Jerry Behn, Rufus Youngblood, Jerry Kivett, John Joe Howl-ett, Robert Steuart, Forrest Sorrels, James Rowley, Arthur Godfrey, and Win Lawson, pretty important Secret Service contacts to the events of 11/22/63, don't you think?).

OK, so what if maybe Mr. Posner chose, for whatever reason, not to reveal his interviews with the former agents in his book (in sharp con-trast to his documentation of every other alleged interview), you say? This is a possibility, right? Well, this is where the matter rested ... until I e-mailed Gerald Posner on 3/4/98 and asked him directly the following two questions:

---

2. On the very same page, Posner also credits Secret Service Archivist Mike Sampson, a young man not even born when the assassination occurred and, to make matters worse, misspells his last name as "Simpson."
3. See author's article in *The Fourth Decade* research journal, May 1995, as well as chapter one of *Survivor's Guilt.*

1) How many former Secret Service agents did you speak to?

2) Specifically, what were their names?

This is the alarming response I received (printed below, exactly as he wrote it):

> Dear Mr. Palamara – Without checking my files (you're asking about research six and seven years ago), I don't remember interviewing any SS agents for the record, and I don't remember off hand even talking to any for background. I am almost certain I merely relied on orig. docs, or the agents' original interviews and/or testimony. Hope it helps, Gerald Posner

"Hope it helps," indeed! This helps demonstrate, once again, some of the tactics used by Gerald Posner for his book. He "contacted" Boring, who told him nothing other than Hamilton Brown's phone number, and then he (presumably) "contacted" Brown, who apparently told him to get lost, if Posner's recent e-mail to me is accurate, which I strongly believe it is. Still, he can technically hold on to the claim that he did indeed "speak," "locate," and "contact" former Secret Service agents (plural: two). Although the fine print is: they told him nothing that made it into his book, despite the obvious attempt to demonstrate the opposite as shown above (*Case Closed*, page 503). Posner's statements to me were later confirmed to researcher W. Tracy Parnell.

Brown was interviewed for the 1999 book *Just Jackie: Her Private Years* by Edward Klein (regarding Clint Hill), *Star* magazine 6/28/94 (regarding agent Jack Walsh), ABC television 1/28/98 (regarding the Seymour Hersh book), and *Dateline* NBC 3/28/98 (again, regarding the Hersh book). Brown also appeared in media stories venting his anger about the Secret Service having to testify during the Kenneth Starr/ Monica Lewinsky matter (and Hersh), an example of which can be found in the *Los Angeles Times* of 1/28/98: "I have a hell of problem with it. It's going to make the job tremendously difficult in the future… The relationship [between the president and his agents] is based on trust and confidence," Brown said. "He has to know he can talk in their presence and have total trust the agents will not pass on anything." Like Jack Warner, Brown became something of a Secret Service spokesman throughout the 1990's and early millennium.

Brown passed away 9/2/2013.

89

JIM JOHNSON

JIM JOHNSON

The *Beaufort Gazette* reported on 2/17/2011:

The Kentucky native attended Centre College and worked for IBM for two years after school. A friend told him about the Secret Service, and he applied. The Secret Service was small back then; there were only about 250 agents across the country. It's best known for the protection division. But when Johnson was accepted, he was placed in the Louisville field division, investigating forgeries, counterfeiting and fraud.

Soon enough, he received a 30-day temporary assignment in Washington, D.C., and in August 1960 got a permanent transfer.

He was assigned to former President Dwight D. Eisenhower. His first trip was to follow the president to Augusta, Ga., for a golf expedition. The next trip was similar -- golf in Palm Springs, Calif.

The trips weren't the most exciting, but, as he recalls, he was just a farm boy from Kentucky and suddenly he was traveling across the country with the president.

Johnson stayed in the White House once John F. Kennedy was sworn in. He has fond memories of the young president. Kennedy was friendly and engaging, Johnson said. He knew the agents by name. He'd strike up conversations on his weekend vacations to Hyannis Port, Mass., asking about families or football. One Christmas, he invited the families of the agents assigned to him to Palm Beach, Fla. There, the Kennedys mingled with the agents' wives and children over punch, wine and cookies.

DECIDING TO LEAVE

The job of a Secret Service agent is inherently stressful. Some of Johnson's days were filled with lots of public interaction, where tense agents scanned crowds while the president reached for outstretched hands. But other times, the job might seem mundane. Johnson would sometimes get stuck on the midnight shift with nothing much to do but patrol the White House grounds. But he was always on alert, even if the setting appeared relaxed to everyone else.

He left Kennedy in August 1963. The job was engaging, but the long weekend trips took a toll.

"I wasn't seeing much of my family," he said. "It was time to move on."

He returned to the Louisville field office. Kennedy was assassinated just a few months later. Johnson and his fellow agents gathered around the television, like millions of their fellow Americans, when they heard the news.

"I was sick," he said.

He received an assignment in the wake of the assassination to head to Texas. Secret Service agents were assigned to protect gunman Lee Harvey Oswald's relatives. Johnson stayed for several weeks with Oswald's wife, Marina, in Carrollton, Texas. The Russian native spoke broken English and was overwhelmed by the situation, Johnson said.

The assignment was rather uneventful. Marina and her children stayed in their house, leaving mostly for dentist or doctor appointments. Once, in their downtime, Johnson talked with Marina about the Russian language. She wrote the Russian alphabet on a ruled sheet of paper. Johnson still has it in a scrap book.

Congress authorized the protection of major presidential and vice-presidential candidates in 1968 after the assassination of Robert Kennedy. Because he had experience, Johnson was regularly called back for special duty. He guarded vice presidential candidates Edmund Muskie and then Shriver. Johnson said Shriver was friendly and talkative – but an absolute pain to guard. He would often go off script. "I've got to meet the people," he'd say and head toward a crowd.

Johnson spent time in the Columbia field office and the D.C. office before retiring in 1986 at age 52. He did some consulting work and helped organize security at the 1988 Republican National Convention.

He moved to Moss Creek about 20 years ago. In his office, he has reminders of his time in the Secret Service, including a few framed Christmas cards from presidents. Also framed on his wall are photos of his son, Larry, with former Presidents Bill Clinton and George W. Bush. He followed in his father's footsteps and became an agent, even getting to White House duty."

90

BILL DUNCAN

BILL DUNCAN

gent Bill Duncan said during his 10/15/05 Sixth Floor Museum oral history that JFK was a "real fine gentleman with a magnetic personality" who was "very friendly" and "very concerned about the people around him – a real pleasure to work with" who was also "easy to work very hard for." Most importantly, the former agent stated that President Kennedy "let you do your job." PRS Agent Dale Wunderlich wrote to me on 2/6/2009 and mentioned Duncan a few times: "I was reading through some of your information on the Internet and in one location where you mention me doing an Intelligence advance in Fort Worth, you indicate that there is no record of me being on that trip. I can assure you that I prepared a report that would have been submitted to SAIC Robert Bouck when I returned from Texas. I traveled to Fort Worth from Washington where I joined Bill Duncan and Ned Hall. The advance man for the Vice President was Jerry Kivett. I was the only person from Protective Research Division and I coordinated the electronic, technical and explosives sweeps with local military agencies at Carswell AFB, the Hotel Texas and for the speech in front of the Hotel Texas the morning of November 22, 1963. I also gathered the names of the people that worked at the Hotel Texas and had them run through Texas state criminal records and NCIC.

In addition, it was my job to issue ID pins for the employees at the hotel. Although Ned is no longer with us, Bill Duncan, Jerry Kivett and Mike Howard (Dallas FO) and myself have often discussed our advance in Fort Worth.[1] I might comment that Bill Duncan (Lead PPD advance) and I remain very good friends and in fact worked together for several years after leaving the Secret Service. The local DNC advance man from Texas that we worked with was Bedford Winn. He was a lawyer from Dallas. On the day after the funeral, I drove from WDC to Dallas and transported a car load of technical equipment for screening mail that was being sent to Marina Oswald and the Dallas Field Office. I assisted with the investigation in various capacities and also served on Marina Oswalds' protective detail. I returned to DC with Marina Oswald on Sunday February 2, 1964 and I believe she testified before the Warren Commission on the following day."

Duncan later became the ASAIC of the White House Detail during the Nixon era, primarily guarding the Nixon family, and was let go via the machinations of Nixon aides Haldeman and Erlichman in 1973.[2] Duncan went on to the Foreign Dignitary Protective Division (FDPD).[3]

---

1. A captioned photo of Agent Bill Duncan can be found in the *Fort Worth Press*, 11/22/63. Interestingly, the Secret Service's Final Survey Report for the Fort Worth leg of the Texas tour lists Agent's Bill Duncan, Ned Hall, and Howard as assisting in the advance arrangements. However, Howard is listed as "James M. Harwood."

2. *Confessions of an Ex-Secret Service Agent*, page 58; *Five Presidents* by Clint Hill, pp. 403-404; see also *Protecting the President*, pp. 217-218.

3. *In The Secret Service* by Jerry and Carolyn Parr (2013), pages 171-173, 175.

91

ED Z. TUCKER

Agent Ed Z. Tucker was a well-respected agent who served on the White House Detail during the Eisenhower and Kennedy eras (at first being a part of the Kiddie Detail[1]) before heading to the Chicago field office.[2] At the time of the assassination, the White House Detail was in a weakened condition due to recent resignations and transfers. Nearly one third of the 34 agents on the White House Detail assigned to protect JFK, including a number of experienced agents, had recently resigned or been transferred.

"In the past two months alone, eleven of the most experienced agents on the Kennedy Detail had been replaced. It had been a purely personal choice by the agents – they'd requested, and had been granted, transfers to field offices … Nearly a third of the agents had decided they just couldn't do it anymore. Too many missed birthdays and anniversaries, too many holidays away from home." (This means that despite several known plots to assassinate the president, the Secret Service nonetheless was permitting numbers of its experienced agents to leave the Detail. Shouldn't it have been obvious under the circumstances that allowing so many experienced agents to depart was unwise?). Based on years of intensive research, here are the experienced veteran agents who left in 1963: Tom Fridley, Bill Skiles, Scott Trundle, Milt Wilhite, Tom Behl, Charlie Kunkel (Summer 1963), Jimmy Johnson (Aug 1963), Ed Z. Tucker (Summer 1963), Jerry Dolan (Fall 1963), Bob Lilley (Fall 1963), Larry Newman (Oct 1963), Anthony Sherman, Jr. (Oct 1963), Thomas B. Shipman (DIED

---

1. *The Kennedy Detail* by Gerald Blaine, pages 49-50; *Secret Service Chief* by U.E. Baughman (1962), page 190.
2. *Daily Herald*, 2/3/75.

10/14/63), and Ken Wiesman (10/23/63). The new agents were Robert L. Kollar, Robert R. Burke (Summer 1963), Radford Jones (Summer 1963), George W. Hickey (July 1963), Robert R. Faison (Sept 1963), William T. McIntyre (Fall 1963), Chuck Zboril (Fall 1963), Henry J. Rybka (Fall 1963), William Straughn (10/17/63), Bill Bacherman (11/10/63), Dick Metzinger[3] (11/10/63), John J. McCarthy (11/10/63), Roy "Gene" Nunn (11/11/63), Gerald W. O'Rourke (11/11/63), Kent D. Jordan (11/15/63), Andrew M. Hutch (11/18/63), Ed Morey (11/20/63), Dale Keaner (11/23/63), Ken Thompson (11/23/63), Glenn Weaver (11/23/63) and Bill Livingood (11/23/63). Also, PRS agent Glen Bennett was made a temporary agent of the WHD on 11/10/63. Agent Tucker was one of the experienced agent who could have helped protect Kennedy on 11/22/63. Interestingly, Tucker was one of the agents involved in the investigation of Oswald's money order for his rifle at Klein's Sporting Goods of Chicago.[4]

Fellow agent David Grant mentioned Tucker during his HSCA testimony regarding JFK's cancelled 11/2/63 Chicago trip: "Mr. Grant stated that his advance work required him to be present a "great deal" at the local Chicago SS office Headquarters. He indicated that while performing his advance duties out of headquarters, he developed several contacts or associations within the SS and with the Chicago P. D. These contacts included making the acquaintance of Chicago-office Special Agents Abraham Bolden, Conrad Cross, and Edward Tucker; they also included working in close professional association with the Chicago office Acting Special Agent in Charge (ASAIC) Maurice Martineau."[5] Tucker himself mentions the Chicago police surveillance of suspect Thomas Arthur Vallee during his 1/19/78 HSCA interview.[6] Fellow Chicago office agent Conrad Cross told the HSCA "the name Thomas Arthur Vallee was familiar and he remembers it was Ed Tucker's case."[7] Fellow Chicago office agent J. Lloyd Stocks told the HSCA on 4/12/78 that he remembered the Vallee incident but did not take part in the investigation (agents Thomas Strong and Ed Tucker handled the case).[8] Agent Gary M. McLeod told the HSCA that he did recall the name Thomas Arthur Vallee and that Agent Ed Tucker was assigned to the Vallee case that involved guns.[9]

---

3. His daughter Julie wrote to me on 6/19/16 and said: "My dad got sent home unexpectedly from the detail the day before Kennedy was shot"
4. http://www.ctka.net/2015/JosephsMOTimeline.pdf
5. 2/3/78 HSCA interview with Grant [RIF# 180-10082-10451].
6. HSCA RIF # 180-10070-10276.
7. HSCA RIF# 180-10104-10324.
8. HSCA RIF # 18010104-10326.
9. 3/6/78 HSCA interview with McLeod [HSCA RIF# 180-10071-10164].

During JFK's earlier Chicago, IL trip of 3/23/63, according to the Secret Service survey report, six motorcycles surrounded limo, agent Don Lawton rode on JFK's side of the rear of limo, the Mayor's follow-up car with four detectives was used in addition to SS follow-up car, the police were facing crowd (not JFK) on the route, no-one was permitted on the overpasses except four policemen guarding them, and the press/photographers were close to JFK. In addition, assistant press secretary Andy Hatcher was with Malcolm Kilduff and PRS found one threat. Tucker was one of the Chicago office agents involved with security.[10] Former agent George McNally wrote: "... during the Chicago visit, the motorcade was slowed to the pace of a mounted Black Horse Troop, and the police got a warning of Puerto Rican snipers. Helicopters searched the roofs along the way, and no incidents occurred."[11]

Fellow Chicago office agent Joseph Noonan (like Tucker, also a former WHD agent) told the HSCA: "He had participated directly in surveillance involving Tom Mosely and Homer Echevarria ... he and [the] other agents were uneasy that the Cubans might have some ties to the CIA ... a little later they received a call from Headquarters to drop everything on Mosely and Echevarria and send all memos, files, and their notebooks to Washington and not to discuss the case with anyone." Noonan also knew about the Vallee case.[12]

Fellow WHD and Chicago agent Abraham Bolden wrote to me: "The senior agents were "party people" (not so with Clint Hill, Ed Z. Tucker, or Bob Foster)."[13] It is clear, even now during correspondence I have had with the former agent, that Bolden still holds Tucker in high regard. In addition, please see Bolden's fine book *The Echo from Dealey Plaza* (pages 22, 38, 92 and 93). Tucker wrote a positive review of fellow agent Gerald Blaine's book *The Kennedy Detail* (in sharp contrast to Bolden's negative review) and also did a Sixth Floor Museum oral history on 5/6/2015.

TUCKER, LIKE MOST Americans, remembers Kennedy fondly, but with sadness. Transferred to Chicago just months before the young President was assassinated, Tucker easily could have been in the motorcade Nov. 22, 1963, in Dallas. He knows several Secret Service men who were there, and at the time, first thought one of them had been killed.

An excerpt from Tucker's 1975 interview from the *Daily Herald, 2/3/75*:

10. RIF #154-10003-10012.
11. *A Million Miles of Presidents*, page 204.
12. 4/13/78 HSCA interview of Noonan Re: Mosely and Echevaria – 12/19/63 USSS report [HSCA RIF # 180-10087-10136], 11/27/63 USSS report (Martineau to Paterni) [HSCA RIF # 180-1008710137], 12/13/63 USSS report [HSCA RIF # 180-10087-10138]. See also HSCA Report, p. 236.
13. Letter from Bolden to the author, 9/10/93.

92

BROOKS KELLER

Without question, Brooks Keller was one of the most colorful characters the Secret Service has ever employed. You know you are colorful when another colorful character, fellow agent Marty Venker, waxes glowingly about you in his book. Venker wrote: "President Kennedy once summoned the agent to Air Force One and demanded to know when Keller was going to invite him to one or his parties. Keller's bosses were less enchanted with him. He earned a record number of suspensions and disciplinary transfers. Still, probably because he had family wealth, Keller never seemed to sweat getting fired."[1]

Venker further wrote: "He was one of the few agents I'd bum around with after work. He had friends who were writers, theater people, artists. He had a mind of his own and a life outside the Secret Service. Brooks was sort of like the Service's roving minstrel show. He'd liven up one field office, then he'd get bored and have himself kicked somewhere else. The Secret Service was free airfare around the world. He said that his father and grandfather, all the men back in his family, all of them had only lived to be fifty. Brooks wanted to have some fun before he joined them."

Fellow agent Dennis McCarthy wrote: "Simply stated, Brooks is a Secret Service legend.... Perhaps since every male member of his family for generations had died before reaching fifty years old, he just decided to pack all the life he could into the time he had. When he died, at forty nine [sic], friends from all over the world came to his funeral." McCarthy

1. *Confessions of an Ex-Secret Service Agent,* page 83; see also *The Secret Service: The Hidden History of an Enigmatic Agency* by Philip Melanson (2005), pages 284-285.

further noted: "Brooks was known as the most transferred agent in the service. Every time he got into trouble with a supervisor, off he would go to another post."[2]

Agent Darwin Horn wrote me on 3/1/2004: "I recall Brooks Keller and he was a character." Agent Walt Coughlin wrote me on 2/29/2004: "Now Brooks was a legend. When told to catch the next available transport back to the USA from Paris (for a discipline problem) he took the *Queen Mary* (8 days)! There are hundreds of stories about Brooks. He used to brag that he applied for a job as a life guard at Ocean City, Maryland and the Secret Service and was turned down by Ocean City!"

Keller had been a Secret Service agent for 19 years, assigned variously at the White House and at field offices in St. Louis, Oklahoma City, Paris and New York, He was a graduate of Duke University and served in the Navy from 1955 to 1957 as a hospital aide.

Brooks Keller died of a heart attack 4/3/78. He was just 44 years old.[3]

---

2. *Protecting the President*, pages 175-181. Keller is mentioned on page 23 of Gerald Blaine's *The Kennedy Detail*.
3. *New York Times*, 4/4/78.

93

BOB FOSTER

BOB FOSTER

From the *Columbus Dispatch* (Ohio), November 20, 1988: "Robert Foster: Today a U.S. marshal for the Southern District of Ohio, Robert Foster is a 1948 graduate of Worthington High School and a graduate of Ohio State University. He was a Secret Service agent for 22 years, before he retired in 1978. During Kennedy's administration, and for a year after the assassination, his main responsibility was the protection of the president's children, Caroline and John. Not surprisingly, he calls the months following the president's death 'the worst year of my life.' Foster, who was given the family's Welsh terrier, Charlie, when Mrs. Kennedy moved out of the White House, says he will never write a book about his experiences. 'We were there by fate,' he says. In a note to him, Jacqueline Kennedy wrote, 'To Robert Foster, who did so much to make our children happy – how grateful the President was to you and how we will miss you.'"

The *Columbus Dispatch* reported on 6/20/2008: "Decades later, when the plane carrying Caroline's brother crashed into the ocean, it was difficult for the man to watch the news reports. He preferred to remember John Jr. as the little boy he held on outings to the park or who laughed at his made-up stories … Foster guarded the Kennedy children from 1961 until 1964. Kennedy's assassination hit him hard, as it did others who worked closely with the family.

"All of us shed tears," said Thomas Wells, also a former Secret Service agent. "The trauma was severe to everyone." Wells, 74, of Saint Augustine, Fla., said he and Foster were among five agents assigned to Kennedy's family. He recalled Foster had a "dry wit and was fun to be around."

Foster's ex-wife, Peggy, who lives in Worthington, recalled a comment by the president's father, Joseph Kennedy: "Mr. Foster, how does a Republican from Columbus, Ohio, wind up guarding my son – a Democrat from Massachusetts?" Andrew Foster said his father never let politics interfere with his duties, a hallmark of the Secret Service.

"It was the most meaningful service that he rendered to the country," Andrew Foster, 44, of Princeton Junction, N.J., said. "He took an enormous amount of pride in his affiliation to the Secret Service."

After Jacqueline Kennedy and her children moved to New York in 1964, Robert Foster took on other Secret Service assignments, including the Democratic convention in 1968 in Chicago. He retired from the agency in 1978 after serving as the special-agent-in-charge of the Columbus office. He was a marshal from 1981 to 1994 and sergeant-at-arms through 2001."

People magazine reported on 8/2/1999: "Caroline and John Jr. were at home with nanny Maude Shaw when their world changed forever, on Nov. 22, 1963, with John F. Kennedy's assassination. Following the funeral mass three days later in St. Matthew's Cathedral in Washington, D.C., the youngest Kennedy became the focal point, a heartbreaking image that sealed him in the nation's memory forever. During the service the boy got fidgety, so Jackie had agent Foster take him to a small room at the back of the cathedral. There, John was entertained by an Army colonel, who described to the boy what each of the medals on his uniform was for. To thank the officer, John saluted him, something he had seen done countless times at the White House. But John used his left hand. Recalls agent Foster: "The colonel said, 'Oh, no, John, that's not the way to salute. You salute with your right hand.' And he showed him how to salute properly. Then, when we went outside, I was standing right there, and Mrs. Kennedy said as the casket passed by, 'Say goodbye to your daddy, John,' and he whipped up that salute the right way, and I just about fell over. It wasn't coached or anything. He just did it."

After the funeral, in keeping with the Kennedy family tradition of getting on with life in the face of tragedy, Jackie and the children returned to the White House to celebrate John's 3rd birthday with a small party. During the next weeks the Kennedy children were gently led to the realization that their father was not coming home. As Jackie was packing to leave the White House, agent Foster took John for one of their last walks outside. "I was getting him a drink out of the fountain," Foster recalls, "and a photographer came up and took some pictures. John looked him right in the eye and said, 'What are you taking my picture for? My daddy's dead.' The poor photographer started to cry. I cried too."

94

JULIA PIERSON

Julia Pierson served as the 23rd Director of the Secret Service and had one of the shortest tenures, serving only from 3/27/2013 to 10/1/2014. She was also the first female Director. 1988 to 2000, she served on the presidential protective details (PPDs) of Presidents George H. W. Bush, Bill Clinton, and George W. Bush. Between 2000 and 2001, Pierson held the position of special agent in charge of the Office of Protective Operations, and then as deputy assistant director of the Office of Administration from 2001 to 2005. From 2005 to 2006 she served as deputy assistant director of the Office of Protective Operations. From 2006 to 2008 Pierson served as assistant director of the Office of Human Resources and Training. In 2008 Pierson received the Presidential Meritorious Executive Rank Award. From 2008 to her appointment as director in 2013, Pierson served as the chief of staff to the director.

Fellow agent Dan Emmett said: "Barack Obama was going to have a female Secret Service director and that was the end of the story. Julia Pierson was a fine agent. We came on the job together, and I consider her to be a friend. But she was not director material. When she got the position, I feared it would not end well, because she lacked a strong sense of being a leader."[1]

---

1. WND 12/7/14.

As the *Washington Post* reported on 10/2/2014: "the ultimate reason [Pierson resigned] was not because an intruder breached the White House, however incredibly concerning that is. It was not, in the end, because an agent reportedly passed out drunk in a hotel hallway in March, raising questions about her success at bringing the agency's frat-house culture in line. And it was not because of recent reports that it took the White House four days in 2011 (before she took the top job) to realize fired gunshots had actually hit the president's residence.

Rather, the deciding reason she lost the confidence of President Obama appears to be that he found out bad news just minutes before it appeared in the media. That, combined with misleading statements the agency made about the Sept. 19 [2014] breach, speak to an overall breakdown of trust in her leadership. And when that happens, it's nearly impossible for most leaders to recover. The end often comes quick."

95

TOM WELLS

Secret Service agent Tom Wells was one of the three primary agents who guarded the Kennedy children (the other two were Lynn Meredith and Bob Foster). "Helicopters and his dad were like two lollipops in his life," said Tom Wells, a Jacksonville native who was one of three Secret Service agents assigned to guard the Kennedy children. Wells appeared with two other Kennedy agents on *20/20*, reliving his memories of the children that he once spent more time with than his own wife, son and daughter.

When President Kennedy flew on Air Force One, he would travel to Andrews Air Force Base by helicopter from the White House, Wells recalled. John Jr. would race across the South Lawn to ride with his father to the Maryland base, returning later by car. "He would be upset if he couldn't make the trip," Wells recalled.

When Wells heard the news that John Kennedy Jr.'s plane had crashed on July 16, he said his heart went immediately to Caroline. "My pent-up emotions are for her," he said. "They were so close." Wells, who guarded the children from November 1962 until August 1964, spent 22 years in the Secret Service.[1]

Wells appeared on *The Kennedy Detail* documentary in 2010 and participated in part of the book tour, as well. Interestingly, Wells seems to leave the door open to the possibility of a conspiracy in the death of JFK in this online comment he made on a video about Clint Hill: "This man was suffering from considerable false guilt. No one could have stopped the shooter *or shooters*. This is a good man. God bless him."[2]

2. http://vincepalamara.blogspot.com/2012/08/jfk-secret-service-agent-tom-wells.html

96

BILL LIVINGOOD

W ilson "Bill" Livingood is a 33-year veteran of the Secret Service who is best known in his role as Sergeant at Arms for the U.S. House of Representatives (the man who shouts "Mr. Speaker, the President of the United States") from 1/4/95 (Clinton) to 1/17/2012 (Obama). Livingood was responsible for ensuring the security of all members of Congress, all Congressional chambers and facilities, continuity and emergency operations for Congress, and command of the US Capitol Police. Livingood made monumental security enhancements post September 11, 2001.

"Bill Livingood has served the House during the most challenging times faced by anyone who has ever held this demanding position," said Speaker John A. Boehner in a statement, citing the 1998 shootings of two Capitol Police officers, the 9/11 terrorist attacks, the anthrax mailings and the shooting of Representative Gabrielle Giffords, Democrat of Arizona, earlier this year [2011], which initiated a new internal scrutiny of member safety. [Boehner continued:] "Bill's hard-earned and well-deserved retirement will be a real loss for the House," Mr. Boehner said, "but we are grateful that he has assembled an outstanding team of professionals who share his dedication to round-the-clock protection of members, staff and visitors here in the people's House."[1]

---

1.   http://thecaucus.blogs.nytimes.com/2011/12/01/houses-sergeant-at-arms-retires-after-17-years/?_r=0

House Minority Leader Nancy Pelosi (D-Calif.) said in a statement that Livingood's retirement "marks the end of an era defined by Bill's dedicated leadership, sound judgment, and laser-like focus on what is best for the institution, its Members, staff, and visitors."

"In some of the most challenging times for the House, such as 1998's deadly attack on the Capitol Police, 9/11, and this year's [2011] horrifying attempt on Congresswoman Giffords' life, Bill Livingood has been a steady hand," Pelosi said. "He's overseen an era of greater security in the Capitol complex and an expansion in the responsibilities of the Capitol Police, always discharging his duties with bipartisanship and the utmost professionalism."[2]

A veteran of the U.S. Navy, he was appointed as a Special Agent at the Secret Service's Dallas Field Office in 1961 and held supervisory assignments at headquarters and on several protective divisions to include the Presidential Protective Division (PPD).

In 1969, Mr. Livingood was promoted to Assistant to the Special Agent in Charge of the Presidential Protection Division. Five years later, he was promoted to Assistant Special Agent in Charge of the Office of Protective Forces. Mr. Livingood was named Special Agent in Charge of the Houston Field Office in 1982 until his appointment as Deputy Assistant Director, Office of Training in 1986. From 1988 to 1995, he served as the Senior Advisor to three Directors.[3] Livingood had been on VP Hubert Humphrey's detail, as well as serving as an advance agent on President Nixon's detail.[4] In fact, his personal highlight was advancing President Nixon's historic trip to China. "It was almost like being in another planet," he recalls. "China hadn't seen an American in 25 years. We couldn't walk anywhere (without getting mobbed)."[5]

Livingood was interviewed for the 1999 book *Just Jackie: Her Private Years* by Edward Klein (regarding Clint Hill). Livingood told researcher Gary Rowell in 1991: "There were no Secret Service agents on the grassy knoll."[6] Livingood, whom I spoke to in November 1992, wrote to me on 11/19/97: "I served on the White House Detail from November [?] 1963(after the assassination of President Kennedy) until 1972. I was in the Dallas Field office from Aug. 8, 1961 until November 1962, at which time I was transferred to the Vice Presidential [LBJ] Protective Division."

2. *Washington Post*, 12/1/2011.
3. http://capitolwords.org/date/2011/12/16/S8726-3_tribute-to-wilson-bill-livingood/
4. *20 Years in the Secret Service* by Rufus Youngblood (1973), pages 199-210, 233.
5. https://msu.edu/unit/msuaa/magazine/s95/wilson.htm
6. Author's article in the Dec. 1994 *Investigator* research journal; author's interview with Bill Livingood, 11/92; author's phone conversations with Gary Rowell.

In 2005, Livingood attended (along with fellow former agent Jerry Blaine) Clint Hill's son's wedding,[7] as well as, more recently, several other events with Blaine, Hill, and other surviving Kennedy Detail agents.

Livingood was the last agent on active duty when President Kennedy was assassinated.

---

7. Author's interview with Jerry Blaine, 6/10/05.

97

REX SCOUTEN

Former agent Rex Scouten served with distinction as the White House Chief Usher from 1969 to 1986 and as the White House Curator from 1986 to 1997. Scouten served in the United States Army during World War II. He graduated from Michigan State University. From 1947 to 1957, he served in the Secret Service. Known for his protection of (and fondness for) President Truman, Scouten appears in the blockbuster Pulitzer Prize-winning book *Truman* by David McCullough, as well as several television programs about the former president. Scouten also protected Vice President Nixon.

All told, Scouten served 10 different presidents (Truman thru Clinton) in his various roles (Secret Service, Assistant Usher, Chief Usher, Curator). The usher, who oversees the physical White House and its staff, helps spruce up and redecorate the presidential mansion for every new occupant. He must often accommodate the most specific and adamant of tastes, within limits. His duties included the smooth running of state dinners and presiding over major refurbishing projects in the 132-room mansion. At times, he held sway over the most sensitive of perks, including who got bumped despite reservations for the White House tennis court.

As assistant Usher, Scouten said that, among the most difficult duties he undertook was a 1961 state dinner thrown for Pakistani President Ayub Khan. President John F. Kennedy and the first lady hosted the event at George Washington's Mount Vernon estate, 16 miles down the Potomac River from the White House.[1] On Nov. 22, 1963, Mr. Scouten was overseeing redecoration of the Oval Office when word reached him that President John F. Kennedy was fatally shot in Dallas. He put the office back in order and made arrangements for visiting world dignitaries. He did not make it home for five days.

Mr. Scouten grew particularly close to first lady Nancy Reagan, who once described him as "the second most important man in my life." They were together in the White House's third-floor solarium on March 30, 1981, when she learned her husband had been shot by a gunman outside a Washington hotel. Not long afterward, Mr. Scouten and White House curator Clement E. Conger guided Nancy Reagan in the first major interior renovation in a decade.[2]

In a letter I received in September 1998, Scouten wrote: "Emory Roberts, a very good friend of mine, died in the late 60's as I recall [actually 10/8/73] – returned home from work one afternoon – laid down on the bed and suffered a major heart attack – and died." Scouten also wrote: "Dear Vince, Stewart Stout, following his retirement from the Secret Service was hired (by me) as an assistant Usher at the White House. He had a heart disorder – suffered a heart attack at the White House and died within a few hours. I believe this happened around 1963-1965."[3] Actually, it was in December 1974.[4]

Scouten also wrote: "Paul Paterni was [my] mentor when I entered the Service in the Detroit field office (1948). I learned so very much from him. Paul was most famous for his OSS work during the war and his undercover work (counterfeiting) in New York City. Upon retirement he moved to Missoula, Montana. He died I think around 1980 [Feb. 1984]."[5]

Rex Scouten- a very good man and great public servant (who perhaps wasn't the greatest when it came to dates).

---

1. *Washington Post*, 2/22/2013.
2. *Washington Post*, 2/22/2013.
3. Letter to author dated 5/28/98.
4. Winston Lawson wrote the author in a letter dated 1/20/04, "Stu Stout died in December 1974, a few years after retiring from USSS. He worked for a while after that in what is called the "usher office," which is adjacent to the large front foyer. He was a good friend and probably the nicest "gentleman" I ever knew. He went into real estate and then died suddenly in December 1974. He had been a state trooper in PA, joined the USSS during WWII, was drafted and came back to USSS. I was on his shift for a few years from probably 1961-1965. He was a wonderful man."
5. Letter to author dated 5/28/98.

DANNY SPRIGGS

A gent Carlton Daniel "Danny" Spriggs is best remembered as one of the heroes of 3/30/81, protecting President Reagan, garnering a Special Act Award from the Department of Treasure in the process. Spriggs was agent Dennis V.N. McCarthy's partner that fateful day and assisted in apprehending the assassin John Hinckley.[1] Spriggs spent 28 years in the Secret Service, starting as a special agent with the Albuquerque, N.M. field office and working his way up to deputy director in Washington, D.C. in 2002. In that role – the No. 2 position in the agency, the assistant director of the Secret Service's Office of Protective Operations, the position he held on 9/11 – he helped carry out the presidential executive order transitioning the Secret Service from the Department of the Treasury to the newly created Department of Homeland Security.

Spriggs also served in Washington and White Plains, New York, before joining the managerial ranks in 1991 as special agent in charge of the Philadelphia office, and advancing to such positions in the nation's capital as deputy special agent in charge of the vice presidential protective division and assistant to the special agent in charge of the presidential protective division. He routinely coordinated with military and law enforcement agencies in other countries when he was engaged in advance security work for trips by the president and vice president as well as visiting foreign heads of state.

Spriggs played for the Dallas Cowboys before joining the Secret Service.[2]

1. *Rawhide Down* by Del Wilber (2011), pages 84-85, 125-126; *Protecting the President* by Dennis McCarthy, page 66.
2. *Washington Post*, 1/7/2001.

BRIAN STAFFORD

Brian Stafford, the 20th Director of the Secret Service (1999-2003) and former SAIC of PPD during part of the Clinton era, presided over a tumultuous time: the post-Lewinsky scandal era of President Clinton, the 2000 presidential election, 9/11, and the beginning rumblings of the Iraq War, as well as all the other noteworthy items of the late 20th/early 21rst century. After earning a Bronze Star in service to his country in Vietnam as a member of the U.S. Army, Stafford joined the Secret Service in 1971. Stafford protected Presidents Nixon thru Clinton and retired as Director during the George W. Bush era.

The *Sharon (PA) Herald* reported Stafford's remarks on 5/29/15:

> "We've had presidents who jog, ride mountain bikes, sky dive and scuba dive," he said. "We've had to adjust." Since President Reagan was a trained equestrian, agents assigned to protect him had to learn horseback riding. It proved adventuresome.
>
> "Our guys were falling off the horses," Stafford noted with a wry smile. "We had to kick it up a notch."

What had to be the most tension-filled moments of his career were during the Sept. 11, 2001, terrorist attacks. He got first reports from the agency's field office in the World Trade Center that the North Tower had been hit by a plane around 8:45 a.m.

"I, probably like everyone else, thought it was an accident," he said.

After the second plane hit the Trade Center he was summoned to the White House for a national security meeting. President Bush, in Florida at the time, tuned in on the meeting by video conferencing. With another plane hitting the Pentagon and another downed in Pennsylvania – Flight 93 – it was clear the nation was under attack.

"I made the recommendation that the president stay away (from the White House temporarily)," Stafford said. "The vice president sided with me."

Later that evening he rousted President Bush and his wife out of bed into safety amid fears another plane might be part of the attack. It proved to be a false alarm.

"He wasn't very happy with me," Stafford said of the president. "It wasn't a very happy day anyways. I told him I wasn't here to make you happy."

In his retirement life, Stafford said he manages to keep in touch with the Clintons. A night before he was to undergo a major surgery, President Clinton called him to boost his morale."

100

LEWIS MERLETTI

L ewis Merletti, the 19th Director of the Secret Service (1997-1999) and SAIC of PPD during part of the Clinton era, will always be remembered as the Director who presided during the Monica Lewinsky scandal involving President Bill Clinton. Like the author, Merletti was born in Pittsburgh, PA and graduated from Duquesne University. Like the author's father, Merletti went to Central Catholic High School. Like Director Stafford, Merletti served in the Army during the Vietnam War and received the Bronze Star.

Merletti joined the Secret Service in 1974 and went on to protect Presidents Ford thru Clinton. During the Clinton impeachment trial in 1998, while Merletti was Director of the Secret Service, Independent Counsel Kenneth W. Starr's prosecutors requested that numerous Secret Service agents testify in the investigation of President Clinton's relationship with Monica Lewinsky."Merletti argued strongly against this, saying: "As law enforcement officers, Secret Service agents would proactively report any crime that they witnessed, however, Secret Service agents assigned to the Presidential Protective Detail should not be subpoenaed as part of a 'fishing expedition.' It is my firm belief, as Director of the United States

Secret Service, that using Secret Service protective personnel as witnesses concerning non-criminal activities of a President will substantially undermine, if not destroy, the relationship of trust and confidence that must exist between the Secret Service and the President in order for the Secret Service to successfully fulfill its mission. If our Presidents do not have complete trust in the Secret Service personnel who protect them, they may push away the Service's 'protective envelope,' thereby making them more vulnerable to assassination."

On May 22, Chief U.S. District Judge Norma Holloway Johnson ruled that since the Secret Service employees are part of the federal law enforcement establishment sworn to assist in criminal investigations, they must testify.[1] The Secret Service appealed her decision and the case eventually made its way to the Supreme Court where the Secret Service lost in a split decision. Scores of Secret Service agents then testified before Starr's Independent Counsel. In the end, Starr and his Independent Counsel were frustrated to learn that the rumor and innuendo that they had been led to believe regarding the Secret Service's involvement with the Lewinsky issue was totally unfounded. The Independent Counsel remarked that the Secret Service turned out to be "a dry well." Merletti felt vindicated and remarked, "It was the fight that mattered, future Presidents would have faith in the Secret Service's motto of being 'Worthy of trust and confidence.'"[2]

Merletti went on to work as head of security for the Cleveland Browns. Merletti later became embroiled in a dispute with a neighbor that made headlines.[3]

Thus ends a look at the who's who of the Secret Service – a truly interesting group of men and women, indeed.

---

1. http://tech.mit.edu/V118/N29/service.29w.html
2. https://en.wikipedia.org/wiki/Lewis_C._Merletti
3. http://www.cleveland.com/naymik/index.ssf/2015/03/onetime_us_secret_service_head.html

APPENDIX I

THE CIA & THE SECRET SERVICE

30 November 1948

Mr. U. E. Baughman, Jr.
Chief, United States Secret Service
Department of the Treasury
Washington 25, D. C.

Dear Mr. Baughman:

I was delighted to learn yesterday of your
becoming Chief of the Secret Service. Please
accept my heartiest congratulations on your promotion.

You may be assured that we will continue to
cooperate to the fullest extent with the Secret
Service under your regime, and do not hesitate to
call upon us for any assistance which we can ren-
der. I know that we can count on receiving from
you the same splendid cooperation which we have
received from the Secret Service in the past.

I am looking forward to seeing you in the
near future. Meanwhile, please accept my renewed
congratulations.

Sincerely yours,

R. H. HILLENKOETTER
Rear Admiral, USN
Director of Central Intelligence

WLPforzheimer:blc
Central Records
Signer
Return to Pforzheimer

Note for Record: Reply (ER 0-2484)
12/10/48: Thank you very much for your
letter of 11/30 congratulating me on my
promotion to the position of Chief,U.S.Secret
Service. Your invitation to call upon you
should you or your staff be able to assist me
in any way is much appreciated. The relationship
between your department and our service has
always been most cordial, and it is my sincere
desire that this pleasant relationship continue."
(Treasury)

The Director of the CIA congratulating Baughman on becoming Chief of the
Secret Service. As we know, Baughman became the Chief via a phone call on
11/22/48.

S1

1ᴸ

8 2 SEP 1958

1 ✓

Mr. U. E. Baughman
Chief, U. S. Secret Service
Treasury Department
Washington 25, D. C.

Dear Mr. Baughman:

Thank you very much for your recent letter concerning the assistance rendered by Mr. John _____ and other CIA personnel in connection with _____

It is most gratifying to receive such comments with respect to the performance of our personnel, and I shall pass along your kind remarks to all concerned.

With best regards,

Sincerely,

Signed

C. P. Cabell
General, USAF
Acting Director

O/DC I/_____ / km

Orig & 1 - Addressee
       1 - DCI
       1 - CI w/Basic - via Reading
       1 - JEC   ST/

NOTE FOR RECORD: Copies of basic forwarded, by memorandum from Acting DCI, same date as above, to _____ (via O/Security) and to DD/P.

Charles Cabell, the number 2 man of the CIA later fired by Kennedy over the Bay of Pigs (and the brother of the Mayor of Dallas), corresponds with Chief Baughman.

11-1299

UNITED STATES SECRET SERVICE

WASHINGTON

U. E. BAUGHMAN
CHIEF

February 27, 1959

Dear Mr. Dulles:

It is again my privilege to express my thanks for the assistance rendered by Messrs.

Our agents have brought to my attention the efficient and quiet manner in which these gentlemen performed their work, which commanded the highest respect and made for the most amicable relationships.

Because of the devotion to duty of these gentlemen and their understanding of our responsibilities, I want to commend them to you for their deportment and congenial attitude during the visit.

Kindest regards.

Yours sincerely,

M B Baughman

Honorable Allen W. Dulles
Director
Central Intelligence Agency
Washington, D. C.

Chief Baughman corresponds with Director Allen Dulles, during the Ike era. Both men would later be fired/ "retired" by JFK around the same time in 1961.

Approved For Release 2002/05/07 : CIA-RDP80B01676R002900140002-6

63 9115

TREASURY DEPARTMENT

UNITED STATES SECRET SERVICE

WASHINGTON, D.C. 20220

OFFICE OF THE CHIEF

December 9, 1963

Mr. John A. McCone
Director, Central
  Intelligence Agency
Washington, D. C.

Dear Mr. McCone:

I was very pleased with the fine cooperation we received from your Agency in implementing the security
provisions for the funeral of the late President
John F. Kennedy, November 25, 1963.   25X1

Through arrangements made with Mr. [   ]   STAT
[   ] agents of your Agency under the supervision of
Messrs. [   ] were imme-   STAT
diately placed at our disposal. Their services
were utilized at St. Matthews Cathedral, Arlington
Cemetery, and all along the route of the funeral
procession from the Cathedral to the Cemetery.

With pressing problems of your own, I can imagine
the difficulty in mustering this group on relatively
short notice. Also, I understand that Mr. [   ]   STAT
had an additional force of men available if they
had been needed.

All of your representatives carried out their assignments with the highest degree of efficiency and
effectiveness.

I am deeply grateful.

                                Sincerely,

                                James J. Rowley

(EXECUTIVE REGISTRY FILE *Treasury*)
(Approved For Release 2002/05/07 : CIA-RDP80B01676R002900140002-6

                                900212

Chief Rowley to CIA Director John McCone regarding security for Kennedy's
funeral 11/25/63.

516.0

TREASURY DEPARTMENT

UNITED STATES SECRET SERVICE

WASHINGTON 25, D.C.

OFFICE OF THE CHIEF

_63-448_

Ref atl:
_63-1081_

January 17, 1963

Honorable John A. McCone
Director
Central Intelligence Agency
2430 E Street N. W.
Washington 25, D. C.

Attention: Technical Services Division

Dear Mr. McCone:

The Secret Service has need for a highly discriminating
voice operated relay unit. Your Technical Services
Division advises that your organization has participated
in the development of such a unit and has contacts with a
source of supply.

If this meets with your approval, will you please arrange
for the purchase of one unit for transfer to this Service,
and advise concerning the procedure for any necessary
transfer of funds.

The equipment will be kept under strict security and any
specific restrictions or security classification you may
wish to impose will be honored.

As a point of contact for further details Mr. Robert I. Bouck,
Room 94, Executive Office Building (EX 3-3300, ext. 2584)
will be available.

Your cooperation and assistance in this matter are appreciated.

Yours sincerely,

James J. Rowley

An important document: Chief Rowley to CIA Director McCone regarding assistance from the Technical Services Division of the CIA.

Approved For Release 2002/03/29 : CIA-RDP80B01676R002900140010-7

63-2899

YR 3-1164

3 April 1963

The Honorable James J. Rowley
Chief, United States Secret Service
Department of the Treasury
Washington 25, D. C.

Dear Jim:

      Following up on our telephone conversation of this afternoon, I send you herewith my most recent memorandum to three of my Deputies on the subject, "The CIA Role in Support of Presidential Trips Abroad." This is an updating of a memorandum I put out on 8 June 1962, and is designed to tell everybody in the Agency what their responsibilities are and to whom. You will of course understand that while our responsibilities to the Secret Service are intimate and compelling as covered in paragraph II D of the attached, we also have responsibilities for pure intelligence aspects and Presidential briefings which must be covered in detail. If you have any suggestions as to where we might improve our coverage, I would be delighted to have them.

      This letter also confirms my telephonic invitation to you and Mr. Campion to have lunch with Lyman Kirkpatrick and me at 12:30 on Friday, 12 April, out here at the pickle factory.

Faithfully yours,

/s/ Pat

Marshall S. Carter
Lieutenant General, USA
Deputy Director

Attachment

      Memo to DD/I, DD/P, DD/S from DDCI dtd 8 Mar 63, Subject:
The CIA Role in Support of Presidential Trips Abroad (ER 63-1664)
MSC:blp
Distribution:
Approved For Release 2002/03/29 : CIA-RDP80B01676R002900140010-7
1 - DDCI w/o att 1 - Executive Director w/o att 1 - ER w/o att

A very important document: Kennedy-era correspondence between Deputy Director Marshall Carter and Chief Rowley regarding the CIA's role in support of presidential trips abroad.

ER 60.2275

R G MAR 196

Mr. U. E. Baughman
Chief, U. S. Secret Service
Treasury Department
Washington 25, D. C.

Dear Mr. Baughman:

Thank you for your recent letters addressed
to Mr. Dulles concerning the assistance rendered
by members of this Agency in connection with the
President's trip to Latin America.

It was most thoughtful of you to write, and
I shall see that those concerned are apprised of
your commendatory comments with respect to their
performance.

With best regards,

Sincerely,

C. P. Cabell
General, USAF
Deputy Director

O/DDCI:KM/26 March 60

Orig & 1 -- Addressee
        1 - DDCI
        1 - ER w/ 4 bsc ltrs*
        1 - C/WH via DDP w/cys 4 bsc ltrs
        1 - D/Sec via DDS w/cy bsc ltr dtd 3/23
        1 - AAB

(EXECUTIVE REGISTRY FILE

*There were four basic letters from Mr. Baughman as follows:
ER 60-1799, dtd 11 March; 60-2027, dtd 22 March; 60-2074,
dtd 23 March; and 60-2095 dtd 24 March. All concerned WH Div.
personnel exclusively except the letter of 23 March, which also
concerned [   ] of Security.

More correspondence between Cabell and Baughman regarding CIA assistance on a presidential trip.

ER 61-5614/a

1 3 JUL 19⬛

Mr. U. E. Baughman
Chief, U. S. Secret Service
Treasury Department
Washington 25, D. C.

Dear Mr. Baughman:

  Thank you very much for your letter of 10 Jul⬛
concerning the assistance rendered by Messrs.

  I am highly pleased to get your kind comments
about their performance, and it was very thoughtful
of you to bring this to my attention. I will be glad
to convey the appreciation of the Secret Service to
them and, as a matter of record, copies of your letter
will be placed in their official personnel folders.

  With kindest regards,

         Sincerely,

         SIGNED

         Allen W. Dulles
         Director

O/DCI/⬛⬛⬛⬛⬛rap(12 July 61)

Distribution:
 Orig - Addressee
 ✓ - DCI
 1 - ER
 1 - AAB
 1 - DD/P w/basic for necessary action
 3 - O/Personnel for filing in the official personnel
   folders of

Correspondence between Dulles and Baughman very shortly before both men were fired/ "retired" by President Kennedy.

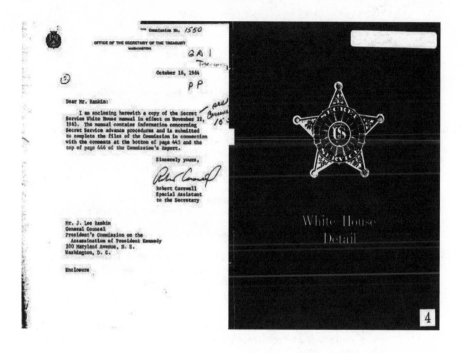

Part 1 of 2: The Secret Service White House Detail manual (Ike era) submitted to the Warren Commission.

- 3 -

VII. AUTOMOBILES

a. Identify cars to be used by President and Secret Service follow-up car
b. Name drivers of Presidential and Secret Service follow-up cars
c. Time and place drivers to report
d. Arrangements made for cars for members of Presidential party
e. Car Assignments for Presidential party

VIII. PRESS AND PHOTOGRAPHERS

a. Indicate whether event is on or off the record
b. State whether Presidential Press Secretary has approved presence of correspondents and photographers and number
c. State whether press and photographers to accompany Presidential motorcade
d. Indicate restrictions on press and photographers, their location during event, whether photographs, newsreels authorized
e. Comment on arrangements for broadcasts, if any

IX. COMMUNICATIONS

a. Describe arrangements for maintaining means of communication, while enroute and at location of event, i.e., radio, special telephone service, etc.
b. Show code to be used if short wave radio communication is employed

X. CONCLUSION

a. Itemize number of personnel from each group to participate in security measures (White House Detail agents, field agents, detectives, uniformed police, military police, National Guard, firemen, etc.)

b. Furnish the name, location, and home and office telephone numbers of the person in charge of the local office of the Food and Drug Administration, Department of Health, Education and Welfare.

c. Name those participating in survey and those rendering assistance to this Service.
d. Attach maps, charts, and diagrams, showing route of travel, physical description of point of departure, place of arrival, place where event will be held, post assignments, restricted areas, and other pertinent points.

Part 2 of 2: Secret Service manual excerpt regarding motorcades. Note press, photographers and personnel to participate in security measures.

CIA HISTORICAL REVIEW PROGRAM
RELEASE IN FULL 1995

-2-

1964

8. Jean SOUETRE aka Michel ROUX aka Michel MERTZ - On 5 March, Mr.
Papich advised that the French had hit the Legal Attache in Paris
and also the SDECE man had queried the Bureau in New York City concerning subject stating that he had been expelled from the U.S. at
Fort Worth or Dallas 48 hours after the assassination.* He was in
Fort Worth on the morning of 22 November and in Dallas in the afternoon. The French believe that he was expelled to either Mexico or
Canada. In January he received mail from a dentist named Alderson
living at 5803 Birmingham, Houston, Texas. Subject is believed to
be identical with a Captain who is a deserter from the French Army
and an activist in the OAS. The French are concerned because of
De Gaulle's planned visit to Mexico. They would like to know the
reason for his expulsion from the U.S. and his destination. Bureau
files are negative and they are checking in Texas and with INS. They
would like a check of our files with indications of what may be passed
to the French. Mr. Papich was given a copy of CSCI-3/776,742 previously
furnished the Bureau and CSDB-3/655,207 together with a photograph of
Captain SOUETRE. WE/3/Duhlie; CI/SIG; CI/OPS/Evans

* of President Kennedy

Document Number 632-796

A French assassin-and mortal threat to the President of France- was in Fort
Worth and Dallas on 11/22/63, as was JFK!

Toledo Blade - Oct 17, 1961   Browse this new

Dallas Coolness To Chief Irks White House Aids

White House staff members are still steaming over the official brush-off President Kennedy received when he flew to Dallas last week to visit Speaker Rayburn in Baylor Hospital there.

Although the President's plan to fly to Texas had been announced hours before his departure, the only public official on hand at the airport to greet him was the Dallas chief of police, who had been called on by the Secret Service for security assistance. Only a few hundred people were gathered at the airport and the hospital to see the President.

Mayor Earle Cabell, brother of Gen. Charles P. Cabell, deputy director of the Central Intelligence Agency, explained that he was too busy to greet the President.

Mayor Cabell was elected on a nonpartisan ballot but he speaks for strongly Republican Dallas, which is represented by Texas' only Republican member of the House, Rep. Bruce Alger.

Cabell became Deputy Director of CIA under Allen Dulles. He was forced by President Kennedy to resign, on January 31, 1962, following the failure of the Bay of Pigs Invasion. Cabell's brother, Earle Cabell, was Mayor of Dallas when Kennedy visited that city and was assassinated, on November 22, 1963

CIA Director Allen Dulles, Ed Lansdale and Charles Cabell:

In a recent discovery, it turns out Dallas Mayor Earle Cabell was a CIA asset! Best-selling author David Talbot wrote: "What a cozy setup the CIA had in Dallas in 1963. Mayor Earle Cabell was not only the brother of Charles Cabell, the former CIA deputy chief who, along with his boss Allen Dulles, was fired by JFK. Now we learn that the Dallas mayor was also a CIA asset! This is part of a pattern: the Texas School Book Depository where Oswald supposedly fired from his sniper's nest was owned by right-wing oilman D.H. Byrd, who also had deep national security connections; the press corps covering the Kennedy motorcade was riddled with CIA assets."[1]

---

1. https://whowhatwhy.org/2017/08/02/dallas-mayor-jfk-assassination-cia-asset/

271

APPENDIX II

OSWALD AND ZBORIL

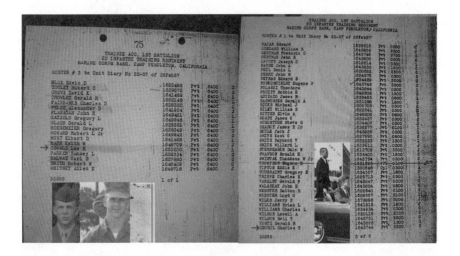

I made a major discovery tonight that is so mind blowing I am having a hard time wrapping my head around it. While doing research for author T.C. Elliott, I decided to peruse a document only released in 1998, the official Marine Corps Unit Diaries, RG 127, Camp Pendleton, CA 1957-01-20 to 1957-02-26. As most people know (so common I grabbed this from an online encyclopedia) "Lee Harvey Oswald was sent to Camp Pendleton for advanced infantry combat training. Oswald completed his training between 20th January 1957 and 26th February 1957 as a member of QUA Company, 1st Battalion, 2nd Infantry Training Regiment, Marine Corps Base, Camp Pendleton, California": one of many true facts no one disputes; in the category of "there is a sun and there is a moon; duh!"

Guess who else was a member of QUA Company, 1st Battalion, 2nd Infantry Training Regiment, Marine Corps Base, Camp Pendleton, California at the very same time and never told anyone, at least not in public for books, articles, or the television interviews he has done: JFK White House Detail Secret Service Agent Charles T. "Chuck" Zboril! Zboril was brand new to the detail, joining in the Fall of 1963. He famously rode on the rear of President Kennedy's limousine in Tampa, Florida on 11/18/63 (the trip *before* the fatal Texas journey) and, infamously and controversially, was allegedly ordered to get off the limo (by JFK, which is bunk, but I digress for now), which is regularly brought up as causing great peril to JFK four short days later... *when his Marine unit "buddy" was allegedly taking aim exactly where Chuck could have and should have been!* What are the chances of this bizarre connection: are we talking DNA numbers?!?! And, again, Zboril, who contributed to Gerald Blaine's *The Kennedy Detail* (doing part of the book tour and local Florida television interviews), a major PBS documentary on the 11/18/63 trip, and several other media outlets, never uttered a *word* about this connection! Zboril served from JFK to Carter on the White House Detail, as well as other details and duties within the agency. I spoke to Zboril at length in 1995 and he never mentioned this (Zboril went on to write a one-star review of my first book. He is not a fan).

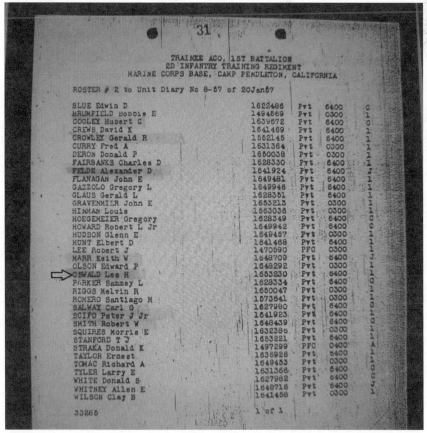

From John Armstrong's work: "On October 24, HARVEY and three other Marine recruits boarded an American Airlines flight to San Diego. Oswald and the three men from Dallas were assigned to Platoon

2060, along with a young man from Wisconsin named Allen R. Felde. Following boot camp these 8 marines from Platoon 2060 were transferred to Camp Pendleton for infantry training. They shared the same tent and Allen Felde and HARVEY Oswald spent a lot of time together. Felde told the FBI that Oswald continually discussed politics, championed the cause of the working man, and was "left-winged." In the fall of 1956, while HARVEY Oswald and Allen Felde were stationed at San Diego, LEE Oswald was at the Marine Corps Air Facility at El Toro, CA, 10 miles south of Camp Pendleton. It was in El Toro that Sergeant Wallace Ransberger first met Private First Class LEE Oswald, and a year later associated with him at Atsugi, Japan. Ransberger and LEE Oswald were assigned to the same unit and their duties were to furnish repair parts for vehicles and generators. In early 1957 Sergeant Donald Goodwin was assigned to Camp Pendleton and supervised a group of 20 men in the 5th Marine division, one of whom was radio communicator LEE Oswald, Private 1st class."

From the Warren Report: "On January 18, 1957, he reported to Camp Pendleton, Calif., for further training and was assigned to "A" Company of the First Battalion, Second Infantry Training Regiment. He was

at Pendleton for a little more than 5 weeks, at the end of which he was rated 4.2 in conduct and 4.0 in proficiency. Allen R. Felde, a fellow recruit who was with Oswald at San Diego and Pendleton, has stated that Oswald was generally unpopular and that his company was avoided by the other men. When his squad was given its first weekend leave from Pendleton, all eight men took a cab to Tijuana, Mexico. Oswald left the others and did not rejoin them until it was time to return to camp. Felde said that this practice was repeated on other trips to Los Angeles; Oswald accompanied the men on the bus to and from camp but did not stay with them in the city. On February 27, he went on leave for two weeks, during which he may have visited his mother in Fort Worth."
HIDELL/ZBORIL?

ACCORDING TO AGENT FLOYD BORING: OSWALD IN D.C. 9/27/63

As researcher Deb Galentine wrote to me: "LHO supposedly arrived in Mexico City on 9/27/63. But this report has him in Washington DC on that date. Ruth Paine had recently returned to New Orleans shortly before this date from the Washington DC area. She had incorporated a visit to CIA headquarters while in the D.C. area in order to "see her sister." I have doubts about Ruth traveling alone on her road trip with two small children. I suspect she took her husband along. So it may be possible that Michael Paine stayed behind in the area. Someone in the D.C./PA/Baltimore area was impersonating LHO in several places during that time frame.

Researcher Carolina Lynn also weighed in on the matter: "This is intriguing on many levels. First, the witness is a chauffeur for Secretary of Agriculture Orville Freeman, a seemingly very credible witness. The driver spoke to a D.C. policeman about the demeanor of the "Oswald" look-alike he encountered. [Sadly, the report says the policeman did not interview or ID "Oswald"]. Second, the report throughout refers to the "suspect" as Harvey Lee Oswald," a switching of the name that author John Armstrong believes is government code to indicate the Russian-native doppelganger of the New Orleans-born Lee Harvey Oswald... "Lee Harvey Oswald" had by the date of this report, Dec. 2, 1963, become the most notorious name in U.S. history, repeated over and over on TV and radio and in newspapers. So it is hard to believe the name reversal could be "accidental." Third, The Warren Omission Report is adamant that "Oswald" was in Mexico City on September 27, 1963, the verified date of the DC incident, so this person was not the same "Oswald" in Mexico!"

Form No. 1140 (Revised)
Administrative Manual
(Rev-8)

UNITED STATES SECRET SERVICE
TREASURY DEPARTMENT

OFFICE: Field	OFFICE: Washington, D.C.	FILE NO. CO-2-6010

TYPE OF CASE	STATUS	TITLE OR CAPTION CO 2-34050 H 650
Protective Research	Pending	Person Identified:

INVESTIGATION MADE AT	PERIOD COVERED	Name : Harvey Lee Oswald
Washington, D.C.	12/2-5/63	Alleged appearance in Washington, D.C., on September 27, 1963

INVESTIGATION MADE BY
Special Agent William H. McClarin, Jr.

DETAILS

SYNOPSIS

Mr. Bernard Thompson, Chauffeur for Secretary Freeman, identified photograph of Harvey Lee Oswald as resembling an individual whom he had a conversation with on September 27, 1963, in front of the Willard Hotel. This individual made several antagonistic remarks regarding the Secretary's car being parked in a no parking area.

(A) INTRODUCTION:

This case originated with information received in this office from Assistant Special Agent in Charge F. W. Boring, White House Detail, on December 2, 1963, that a personal acquaintance of his, Mr. Bernard Thompson, 2104 Shiply Terrace, S.E., Apartment 203, telephone #562 3450, office telephone # DU 8 5092, a Chauffeur for Secretary of Agriculture Freeman, had reported to him that he had a conversation with Oswald regarding the Secretary's car in front of the Willard Hotel in the latter part of September 1963.

(B) GENERAL INQUIRIES:

On December 2, 1963, ASAIC Boring was interviewed and related that Mr. Bernard Thompson, whom he has known for some time and who is employed as a Chauffeur for Secretary Freeman, had informed him on December 1, 1963, that he believed he had seen Harvey Lee Oswald in front of the Willard Hotel in the latter part of September of this year. Thompson told Mr. Boring that a stranger had walked over to the Secretary's car which was parked in front of the Willard Hotel and demanded to know whose car it was. Mr. Thompson refused to tell him anything except that it was a Government car and thereupon moved the car around the corner, and this individual again approached him and asked him the same question.

DISTRIBUTION	COPIES	REPORT MADE BY		DATE
Chief	Orig & 2cc	[signature] William H. McClarin, Jr.		12/11/63
Washington	2cc	APPROVED [signature]		DATE
		650 Harry W. Geiglein		12/11/63
WHM:beg		LOCAL AGENCY CHECKED		

(CONTINUE ON PLAIN PAPER)

CO-2-601.0
Page 2

Mr. Boring said that Mr. Thompson was quite concerned about this matter at the time because he did not believe this individual was acting in a usual manner and that this matter had been preying on his mind for some time; that when the pictures of Oswald appeared in the paper after the President's assassination, Mr. Thompson thought that he recognized Oswald as being this same individual. Mr. Boring stated that Mr. Thompson is not a crank and that he has a sincere desire to give information which he believes to be of value in our investigation.

On December 3, 1963, a photograph of Harvey Lee Oswald was obtained from the Protective Research Section. The following known aliases of Harvey Lee Oswald were also obtained at that time: O. H. Lee, A. J. Hidell, Alek J. Hidell, Alex James Hidell, A. Haidell.

On December 3, 1963, Mr. Thompson was interviewed in the Washington field office. He stated that in the latter part of September, around the 25th of the month, at about 3:10 P.M., he arrived at the north entrance of the Willard Hotel which would be the corner of 14th & F Streets; that he parked in the no parking zone in front of the hotel entrance, as he was expecting Mrs. Freeman to come out of the hotel where she was attending a function; that an individual whom he did not know came out of the hotel entrance, walked directly to his car and demanded to know "Whose car is this." Mr. Thompson said that he replied that it was a Government car. Mr. Thompson said that this individual then said to him, "This must be some big official's car. This is a no parking zone. You have no right to park here." Mr. Thompson said that this man did not say this in a conversational type of tone, or a friendly tone in any sense, but that he appeared to be highly antagonistic and Mr. Thompson classified him as the "rabel rouser type." Mr. Thompson then said that rather than to get in an argument with this man, he drove slowly around the block again returning to the F Street side, but rather than parking directly in front of the hotel entrance, he parked nearer to 15th Street. The same individual who had accosted him before spotted the car, walked down the sidewalk from in front of the hotel entrance and stood opposite the car, staring at Mr. Thompson; that Mr. Thompson became concerned as he did not think this appeared as normal behavior. He noticed that a White House car was parked directly in front of him and he thereupon spoke with the driver whose first name he recalls as George, and told him of the actions of this individual. He requested the White House driver to take a good look at this man and keep his eye on him while he, Mr. Thompson, went over and spoke with the policeman at the 14th Street inter-

CO-2-601.0
Page 3

section about this man. Mr. Thompson said that he spoke with this officer and advised that this individual had done and also requested permission from the officer to park in the entrance of the hotel while waiting for Mrs. Freeman. He said that the officer told him it was alright to park there while waiting for Mrs. Freeman and also that the officer walked with him down the sidewalk and took a good look at the man, however, the police officer did not stop and question the individual, but merely walked on down the sidewalk.

Mr. Thompson said that he was concerned about this incident and when he returned to the Agriculture Department, he informed his supervisor about it and also Mr. Thomas Hughes, the Secretary's Executive Officer.

At this point, Mr. Thompson examined a spread of photographs containing one of Oswald. After examining each photograph, he picked the photograph of Oswald as most resembling the individual involved in the incident described above. Mr. Thompson described the individual whom he saw as a white American male, early 20's, 5'7" tall, 130-135 lbs., slender build, dark hair, either black or brown, combed straight back with a slight wave, wearing a sport shirt and light colored trousers with narrow cuffs.

Mr. Thompson said that the only picture he really has looked at since the President's assassination, was a picture in the newspaper taken at the time Oswald was shot by Ruby in the Dallas Police Station, and that he felt that Oswald very closely resembled the individual described in the incident above.

On the same date, while Mr. Thompson was in the office, he telephonically contacted Mr. Thomas Hughes, Executive Officer to Secretary Freeman, in an effort to establish the date on which the foregoing incident occurred. Mr. Hughes checked Mrs. Freeman's social calendar and determined that the date was September 27, 1963.

On this same date, I spoke with Inspector Thacker in the Protective Research Section, in an effort to determine whether or not Oswald's movements and whereabouts on September 27 were known. Inspector Thacker informed me that Oswald's movements between September 23 and October 4, 1963, were still not definitely established. He advised me that new information on his whereabouts during this period was arriving, and that perhaps he would shortly be able to furnish information as to Oswald's whereabouts on September 27, 1963.

MICHAEL PAINE/ LEE HARVEY OSWALD:

APPENDIX IV

THE SECRET SERVICE FAILED PRESIDENT KENNEDY

I magine this stunning scenario- President Kennedy survives Dallas on November 22, 1963. There is no Vietnam War as we know it today; no ground troops– merely a few thousand advisors as the low-key conflict grinds to a halt and fades away like a poor man's Korean Conflict, at best. In turn, imagine no civil unrest, no drug culture, no prolonged Cold War, no J. Edgar Hoover reigning for another decade, no 1968 Democratic National Convention violence– without the Vietnam War, there is no real reason to protest the government now, is there? With JFK alive to fulfill a second term, there is no LBJ presidency, no Nixon revival (and, thus, no Watergate, the other historical event, like the JFK assassination and the Vietnam War, that tore the country apart and created decades of mistrust in government); no Ford Presidency (no Nixon– no Ford), thus, no reason for a "protest" Carter vote; presidents Reagan thru Trump may or may not have ever happened.

I am not saying it would have been utopia … it wouldn't have been.

I am not saying President Kennedy was a God, a saint, or an unflawed man … he clearly was not.

What *I am* saying is this: if the Secret Service would have done their usual, thorough, 1963-era standard job, *President Kennedy survives Dallas and probably doesn't even become wounded in an attempted attack!*

So, the next time someone says "Oh, c'mon now – it's over 50 years later; a new century; post 9/11– what does it all matter now?" Tell them no Vietnam War, no Watergate, the large mistrust in government probably never would have reached the levels it has today (or, at least, as soon), the Cold War would have ended long ago, and, perhaps – perhaps: the need to keep the military-industrial "war machine" going wouldn't have led to our heavy hand in the Middle East and all the inherent problems that have arisen from it – 9/11, the war on terror, the draining of our economy, etc.

The *real* "domino theory" came to fruition – with the death of JFK, several presidencies were spawned that never would have happened (again, at least LBJ thru Carter, at a minimum) and the respect and trust in government would have been felt for a far longer time. The scars from the JFK assassination truly are with us today. Keep in mind – President Kennedy was our last assassinated president and only 10 presidents ago; in the big scheme of things, with new best-selling books and audio/visual reminders plentiful on the internet and shared by millions, *not* ancient history.

As for myself, my interest in President Kennedy, the Secret Service and the JFK assassination began at the age of 12 in 1978, coinciding with both the HSCA re-investigation of the assassination and reruns of the classic fictional television series about the Secret Service of the 19th century, *The Wild, Wild West*. Coupled with two parents who (still today) are rabid Kennedy fans and you have a most interested son in myself.

My original research truly took off shortly after 1988, the 25th anniversary of the assassination. I started to key on the Secret Service, especially in comparison to the assassination attempt on President Reagan on March 30th, 1981. I said to myself: "Hmmm – theories about the Mafia, the CIA and other possible culprits are all fascinating, but what did the Secret Service agents do to try to *prevent* the assassination? *Why* was the assassination a success?"

In 1991, at the age of 25, I made my first major presentation at Jerry Rose's "Third Decade" conference in Fredonia, New York and, if I do say so myself, amazed an audience of 60 older authors and researchers, many of whom admitted they really didn't pay the Secret Service any mind – as Robert Groden told a friend of mine, "I guess that is why the Secret Service is secret." I was the first to popularize the *fact* that the driver of JFK's limousine, Bill Greer, turned around not once but *twice* during the shooting, slowing the limousine down to a near stop; disobeyed common sense, training and a direct order from his superior, fellow agent Roy Kellerman, to get out of the line of fire; and was chiefly responsible for the success of the assassination no matter *who* was the shooter and no matter *who* was behind the murder. The reaction from the audience, which included authors Harrison Livingstone, George Michael Evica, and Bob Cutler, among others, made me realize that I was on to something. With their encouragement and inspiration, I went further than mere photo and film analysis and secondary sources. In short, my goal was to do something unique: attempt to interview and/or correspond with every former agent and surviving family member I could find.

From 1991 until the present time, this is what I have done.

I am now the author of four books on both the Secret Service and the assassination; I have a major part in both part seven of *The Men Who Killed Kennedy* from 2003 (a major ratings success and popular DVD) and the recently-released DVD/Blu Ray called *A Coup In Camelot*. I have appeared in over 120 other author's books ... and so on and so forth.

I have interviewed and/corresponded with over 80 former agents, White House aides and sundry other important people, far more than the Warren Commission, the HSCA or the ARRB. In fact, I am in the ARRB's final report and the Board was inspired by me to go interview a couple important former agents, but I digress.

But enough about my background – this is all a labor of love and a commitment to truth and history; I have a life and a job; not in this for the money, folks– far from it. So, what is the bottom line from all my research and hard work?

Here it is: *President Kennedy should have survived Dallas and the Secret Serive agents truly are the men who killed Kennedy!*

No, there was no agency plot, per se, and many of these men – the vast majority – were merely following orders or, at most, were negligent. I have three – just three – major suspects who I feel crossed the line into (at the least) gross negligence and (at most) actual participants in aiding the success of the assassination (I will get to them in a moment). Sure, there are a very small handful of other agents I am suspicious of regarding the assassination and/or the cover-up, but, again, we are talking a very small number. Other parties were the shooters, masterminds and power brokers ... what the agency provided was *action through inaction* – no pulling of triggers or firing of bullets, but *allowing* those triggers and bullets to act in an unimpeded fashion. All it takes is a few precious seconds, folks, and we had both a dead president as well as a dead president *who cannot defend himself* against claims that he brought it on himself (the old blaming-the-victim mythology– I will also get to that in a moment).

So, from about 1991 to 2005, I worked hard on my research part time as I pursued a working career and other interests.

However, 2005 was a watershed moment.

Via a tip from former agent Lynn Meredith, I was able to obtain the unlisted address and number for former agent Clint Hill, a very reclusive man who, up to that time, testified to the Warren Commission but not the HSCA or the ARRB, spoke to author William Manchester but no other author and, other than an iconic *60 Minutes* interview and a couple Secret Service television programs, pretty much became the Howard Hughes of the Secret Service – again, reclusive and never granting private researchers and authors any interviews. After all, as I said, he had an unlisted address and phone number and, if you notice, he only spoke to official bodies and spouted pretty much official history – just "name, rank and serial number" and a few other notions ... that was it.

Then in 2005 came my 22-page, registered, signed-receipt-required letter to Hill, summarizing my work up to that time, basically saying that the agents were handicapped that fateful day in Dallas because a couple senior agents laid down the law – thru actions and words – that hampered the agent's abilities to do their jobs while, at the same time, falsely blaming JFK for these so-called handicaps. In addition to all the other former agents I spoke to, I also contacted former agent Gerald Blaine. This will become important momentarily.

In a nutshell, one of my major discoveries was the fact that, despite official mythology, President Kennedy did *not* order the agents off his limousine, nor did he order the agents to do anything else! This I learned via many interviews and correspondence with dozens of actual former agents and White House aides who would most certainly know first-hand. The list includes the head of the White House Detail, Gerald Behn; his top assistant, Floyd Boring; one of the three Shift Leaders, Art Godfrey; the driver of the follow-up car in Dallas, Tampa, and many other trips, Sam Kinney; JFK's good friend and aide, Dave Powers; and many more. This was all a huge surprise to me – although I focused on Secret Service negligence, I more or less reluctantly bought the "JFK-as-scapegoat" myth from roughly 1988 until 9/27/92, when I spoke to the number one agent, the aforementioned Gerald Behn, who demolished this notion in no uncertain terms.

Back to the matter at hand: I included a self-addressed, stamped envelope with my bold letter to Clint Hill, encouraging him to contact me with comment. It was a pipe dream, I knew, but, hey – nothing ventured, nothing gained. Having heard nothing from him, I decided to call him ... and, boy, was he livid! The conversation was short, sweet and awkward – Hill denied receiving my letter, although I was staring at his signed receipt, then, after an equally awkward pause wherein I asked him if he was still on the other line, he ended the conversation with "Yes, I am still here. I just have no interest in talking to you." Ouch.

Through happenstance, I spoke to the aforementioned Gerald Blaine the next day and he shocked me by bringing up my private letter to Hill and quoting from a segment from it! It turns out the two long-retired men were dear friends for decades (since the 1950's) and, in fact, Blaine had just attended Clint Hill's son's wedding (along with fellow former agent Bill Livingood, the former Sergeant at Arms for the House of Representatives who you are actually all familiar with – if you watched any of the State of the Union addresses for Presidents Clinton, Bush or Obama from about 1995 to 2012, he was the man who shouted "Mr. Speaker- the President of the United States!" Small world, indeed ... and, yes – I had also spoken to and corresponded with Livingood previously, but, again, I digress).

Up to this time, my first book was a self-published affair and, although I was stunned by these developments regarding Hill and Blaine, I thought that was basically it. I would have my blogs and appearances in other people's books to spread the word, but I thought, at the time, it was the end of the road.

Boy, was I wrong.

In late 2009, I received word that *Gerald Blaine* of all people – yes, him: Clint Hill's good friend whom I spoke to and who quoted from my letter to Hill! – was coming out with a book about the Kennedy Detail (which turned out to be the title of the book: *The Kennedy Detail*). It went from initially being just a small publishing house affair into a huge Simon and Schuster release with all the inherent huge publicity machine, no mean feat for a first time, very obscure agent turned author. I then received a letter from Gerald Blaine's attorney, asking me to take down my one blog post wherein I mentioned his upcoming book – they thought I was trying to say I was the *co-author* of the book, an asinine notion that was the farthest thing from the truth. They threatened me with obtaining a court order to remove my little blog, so I decided to let them have their way – for the moment. But why little ole (ok, big ole) me ... and why Blaine, a very obscure agent who was on the Texas trip but not the Dallas stop that next-to-no-one had ever heard of? Why, indeed.

No sooner could I digest all these bizarre out-of-the-blue happenings then I found out Clint Hill – yes, him: the reclusive agent with the unlisted address and number I had boldly sent that alarming letter to – was writing the foreword to Blaine's book, as well as contributing to its contents, appearing on the inherent media blitz (MSNBC, Fox – you name it), and also appearing in the *Kennedy Detail* television documentary.

These two men (one famous, one very obscure) were long retired and had no compunction to write a book, let alone appear in public again. In fact, Sam Kinney proudly told me "All of us old timers would never sell out or write a book for any amount of money – I am taking Clint Hill, me and all my buddies. This is the old school of 'no kiss and tell.'" In the interest of time, read my first book and see my CTKA review of Blaine's book, as well as all my reviews at CTKA regarding the Hill and Blaine books – no delusions of grandeur here: it *was* my 22-page letter to Hill that awakened a sleeping giant, so to speak. In 2010, when Blaine's book came out, I discovered much of it was a direct response to my work, including Blaine sarcastically calling me a Secret Service expert on pages 359-360. Also in 2010, both Blaine and Hill would appear on C-SPAN with network CEO Brian Lamb and mockingly discuss my work, even showing a You Tube video of me speaking – little ole me of all people! Why? Why, indeed. If it isn't obvious by now, you haven't been paying attention.

Events would springboard from here: Co-author Lisa McCubbin would go on to help in the writing of the *Kennedy Detail*, but also all of Clint Hill's books; all three of them. No TMZ tabloid tidbit here – a factual truth they both admit to: 84 year old Hill left his wife of 50-plus years (although they are still legally married to this day) for 52 year old McCubbin, also married with kids at the time (McCubbin had gone to the prom with Blaine's son years ago, but I digress. All this information is easily verifiable via You Tube and, of all things, the *Irish Times*. McCubbin lived in Qatar in the Middle East during the early millennium, was sought out by the Saudi government to help them in dealing with the Western press – no joke! – and scored an exclusive interview with George Bush, all before the age of 37; despite her relatively young age, no spring chicken here, if you catch my drift. Interestingly, a *John* McCubbin was head of the White House Police in the 1920's and was from Lisa's same home state of Virginia).

The following events occurred not long after Blaine's book came out – Hill would appear on C-SPAN with network CEO Brian Lamb in 2012 discussing *Hill's* first book in his own right and – you guessed it – I was mentioned out of the blue once again (yep, little old me, the as-yet-unpublished researcher at that time [Hill also mentioned on the same program that he burned all his personal notes in 2005 – what? As a reaction to my letter sent the same year?]); I was then harassed at my prior place of employment from a good friend of Blaine's; and, most important of all, Blaine and Hill would do their best to propagate the myth that President Kennedy had it coming and ordered them off the limousine, despite what Blaine told me in 2004 and 2005 that greatly contradicts this false notion.

You can thank me or curse me – take your pick. I am responsible for both Hill and Blaine coming out of the woodwork, writing their huge *New York Times* best-selling books for the biggest publishing house in the world that has garnered them all quite a bit of money, appearing on television numerous times since (include the Emmy-nominated documentary they made) and, sadly, reinvigorating the false debate about blaming JFK for his own death.

It probably would have ended there around 2012 or 2013, but I had a big surprise for them – I obtained a publisher for my first book, Trine Day, and it was released in time for the 50ᵗʰ anniversary. That is when the harassment at work began, my blogs and Amazon reviews started getting hacked, and another obscure agent and dear friend of Hill and Blaine, Chuck Zboril, would go on to write a one-star review of my book (while McCubbin also gave my book a one-star on GoodReads, with Blaine marking it as a "to-read" item), no doubt all with the goal of suppressing what I had to say … because it is very damaging – for them. It shows they are liars profiting on the death of the man they failed to protect. In addition, nine agents drank the night before the assassination … guess who one of them was? *Clint Hill*, the same man who had the audacity to criticize the *nine* agents who drank in Cartegena, Columbia in 2012 when another President was scheduled to appear and who now goes around telling people who want his autographed books that he did not drink the night before, despite his official report in the Warren Commission volumes, and his prior statements, stating the exact opposite. But President Obama lived and wasn't blown away like he was under your watch now, was he, Clint Hill? Hill is a false hero – what I call the Jessica Lynch of the Secret Service: he got to the limousine when the shooting was all over and done with; he did not protect JFK and, furthermore, Jackie got in and out of the limo of her own volition; they never even touched. Hill performed the equivalent of a foul tip out in baseball or even striking out swinging; he made an attempt to do something, albeit too late.

Hill would go on to receive a medal for this attempt from LBJ for this so-called heroism (never mind the drinking incident which Secret Service regulations show were grounds for *removal* from the service! Yes – him, Paul Landis, Jack Ready and Glen Bennett – all in the follow-up car – and five other agents drank hours before Kennedy got his head blown off. Alcohol consumption and sleep deprivation wreak havoc on even the best trained reflexes. They all went to bed between 2 and 5:30 AM and had to report for active duty at 8 AM! For his part, Gerald Blaine was there, too, but claimed to have only drank fruit juice, if he can even be believed.)

See, for me, this is most certainly NOT a 50-plus year old murder mystery. In addition to how history was changed and how it all affects us today, you have two old men traveling the world, smiling widely, making very big money (a Hill book movie is allegedly in the works), and peddling lies against the man they failed to protect; Hill even rode in an open limousine down Elm Street in one program without breaking a sweat; so much for being traumatized by the event. In effect, JFK was assassinated three times: his actual murder, the character assassination regarding his private life (to which several agents held him in contempt) and this blame-the-victim mythology.

Now, after providing you with the background, here is the foreground-the details; the nuts and bolts):

1) **A major discovery of mine in two parts:** *President Kennedy did not order the agents off his limousine* in Tampa four days before his death, there is zero evidence this was even invoked for Dallas in any case, and agents on or near the rear of the limousine would have saved the presidents life. The lack of agents on or near the limo was a secret service decision. Many times, agents walked, ran or jogged near the rear of his limo and/ or rode on the rear of his limo. **The second major discovery, one touched on in my first book and expanded in my next book:** *the Secret Service is the boss of the president, not the other way around. Even if a president wanted to order the agents around, they would ignore him.* Take, for example, an Associated Press story from November 15, 1963: "The (Secret) Service can overrule even the President where his personal security is involved." Shockingly, perhaps with an eye toward real history after he is long gone, Hill admitted in 2010 in his Sixth Floor oral history, with Blaine right by his side: "[The president] can tell you what he wants done and he can tell you certain things but that doesn't mean you have to do it. What we used to do was always agree with the President and then we'd do what we felt was best anyway."

2) President kennedy had *nothing* to do with the limiting or placement of motorcycles by his limousine as has been alleged by some. Three to six motorcycles normally rode on each side of his limousine, as had been the case on the prior stops on the Texas trip, the Florida trip and countless other trips. This was a Secret Service decision to limit their use in Dallas, something the HSCA rightfully said was "uniquely insecure."

3) President Kennedy had *nothing* to do with another major discovery of mine- the lack of security covering multi-story buildings along the parade route. It was common practice from the FDR era thru and including the JFK era (and beyond) to have agents and/or police and/or a branch

of the military to guard and monitor buildings, sometimes even using a helicopter to help monitor both the route and the buildings themselves. This does not mean just watching the windows as the cars passed but by stationing men on the rooftops themselves, as was the case in san antonio, florida, nashville, germany, ireland, and many other trips.

I corresponded twice with former Secret Service Chief Inspector Michael Torina. The position of Secret Service Chief Inspector was very influential – *it was Torina himself who actually completed the Secret Service's Manual*. Torina contributed significantly to a book by author Wayne Hyde written in *1962* in which it is plainly stated: "If the President is to appear in a parade, agents and policemen are assigned posts atop buildings and on the street along the parade route." *This lack of coverage in Dallas was a Secret Service decision*. We would learn even more from Secret Service records of the era except for one thing – the ARRB noted in their final report from 1998: "Congress passed the JFK Act of 1992. One month later, the Secret Service began its compliance efforts. However, in January 1995, *the Secret Service destroyed presidential protection survey reports for some of President Kennedy's trips in the fall of 1963.*"

4) Agent Sam Kinney *was adamant to me, on three different occasions, that he was solely responsible for the bubbletop's removal on 11/22/63* – JFK had nothing to do with it. It was briefly on the car on 11/22/63 and was then removed. Although not bulletproof or bullet resistant in the traditional sense, many people thought it was, thus making it a psychological deterrant: would someone fire onto the car with it on? In addition, many agents thought it would deflect a bullet and/or shield the president via the sun's glare off the top. Many times, the top was on the car in either full or partial formations (meaning, just the front and rear pieces were used so the president could stand intermittently and offer some semblance of protection at the same time, similar to the famous Eisenhower bubble). In addition, the top was used in bright, no-rain conditions: I found it was used on approximately 25 good weather trips, roughly a third of all JFK-motorcades.

5) Normally, a flatbed truck (sometimes two) carrying still and motion photographers from the press was used in motorcades and rode in front of the presidential limousine, as it was used on the prior trip in Florida and many other occasions. It was cancelled at the last minute by the Secret Service at Love Field;

6) SAIC Behn or his immediate assistant, #2 man Floyd Boring, accompanied the president on trips outside of Washington. Behn took his

first vacation of the JFK era coinciding with both the Florida and Texas trips, while number two assistant Boring manned the Florida trip, yet was absent from the Texas trip, allowing a third-stringer, Roy Kellerman, to make only his *second* major trip without either Behn or Boring (there is a possibility Texas was the very first, as it is unclear if Behn was also on a part of the Nashville trip, possibly Kellerman's first trip alone with JFK). However, there were stark contrasts between Nashville in May 1963 and Dallas in November: building rooftops were guarded and a helicopter guarded the motorcade, as well as other strict security measures were invoked.

7) The Secret Service knew of prior threats to the president's life in the month of November in Chicago (that trip was cancelled at the last minute) and Florida, yet the Dallas trip went forward as scheduled, despite all the warnings from Senator J. William Fulbright and others.

8) With regard to these threats, **another major discovery of mine was the existence of two major agency covert threat monitors on the Texas trip that they did not admit to: PRS agent Glen Bennett, riding in the follow-up car, and fellow PRS agent Howard K. Norton, on the Austin trip.** Bennett was temporarily added to the White House Detail on 11/10/63, the day after the infamous Joseph Milteer tape was made, an investigation the Secret Service was very much aware of. Bennett lied under oath to the HSCA, saying he was not on the Florida trip, while *not* volunteering that he was also on the 11/14-11/15 New York trip. Secret Service records released only in the late 1990's, as well as agency identification of Bennett's appearance in photographs, conclusively proves that Bennett was indeed on the New York, Florida and Texas trips – *every stop*– often riding in the follow-up car. The aforementioned Howard Norton was also on the Florida trip and his background was only made known to me via an interview with fellow PRS agent Dale Wunderlich. When I tried to obtain more information on Bennett and Norton, former agent Jerry O'Rourke told me: "I don't want to do it. I don't want to do it. I'm afraid for my agency." Bennett passed away in 1994 and Norton's current whereabout are unknown. I contacted the Secret Service and, after a check of records, they could not even tell me how long he served in the agency! This is in addition to the presence (or lack thereof) of military intelligence operatives in Dealey Plaza, including James Powell, who took a photo of the Texas School Book Depository after the shooting.

9) SAIC Behn confirmed to me that the route was changed for the Dallas trip! He gave me no details other than to say "I know it was changed

but why– i have forgotten completely – I don't know." Needless to say, the Secret Service was responsible for the terrible route JFK took that fateful day in Dallas and there *were* alternate routes, as agents Sam Kinney, Win Lawson, and others confirmed, including the one going from Main to Industrial Boulevard, a route that would have bypassed Elm Street altogether and had the limo moving further away from the knoll and the Depository (and moving at a faster rate of speed, as well). Straight down Main Street is the route FDR took in 1936; it was also the ceremonial route, as Governor Connally admitted under oath.

10) As most people are aware, Sheriff Bill Decker ordered his men not participate in the security of the motorcade, as verified by Deputy Sheriff Roger Craig. Decker said this after agreeing to offer security to Secret Service agent Forrest Sorrels the previous day. Not enough police were guarding the route; the sheriff's department weren't doing their jobs; and no branch of the military augmented security, as was standard procedure (you see, agents weren't *always* on the back of the car and they *were* often short-staffed back then – *this* is why they relied on the local police and the military to help them out).

11) Godfrey McHugh, military aide to President Kennedy, said he was told, *for the very first time, to not ride* in the presidential limousine. Who told him not to ride there? The Secret Service. He said that he normally rode between the driver and senior agent in the front seat observing and taking notes.

12) In conjunction with the above, Dallas Police Chief Jesse Curry and Dallas Chief of Homicide Will Fritz each *wanted a car full of policemen in the motorcade* and these requests were nixed by – you guessed it – the Secret Service, yet, not only did they originally agree to their presence in the motorcade, there was a precedent for their usage, as previous motorcades usually had a police and/or a detectives car in the motorcade, in addition to the Secret Service follow-up car;

13) The overpass in Dealey Plaza *was not cleared* of spectators as it should have been.

14) As mentioned previously, nine agents drank the night before and morning of the assassination, including four agents in the follow-up car.

15) JFK, the president, and LBJ, the vice president, were in the very same motorcade in open cars moving at a slow pace – this never happened before and hasn't happened since.

16) The presence of fake *or unauthorized* Secret Service agents in Dealey Plaza when, officially speaking, no agents were there.

17) **Another major discovery of mine: one of two main drivers of JFK's limousine, Secret Service agent Tom Shipman, passed away suddenly of an alleged heart attack at, of all places, Camp David on 10/14/63.** He was buried quickly and no toxicology tests were given. I have much more on Shipman in this book, as I tracked down several surviving family members. One wonders what would have happened if Shipman – and not Greer – drove the presidential limousine.

18) **Suspect number one:** ASAIC Floyd Boring, the number two agent of the White House Detail, was (as I discovered and as documents and interviews confirm) the actual planner of the Texas trip from the Secret Service's point of view. He gave out the assignments of advance agents and so forth and was responsible for what did – and did not – happen, security-wise, in Dallas. He was the originator of the myth that JFK did not want agents on the rear of his limousine and that President Kennedy allegedly told him this in Tampa. Clint Hill testified that, during the period from *11/19 to 11/21/63 (note the time frame!),* Boring told him and other agents of this alleged request. Yet, Boring was adamant to me – on three different occasions, not to mention his 1976 JFK library oral history – that JFK was very cooperative and did not order the agents off the limo (debunking the Manchester book on this score in the process), while *also* telling the ARRB that there was "no policy change" and he was merely conveying an anecdote of "kindness and consideration" from the president that the agents need not stand on the rear of the car if the crowds were sparse.

Yet, not only did Congressman Sam Gibbons, who rode in the car inches away from JFK, state to me that there was no order from JFK in Tampa, Tampa motorcycle police officer Russell Groover agreed with Gibbons and further told me that agents *were* on the rear of the car for the whole trip (as many films and photos confirm) except for the very end of the trip when the public motorcade was essentially over and the cars were on their way to the airport, travelling at a high rate of speed! In other words, JFK had zero to do with the agents not being there at this final part of the motorcade – they weren't there because of the speed of the cars on the highway heading home, so to speak. What's more, he confirmed (as the Secret Service's final survey report also confirms) that multi-story buildings were guarded during this very long motorcade, the longest domestic motorcade JFK ever undertook (far longer than Dallas) and that police and military units lined the streets and faced the crowds, in addition to the high volume of flanking motorcycles, his own cycle included.

Boring passed away in 2008. I had the ARRB contact him. He told the ARRB the same bizarre thing he first told me: "I didn't have anything to do with it and I don't know anything." Boring rose to the coveted position of Inspector and retired in 1967. I was the first private researcher to talk to him about JFK.

19) **Suspect number two:** Driver William Greer, having no competition from the dead Thomas Shipman, turned around during the start of the shooting, either braking and/or taking his foot off the gas pedal, and looked directly at JFK; this is his first turn to the rear. Kellerman then ordered him to get out of line ... Greer disobeyed a direct order (and his own training and common sense) and turned around for the second time to stare directly at JFK until the fatal head shot occurs. Only after this did he face forward and hit the gas pedal. Greer denied under oath that he ever turned around to see JFK, let alone twice. As Kellerman told Manchester: "Greer then looked in the back of the car: maybe he didn't believe me."

Yet, Greer, after initially giving the impression of guilt and remorse for his horrific actions and inactions, told the FBI the night of the murder that the president sometimes told him to slow down, agent number two who propagated the "blame the victim" mythology (Boring, as we saw before, was first, pre-dating the actual assassination!). Greer retired in 1966, serving LBJ, a president he allegedly despised, for several years after the assassination. Greer died in 1985. When I spoke to his son in 1991, I asked him "What did your father think of JFK?" A very innocent question, to put it mildly. He avoided the question ... so I asked him again. He then answered: "Well, we're Methodists and JFK was Catholic"!! It is important to note that Bill Greer was born and raised in County Tyrone, Ireland, a country infamous for its religious wars, coming to this country around the age of 18 and later serving Henry Cabot Lodge, Jr., JFK's two-time political opponent and, later, ambassador to Vietnam;

20) **Suspect number three:** Shift leader Emory Roberts. As *I discovered and popularized way back in 1991 and have demonstrated at conferences since 1995* (and, later, on *The Men Who Killed Kennedy* and *A Coup In Camelot*), Roberts rises in his seat during the start of the motorcade rolling out at Love Field airport and recalls agent Don Lawton, who stops in his tracks and raises his arms three different times in disgust. Paul Landis makes room for Lawton on the running board of the car, yet Lawton does not budge. Previous to Lawton's recall (literally only moments before), another agent, Henry Rybka (as seen in films and photos and as verified

in his report) joined Lawton in walking/jogging beside JFK's side of the limo, only to walk away, no doubt also a victim of shift leader Roberts' order (interestingly, Rybka was "accidentally" placed *in* the follow-up car in three different reports after the fact, only to be corrected later, as Rybka and Lawton remained at Love Field). As a side note, as with the death of Shipman, I have more on Lawton in my books, but I can add here that he told me in 1995 that the agents had regrets about 11/22/63 and quote: "Who knows – if they had left guys on the back of the car. You can hindsight yourself to death." Notice he did not blame JFK for the agent's removal and the "they" he referred to was the Secret Service.

Lawton told a trusted colleague shortly after the assassination that, quote, "I should have been there" (on the back of the limo). Indeed. Lawton rode on the rear of the limo in Chicago in March of 1963 and in Tampa four days before Dallas. Returning to Roberts, he went on to recall agent Ready who made some forward movement toward Kennedy during the assassination and, much more importantly, ordered the agents not to move during the shooting, as confirmed by an agent sitting inches away from him, driver Sam Kinney (see *A Coup In Camelot* for more on this). Incredibly, Roberts achieved infamy after the assassination as the only agent to ever become appointment secretary to a president (in this case, LBJ, fulfilling the role once accomplished by Dave Powers), also rising to the level of Inspector, receiving a medal in the process and, as I demonstrate, being the object of an attempt by LBJ himself to name him to the federal parole board – why? To make sure LBJ and his cronies were safe?

With regard to motive, I believe it was a combination of a couple major factors: some of the agents (notably, follow-up car agents Tim McIntyre and Emory Roberts, among others) were angry and disgusted with President Kennedy's private life, while others, such as Forrest Sorrels and Elmer Moore, were angry at President Kennedy for his foreign policy views. Chief U.E. Baughman, like Allen Dulles, was fired by the Kennedy brothers – in Baughman's case, the reason was because he did not believe the Mafia existed, a view shared by J. Edgar Hoover of the FBI. Baughman was made the Chief on November 22 ... of 1948. Interestingly, the following agents and White House aides believed (or, in some cases, *knew*) that there was a conspiracy: Abraham Bolden, Maurice Martineau, Sam Kinney, Bill Greer (yes-him), Roy Kellerman, Robert Bouck, Gerald O'Rourke, John Norris, Marty Underwood, and John Marshall. A few other agents – Forrest Sorrels, Lem Johns and Paul Landis- believed at least one shot came from the front.

See, that is all it took – not an agency "conspiracy"; not many men; not dozens of men ... three – the driver of the limousine, the shift leader who was the commander of the follow-up car agents, and the planner of the Texas trip. It is *action thru inaction*– by *not* doing certain things (hitting the gas pedal, having agents on or near the rear of the limousine, and blaming JFK for the lack of security, among other items), the agency was made to purposely fail and, thus, had to run with this *JFK-is-to-blame* myth to cover up and hide their gross, purposeful negligence or face the consequences – Congressional hearings, press inquiries, loss of pensions, prosecutions, and the end of the agency, at least their role as protectors of our nation's highest officials. Further, by covering up the drinking incident (as Rowley testified, he didn't want to stigmatize the agents, never mind that they broke a sacred rule that was grounds for dismissal *and they lost a president*) and giving out two awards (one arguably undeserving – to Hill, the other dubious – to agent Youngblood, who allegedly covered LBJ a little sooner than even Youngblood believed was possible), the agents got away with a verbal slap on the wrist coupled with great praise for their heroism and courage. In an age before Watergate and true investigative journalism, with a dead president unable to defend himself and a naïve and trusting public, should we have expected anything else?

And, when a certain amateur researcher, on his own time and his own dime, started asking the hard questions, should we be surprised when he was subjected to harassment, ridicule and a campaign by two sad old men to blame the president they failed to protect for huge profit, all the while feeding a gullible public seeking their books and the autographs that they willingly and sickeningly affix to autopsy photos and assassination scenes?

Index

K

L

S

TrineDay's Featured Titles

About Political Intrigue

Dr. Mary's Monkey
How the Unsolved Murder of a Doctor, a Secret Laboratory in New Orleans and Cancer-Causing Monkey Viruses are Linked to Lee Harvey Oswald, the JFK Assassination and Emerging Global Epidemics

BY EDWARD T. HASLAM, FOREWORD BY JIM MARRS

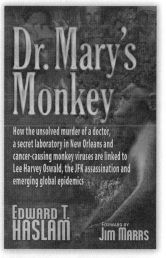

Evidence of top-secret medical experiments and cover-ups of clinical blunders
The 1964 murder of a nationally known cancer researcher sets the stage for this gripping exposé of medical professionals enmeshed in covert government operations over the course of three decades. Following a trail of police records, FBI files, cancer statistics, and medical journals, thisscontaminated polio vaccine, the genesis of the AIDS virus, and biological weapon research using infected monkeys.

Softcover: **$19.95** (ISBN: 9781634240307) • 432 pages • Size: 5 1/2 x 8 1/2
Hardcover: **$24.95** (ISBN: 9781937584597)

Me & Lee
How I Came to Know, Love and Lose Lee Harvey Oswald

BY JUDYTH VARY BAKER
FOREWORD BY EDWARD T. HASLAM

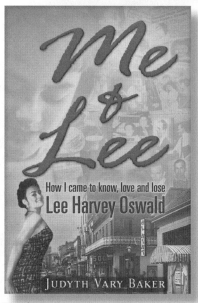

JUDYTH VARY WAS ONCE A PROMISING science student who dreamed of finding a cure for cancer; this exposé is her account of how she strayed from a path of mainstream scholarship at the University of Florida to a life of espionage in New Orleans with Lee Harvey Oswald. In her narrative she offers extensive documentation on how she came to be a cancer expert at such a young age, the personalities who urged her to relocate to New Orleans, and what lead to her involvement in the development of a biological weapon that Oswald was to smuggle into Cuba to eliminate Fidel Castro. Details on what she knew of Kennedy's impending assassination, her conversations with Oswald as late as two days before the killing, and her belief that Oswald was a deep-cover intelligence agent who was framed for an assassination he was actually trying to prevent, are also revealed.

JUDYTH VARY BAKER is a teacher, and artist. Edward T. Haslam is the author of *Dr. Mary's Monkey*.

Hardcover • $24.95 • Softrcover • $21.95 ISBN 9780979988677 / 978-1936296378 • 608 Pages

A Secret Order
Investigating the High Strangeness and Synchronicity in the JFK Assassination
by H. P. Albarelli, Jr.

Provocative new theories that uncover coincidences, connections, and unexplained details of the JFK assassination

Reporting new and never-before-published information about the assassination of John F. Kennedy, this investigation dives straight into the deep end, and seeks to prove the CIA's involvement in one of the most controversial topics in American history. Featuring intelligence gathered from CIA agents who reported their involvement in the assassination, the case is broken wide open while covering unexplored ground. Gritty details about the assassination are interlaced throughout, while primary and secondary players to the murder are revealed in the in-depth analysis. Although a tremendous amount has been written in the nearly five decades since the assassination, there has never been, until now, a publication to explore the aspects of the case that seemed to defy explanation or logic.

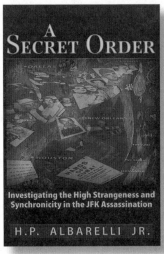

H. P. ALBARELLI JR. is an author and reporter whose previous works can be found in the Huffington Post, Pravda, and Counterpunch. His 10-year investigation into the death of biochemist Dr. Frank Olson was featured on A&E's Investigative Reports, and is the subject of his book, A Terrible Mistake. He lives in Indian Beach, Florida.

Softcover • **$24.95** • ISBN 9781936296552 • 469 Pages

Survivor's Guilt
The Secret Service and the Failure to Protect President Kennedy
by Vincent Michael Palamara

The actions and inactions of the Secret Service before, during, and after the Kennedy assassination

Painstakingly researched by an authority on the history of the Secret Service and based on primary, firsthand accounts from more than 80 former agents, White House aides, and family members, this is the definitive account of what went wrong with John F. Kennedy's security detail on the day he was assassinated.

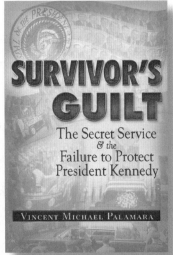

The work provides a detailed look at how JFK could and should have been protected and debunks numerous fraudulent notions that persist about the day in question, including that JFK ordered agents off the rear of his limousine; demanded the removal of the bubble top that covered the vehicle; and was difficult to protect and somehow, directly or indirectly, made his own tragic death easier for an assassin or assassins. This book also thoroughly investigates the threats on the president's life before traveling to Texas; the presence of unauthorized Secret Service agents in Dealey Plaza, the site of the assassination; the failure of the Secret Service in monitoring and securing the surrounding buildings, overhangs, and rooftops; and the surprising conspiratorial beliefs of several former agents.

An important addition to the canon of works on JFK and his assassination, this study sheds light on the gross negligence and, in some cases, seeming culpability, of those sworn to protect the president.

Vincent Michael Palamara is an expert on the history of the Secret Service. He has appeared on the History Channel, C-SPAN, and numerous newspapers and journals, and his original research materials are stored in the National Archives. He lives in Pittsburgh, Pennsylvania.

Softcover • **$24.95** • ISBN 9781937584603 • 492 Pages

In the Eye of History
Disclosures in the JFK Assassination Medical Evidence
SECOND EDITION
BY WILLIAM MATSON LAW

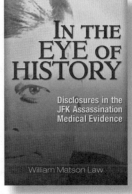

An oral history of the JFK autopsy

Anyone interested in the greatest mystery of the 20th century will benefit from the historic perspective of the attendees of President Kennedy's autopsy. For the first time in their own words these witnesses to history give firsthand accounts of what took place in the autopsy morgue at Bethesda, Maryland, on the night on November 22, 1963. Author William Matson Law set out on a personal quest to reach an understanding of the circumstances underpinning the assassination of John F. Kennedy. His investigation led him to the autopsy on the president's body at the National Naval Medical Center. In the Eye of History comprises conversations with eight individuals who agreed to talk: Dennis David, Paul O'Connor, James Jenkins, Jerrol Custer, Harold Rydberg, Saundra Spencer, and ex-FBI Special Agents James Sibert and Frances O'Neill. These eyewitnesses relate their stories comprehensively, and Law allows them to tell it as they remember it without attempting to fit any pro- or anticonspiracy agenda. The book also features a DVD featuring these firsthand interviews. Comes with DVD.

Softcover: **$29.95** (ISBN: 9781634240468) • 514 pages • Size: 6 x 9

JFK from Parkland to Bethesda
The Ultimate Kennedy Assassination Compendium
BY VINCENT PALAMARA

An all-in-one resource containing more than 15 years of research on the JFK assassination

A map through the jungle of statements, testimony, allegations, and theories relating to the assassination of John F. Kennedy, this compendium gives readers an all-in-one resource for facts from this intriguing slice of history. The book, which took more than 15 years to research and write, includes details on all of the most important aspects of the case, including old and new medical evidence from primary and secondary sources. JFK: From Parkland to Bethesda tackles the hard evidence of conspiracy and cover-up and presents a mass of sources and materials, making it an invaluable reference for anyone with interest in the President Kennedy and his assassination in 1963.

Softcover: **$19.95** (ISBN: 9781634240277) • 242 pages • Size: 6 x 9

The Polka Dot File on the Robert F. Kennedy Killing
Paris Peace Talks connection
BY FERNANDO FAURA

"THE POLKA DOT FILE IS A GEM IN THE FIELD OF RFK ASSASSINATION RESEARCH. READ IT AND LEARN."
—JIM DOUGLASS, AUTHOR, *JFK AND THE UNSPEAKABLE*

The Polka Dot File on the Robert F. Kennedy Killing describes the day-to-day chase for the mystery woman in the polka-dot dress. The book comments on but does not dwell on the police investigation, and reads like a detective thriller instead of an academic analysis of the investigation. It incorporates actual tapes made by an important witness, and introduces the testimony of witnesses not covered in other books and it is a new take on the assassination and the motives for it introduces a new theory for the reasons behind the assassination. Original and highly personal, it reaches a startling and different conclusion not exposed by other books.

FERNANDO FAURA graduated cum laude with a degree in journalism from the California State University. In 1967 he joined *The Hollywood Citizens News*. Fernando has won awards from the Press Club, the National Newspaper Publishers Association, and was nominated for a Pulitzer Prize.

Softcover: **$24.95** (ISBN: 9781634240598) • 248 pages • Size: 6 x 9

From an Office Building with a High-Powered Rifle
A report to the public from an FBI agent involved in the official JFK assassination investigation

by Don Adams

An insider's look at the mysteries behind the death of President Kennedy

The personal and professional story of a former FBI agent, this is the journey Don Adams has taken over the past 50 years that has connected him to the assassination of the 35th president of the United States. On November 13, 1963, Adams was given a priority assignment to investigate Joseph Milteer, a man who had made threats to assassinate the president. Two weeks later John F. Kennedy was dead, and Agent Adams was instructed to locate and question Milteer. Adams, however, was only allowed to ask the suspect five specific questions before being told to release him. He was puzzled by the bizarre orders but thought nothing more of it until years later when he read a report that stated that not only had Joseph Milteer made threats against the president, but also that he claimed Kennedy would be killed from an office building with a high-powered rifle. Since that time, Adams has compiled evidence and research from every avenue available to him, including his experiences in Georgia and Dallas FBI offices, to produce this compelling investigation that may just raise more questions than answers.

DON ADAMS is a former FBI agent who participated in the investigation of the assassination of John F. Kennedy. He is the author of numerous articles on the subject and is considered a respected authority on the topic. He lives in Akron, Ohio.

Softcover • **$24.95** • ISBN 9781936296866 • 236 Pages

Betrayal
A JFK Honor Guard Speaks

by Hugh Clark

with William Matson Law

The amazing story that William Law has documented with his historical interviews helps us to understanding our true history. This compelling information shreds the official narrative.In 2015, Law and fellow researcher Phil Singer got together the medical corpsman, who had been present at Bethesda Naval Hospital for President Kennedy's autopsy with some of the official honor guard, who had delivered the president's coffin. What happened next was extraordinary. The medical corpsmen told the honor guards that they had actually received the president's body almost a half-hour before the honor guard got there. The honor guard couldn't believe this. They had met the president's plane at Andrews, taken possession of his casket and shadowed it all the way to Bethesda. The two sides almost broke into fisticuffs, accusing the other of untruths. Once it was sifted out, and both sides came to the understanding that each was telling their own truths of their experience that fateful day, the feelings of betrayal experienced by the honor guards was deep and profound.

HUGH CLARK was a member of the honor guard that took President Kennedy's body to Arlington Cemetery for burial. He was an investigator for the United Nations. After Hugh left the service he became a New York City detective and held that position for 22 years.

WILLIAM MATSON LAW has been researching the Kennedy assassination for over 25 years. Results of that research have appeared in more than 30 books, including Douglas Horne's magnum opus Inside the Assassination Records Review Board. Law is the author of In the Eye of History and is working on a book about the murder of Robert F. Kennedy with the working title: Shadows and Light. He lives with his family in Central Oregon.

Softcover • **$19.95** • ISBN 9781634240932 • 144 Pages